Life Matters

by

Adrian Ebens

ASPECT Books
www.ASPECTBooks.com

World rights reserved. This book or any portion thereof may not be copied or reproduced in any form or manner whatever, except as provided by law, without the written permission of the publisher, except by a reviewer who may quote brief passages in a review.

The author assumes full responsibility for the accuracy of all facts and quotations as cited in this book.

Copyright © 2011 Adrian Ebens
ISBN-13: 978-1-57258-670-3 (Paperback)
ISBN-13: 978-1-57258-671-0 (E-book)
Library of Congress Control Number: 2011904082

Published by
Aspect Books

Dedicated to my dear friend and colleague

Matthew Sweeny

Whose life was cut tragically short.

www.life-matters.org

Table of Contents

Chapter 1	Building a Family Treasure	1
Chapter 2	Life Source Systems	6

    a. Western Christian Thought
    b. Eastern Thought
    c. Scientific Thought
    d. Comparing Life Source Models
    e. Impact of Life Source Views on Relationships and Value Systems
        i. Potential Impacts of Believing Man is Inherently Divine (Model 1)
        ii. Potential Impacts of Believing Man has Gifted Immortality (Model 2)
        iii. Potential Impacts of Believing Man is Mortal (Model 3)

Chapter 3	A Bible View of Life Source	17
Chapter 4	Connecting to and Maintaining Relationship with the Life Source	21

    a. Submission: The Key Principle
    b. The Vital Example of Submission: Christ
    c. Secondary Examples of Submission
        i. Husband and Wife Relationship (Space Example)
        ii. The Tree of Life (Space Example)
        iii. River System (Space Example)
        iv. The Sabbath (Time Example)

Chapter 5	Receiving Value Through the Life Source	29

    a. The Glory of Children is Their Father
    b. My Beloved Son
    c. The Blessing

Chapter 6	Developing the Life Source – Seed and Nurture Principles	36

    a. The Vital Female Role of Nurturing Submission
    b. The Defining of Equality

Chapter 7	The Origin of Inherent Life Source Models	43

    a. The Tree of Knowledge
    b. The Serpent's Origins
    c. The Rejection of Wisdom
    d. Why Was Satan Allowed to Live?

  e. The Creation of Mankind Provides Answers for the Angels
  f. Humanity Embraces the Inherent Life Source System

Chapter 8   The Origin and Impact of Performance Based Value Systems 53

  a. The Origin of Worthlessness
  b. Impact of Inherent Life System Model on Family Relationships and Structure

Chapter 9   Blessed Enmity 59

  a. The Extent of the Problem
  b. The Solution

Chapter 10   The Development of the Two Life Source Systems 65

  a. The Rise of the Tyrant
  b. Ham Develops the Seed of Babylon
  c. The Spiritual Foundations of Babylon
  d. The Calling of Abraham and the Recovering of the Family System
  e. The Lesson of Sodom

Chapter 11   Underlying Belief Systems of the Two Kingdoms 76

  a. Faith versus Fear
  b. Family Focus versus Individual Focus
  c. Worship as Expressed Through the Sabbath versus Sun-day
  d. Resurrection versus Immortality

Chapter 12   Trials and Triumphs of God's Earthly Family in Genesis ...82

  a. The Challenge of Association and Environment
  b. The Test of Riches
  c. The Test of Marriage – Headship and Submission
    i. Abraham's First Failure in Egypt Causes Vulnerability in Sarah
    ii. Abraham's Second Failure in Hearkening to the Voice of Sarah
  d. God Teaches Abraham Concerning the Vital Nature of Family Structure
  e. The Birthright to Bless

Chapter 13   The Channel of Blessing Lost and Restored Through Egyptian Pilgrimage 105

  a. God Seeks to Reach the Egyptians and Test the Israelites
  b. Egypt and Israel Seduced by Blessings of Wealth and Prosperity
  c. The Lie of Inherent Power Produces Insecurity in Egypt and the

                 Need for Control and Achievement
         d. Pharaoh Undermines the Channel of Blessing to Israel
         e. The Deliverer – The Call of Moses to the Prophetic Office
         f. The Plagues of Egypt – Reveal the Lie of Inherent Power in Nature
         g. Israel Delivered and the Channel of Blessing Restored

Chapter 14   The Protection of the Channel of Blessing 119

         a. Clear Identity Roles are Vital
         b. The Ten Commandments Define Identity of God and Man
         c. The Ten Commandments Twisted by the Lie of the Serpent

Chapter 15   The Journey from Tables of Stone
                      to the Tables of the Heart 129

         a. The Desolating Effects of the Serpent's Lie
         b. The Sanctuary System
         c. The Journey is a Love Story

Chapter 16   A Highway in the Desert 139

         a. The Mountains and the Valleys
         b. Breaking the Cycle
         c. Clinging to Sonship by Faith
         d. His Victory is Ours

Chapter 17   Give Us a King, Like the Other Nations 147

         a. Detailed Instructions to Protect the Family Structure
         b. Israel Turns Away From God
         c. Israel Enshrines the Inherent Power Belief System
         d. The Kings of Israel

Chapter 18   The Rise and Tyranny of World Empire 159

         a. The Battle Between the Two Seeds, Two Women, Two Cities
         b. Satan's Seed Rules the World
         c. Messiah the Prince Comes to His People

Chapter 19   The Greatest Teacher the World Has Ever Seen 172

         a. Delivering the Captives
         b. Re-establishing the Channel of Blessing
         c. Re-establishing the Law – The Channel Protector
         d. Re-establishing the True God as Father
         e. Re-establishing the Correct View of the Sabbath
         f. Re-establishing Submission Principles
         g. Re-establishing the True Purpose of the Sanctuary
         h. Re-establishing the Truth about Death and Life Only in Christ

	i. Re-establishing the True Nature and Purpose of Prayer
	j. Re-establishing the Dignity of Women
Chapter 20	Transition to the Invisible 188
	a. Relationships are Invisible
	b. The Serpent's Lie Shifts Focus to the Visible
	c. The Journey Towards the Invisible
	d. Satan Seeks to Shut the Door to the Invisible
	e. The Followers of Christ Make the Shift from Earthly Symbols to Heavenly Realities
Chapter 21	The Heavenly Sanctuary and Work of Jesus Trodden Under Foot 199
	a. The Priestly Ministry of Jesus in Heaven
	b. The Spiritualization of Rome
	c. Attack on the Heavenly Sanctuary
	d. The Horn Power Attacks the Family Kingdom
	e. Plagues of Judgment Sent to Release the Woman
Chapter 22	The Gathering of Israel the Second Time – Rise of the Advent Movement and The Elijah Message....207
	a. The Reformation Starts Recovery of the Invisible View
	b. The Scattering, Indignation and Gathering of God's People
	c. The Rise of the Advent Movement
	i. Restoration of the Heavenly Sanctuary
	ii. Restoration of the Law of God
	iii. Restoration of the Sabbath
	iv. Restoration of the State of the Dead and Second Coming
	v. Restoration of the Father and Son Relationship
	d. A Solid Platform
Chapter 23	The Marriage in the Most Holy Place – The Judgment.....224
	a. The Marriage Fully Opens the Channel
	b. Many Reject the Wedding Invitation
	c. An Investigation of Worthiness
Chapter 24	The Last Day War on the Family – the Remnant of God's Family Kingdom 230
	a. Family Unit versus the New World Order
	b. The Orchestrated Demolition of the Family
	i. The Education Revolution
	ii. The Music Revolution
	iii. The Feminist Revolution
Chapter 25	The Return of Elijah 237

     a. Turning the Hearts of the Children to the Fathers
     b. The Three Angel's Messages
     c. The Revelation of the Father in the Flames of Hell

Chapter 26 Family Reunion – The Second Coming (The Stone).........247

     a. The Manner of Jesus' Return
      i. A Visible Event
      ii. A Glorious Event
      iii. A World Changing Event
     b. God Claims His Faithful Children
     c. God's Children Permanently Connected to the Life Source

Chapter 27 Living in God's Family Kingdom in the Last Days 252

     a. The Husband and Wife Relationship
      i. The Husband and Father
      ii. The Wife and Mother
     b. Special Blessing Times and Events
      i. Conception and Pregnancy
      ii. Birth
      iii. Toddler and Early Years
      iv. Adolescence
      v. Adulthood
      vi. Marriage
      vii. Grandchildren
     c. Country Living
     d. A Treasure of Family Memories

Appendix A William Miller's Rules of Interpretation..........................264

Chapter 1

Building a Family Treasure

As I entered the house, stale musty air filled my senses and quickly revealed that no one had been living there for some time. After opening a few windows I sat in a lounge chair and surveyed the scene. The grandfather clock in the corner beckoned and reminded me of times past by a flood of memories that were released in my mind. I closed my eyes and 35 years were erased in a moment. The room was suddenly alive with sound, my grandparents, parents and many uncles, aunts and cousins were all there. We were eating sweet cake and biscuits, laughing, telling jokes and stories. I could see their faces so clearly and I chuckled as the film played on. Then without warning a tide of emotion swept over me with a deep, deep yearning that induced tears. Take me back grandfather clock, wind back your old black hands and let me once again revel in the innocence of childhood. The happy faces, the laughter, the innocence – the sense of belonging – oh what a treasure it was.

I was transfixed by the emotion and I knew it was a ritual I must complete. I went to each room, sat down and the film would start again, the faces, the laughter, the belonging, the hunger to go back. It was a way of saying goodbye.

This old house owned by my grandparents was the only thing in my life that had not changed. It was the one constant and though old and musty and slightly run down, it held a treasure of memories that I needed to relive. My grandfather had died and my grandmother had just been moved to a place where she could receive proper care, so the house was soon to be sold.

I have often found myself chasing this treasure of memories. I recently travelled to a place I lived when I was a child and I just soaked up the sights and the sounds, visited my old home and relived the memories. Memories of Dad and Mum, my sister and I, sitting around the lounge, memories of going running with my Dad, memories of playing with my friends in the creek, climbing trees and riding bikes. I know that the memories are slightly 'rose glass tinted' and there is an incredibly strong bias to only remember the good times, but it feels so good and satisfying.

Building and protecting this kind of treasure safeguards the health of communities and gives hope to generations yet to emerge. The treasures of love and affection, sweet memories laid down in family rituals and experiences are the fabric of life. Without this treasure, life has no heart and soul and is reduced to the drudgery of survival. Without a series of warm memories connected to special relationships – life is meaningless. No person can centre and stablise themselves without some place they can point to with warmth and call *home*.

WR was a 19-year old engineering student at a large, competitive, public university. He committed suicide on an early May afternoon by jumping without warning from the tenth floor of his residence hall room.

WR's suicide appears to have been related to his involvement in an automobile accident approximately thirty minutes before his death. WR was ticketed for following too closely – his third traffic offense, thereby making him ineligible to drive. The other driver suffered a minor whiplash injury, and was visibly "in pain and nervous" while being prepared for transport to the hospital. Damage was done to the front of the car WR was driving. That car belonged to his sister; WR's mother had told him not to drive it.

While we can understand someone being upset about having their license cancelled and being in big trouble for driving his sister's car when he was asked not to, why would WR kill himself? How can life get so bad that you want to end it?

WR had kept a diary while at university and it gives a deeper picture of what was really going on. Let's look at some of the entries:

> The feeling in my stomach is one of turning, grinding. I can't feel more sorry for myself. Yet I want to blame my failures on others. I refuse to accept the fault as mine. I hope I'll turn to hate the other members of my class, to punish them and myself, and to come out of this. Today I felt like quitting. Tonight I'll fight on re-enforced ground and I need confidence in a victory.

Help, I'm scared. Oh, I'm scared! I don't want to lose.

Afraid to talk in class . . . Must impress others. Need to prove myself.

Fear!! Put there by yourself. . . You can't do it?

Don't stagnate, go forward, improve.

Reality confronts the 'bottom people.' They often quit school, join the army, or find a job. Admitting the plight of being unable to handle the school system's competition requires courage; and parental or administrative psychological guidance should be available to help recognize the problem.

WR had a speech problem that was intensified by fear. Notice the following comments in his diary:

When I talk it's always bad. So I hide away.

Sitting in class the other day, alone, I realized I could say anything I want. In the presence of others I block myself, I hold myself back.

After my father ordered me to stop talking spastic I felt ashamed and guilty to stutter.

WR's inability to perform correctly in his society began to make him turn in on himself. He began to suffer from loneliness, depression, guilt and anger.

I am alone and bored.

Don't get disillusioned, talk to no one.

Problem exists. Worried, upset, eating a lot, depressed.

If the right people approach me presently I may turn God-squad.

In my room-guilt. Family did not accept.

I still get selfish moods, but now I try to catch myself.

If we look closely at WR's value system, he had a belief that achievement meant acceptance and failure meant rejection. He appears to have had limited support from his family. His father's comments about his inability to talk made him feel ashamed and guilty. Firstly, can we assume that WR took things too seriously and that his suicide was unfortunate but simply part of our environment and that you just have to learn to cope?

It might be easy for some to assume that WR was simply weak-minded but

when you look at the statistics on depression and suicide, it begs us to look a little deeper. Have a look at the following statistics from 1998:
- 1 million suicides every year
- 10 to 20 million attempts every year or up to 38 attempts every minute
- Suicide in the US for males between the ages of 35-49 is the number three cause of death
- Australia's youth suicide rate is the highest in the world.

WR did not have a family treasure of memories to provide a buffer for him during a difficult period, in fact his whole approach to life was driven by achievement based outcomes that he expected would grant him acceptance and good relationships.

The question that must be asked is, what is driving these trends? What principles are at play in society that is causing this breakdown in building a family treasure of memories? What is driving the rising levels of isolation, depression and suicide? We might offer some surface level response of needing to spend more time together and I could give you a list of things to do (which you already know) that could greatly benefit your family treasure building but I guess that would be like offering a mop to clean up the mess rather than pointing to the place to turn off the tap. I believe the issues are much deeper than a simple list of things to do.

How do we build a value system in society that will enhance family relationships and friendships and minimize the negative impacts of failing to achieve goals and performance based outcomes? Our journey begins with our assumptions about life source. We will look at this extensively in the next chapter. But for now we will lay some foundations. When thinking about value systems I believe there is one main ingredient we need to consider that immediately brings two other ingredients:

Main Ingredient:
- **Life or power source** – Life physical, mental and spiritual. This is the essence of being. Where does life come from and how do we engage it? How do we live a life that is full and meaningful?

Secondary Ingredients:
- **Relationships** – the very nature of birth and infancy demands that people engage in some form of relationship. In our human

existence, life is conceived via relationships. We also see the drive for relationships and intimacy due to the great aversion most people have to being alone. Life without intimacy is empty.
- **Value or worth** – a healthy self concept, a sense of purpose and destiny. Without this sense of purpose life becomes meaningless and the desire to preserve it is destroyed. Life without value is meaningless.

How do we connect these ingredients to build stronger relationships with an ocean full of family memory treasures? We state the obvious when we say that relationships and value cannot occur without life, but in stating this fact we see that the nature of our value and relationships are governed by the nature of our life, or in other words, where we understand life comes from.

Chapter 2

Life Source Systems

Answering the question of where life comes from and how it comes to us is one of the most fundamental questions of – well – life. It really defines what kind of beings we are. It also defines the nature of our relationships and our value systems as we discussed at the end of the previous chapter. Considering the priority of this question I find the following statement from Wikipedia under the title "Origin of Life" quite amusing:

> Origin of life studies is a limited field of research despite its profound impact on biology and human understanding of the natural world. Progress in this field is generally slow and sporadic, though it still draws the attention of many due to the eminence of the question being investigated. One plausible reason for the slow rate of progress is that it is difficult to obtain funding for research in this area, since practical commercial applications for the research are difficult to foresee.[1]

So it appears one of the main reasons we still have trouble with this question is that we need more funding for research. ☺ Of course there are many theories and ideas that are passionately promoted claiming to hold the answer to this question. My purpose in this chapter is not to try and answer that question but rather think about the impacts of various life source systems on the ability to build family treasures, strengthen relationships and help our children to have a healthy sense of their own value.

a. Western Christian Thought

Western thought is heavily influenced by the Greek philosophers such as Plato and Aristotle. Plato stated "The soul of man is immortal and

---
1   www.wikipedia.org – Origin of Life

imperishable."[2] A number of Christian church leaders in the first few centuries after the time of Christ were influenced by these views and introduced them to the church. If you notice the latest Catholic Catechism it states the following:

> III. How can we prove that the soul of man is immortal?
>
> We can prove that the soul of man is immortal because man's acts of intelligence are spiritual; therefore, his soul must be a spiritual being, not dependent on matter, and hence not subject to decay or death.[3]

Christians generally accept the immortal soul's presence with no fixed view as to when it becomes part of them. However, it has been a topic of dispute through the centuries. Creationism for example, states God creates a new soul for each at birth (Jerome, Calvin). Traducianism teaches that the soul and body are created by propagation (Tertullian, Leo, Luther). "I may use the opinion of Plato when he declares 'every soul is immortal'" – Tertullian.

The church became so keen on the idea that in 1513, The Lateran Council condemned to be punished as heretics those who "...insist that the intellectual soul is mortal".[4]

There are a small number of Protestant churches that hold the idea that man is mortal and totally dependent on God for life.[5] This idea places life outside of man and something that he only possesses in a relationship with God.

b. Eastern Thought

If we look at eastern concepts of human life we observe the following from a Hindu perspective:

> The greatest exponent of the philosophy of the Vedas, which is also called Vedanta, man is Divine.[6]

Many eastern ideas revolve around the concept of re-incarnation and the progress and development of the soul towards spiritual perfection and the release from earthly pleasures and pursuits. The followers of New Age ideas

---

2   Plato, *The Republic,*, Book X, 608-D
3   Latest Catholic Catechism Appendix 1
4   5th Lateran Council, Session 8 December 19, 1513. http://www.dailycatholic.org/history/18ecume2.htm
5   Seventh-day Adventists are the largest protestant group to hold this view. See www.adventist.org
6   http://www.sriramakrishnamath.org

appear to combine western and eastern thought with the idea that man is divine or part of God.[7]

The concept that man is immortal or divine makes life something that is firmly inherent in man. It is something that we possess within ourselves. While ideas vary as to how we come into possession of that life, the essential theme is that life is a power that we inherently possess.

c. Scientific Thought

Modern science sees life as essentially a chemical process that occurred by chance. "Plausible pre-biotic conditions result in the creation of certain basic small molecules (monomers) of life, such as amino acids."[8] From this perspective science offers us the idea that life is accidental and random but it is something that we possess chemically and in that see it is something we possess inherently but carries no notions of divinity or immortality.

d. Comparing Life Source Models

It is interesting to observe that the place where life originates is the place we typically refer to as 'the divine'. Summing up the various life system concepts, we can express them in three basic ideas. Man has life in himself or has the capacity to produce it himself; or he receives it as a one-time package from someone who can produce it; or he receives it moment by moment from someone who can produce it.

We can summarize this in the following chart:

Model 1	Model 2	Model 3
Man has an inherent life source (the divine) that originates within himself.	Man is given a life source by God (the divine) that he possesses within himself.	Man receives life through a relationship with God (the divine) outside of himself.
MAN IS DIVINE	**MAN IS IMMORTAL**	**MAN IS MORTAL**

---

7   www.newageforum.net
8   www.wikipedia.org – Origin of Life

If we place these three models in a diagram, it could look something like this:

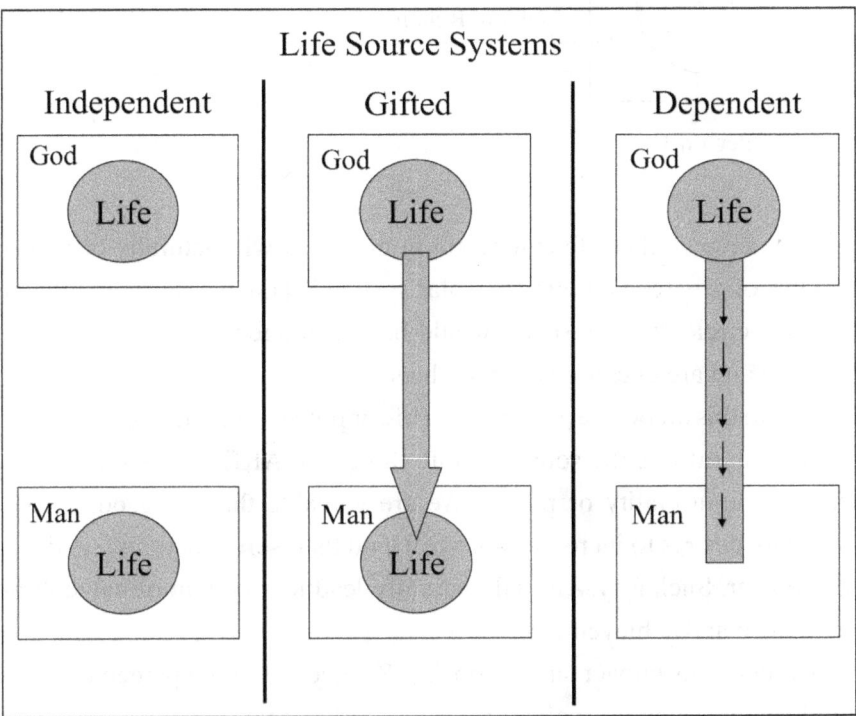

e. Impact of Life Source Views on Relationships and Value Systems

With reference to these three life systems let us explore how they might affect the nature of relationships and value, the secondary ingredients of building a family treasure of memories.

i. Potential Impacts of Believing Man is Inherently Divine (Model 1)

Let us firstly look at a life system where it is perceived that life originates within man. Notice the following diagram:

Life Matters

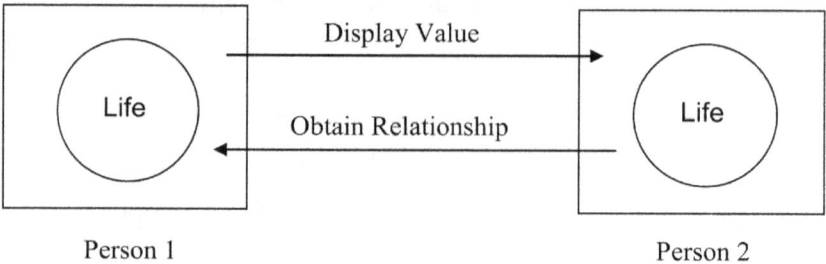

If we perceive that life is inherent in man, self will naturally be placed at the centre of a perceived human "solar system." This would only be natural. As planets circle the sun, so we would be encouraged to see other people as circling us and are essentially for our benefit.

Since in this model we perceive that life or power is our inherent possession, then this naturally is the source of our value. We ARE valuable through our divinity or immortality or power. We are valuable through a possession of power. Any desires to increase value will lend themselves naturally to displays of this power. Such a system will naturally lead to a system of value through performance and achievement.

How does this impact on relationships? Since we would perceive that other individuals also possess power, we could either seek out those who appear most powerful (attractive) and engage (manipulate) them in a relationship or seek out those weaker than ourselves to control them, usually we try to do both. Such relationships enhance our own power or life. This would be a natural playing out of an attempt to live life to the full or to pursue happiness. In this way relationships are primarily engaged to enhance and extend self power. We seek out the most attractive, the wealthiest, the most influential or the most useful and through a display of our power, we attract them to ourselves so that we can possess, use and obtain their power. How many times have we witnessed a wealthy old man marrying a beautiful young lady 30 or 40 years his junior? The optimists proclaim this as the breadth of love while the skeptics call it a very expensive form of prostitution. Regardless of what we think, in this system, beauty is in the eye of the beholder and many people will spend a fortune for the beautiful, so these examples are perfectly normal. Conversely how many times have we seen a dictator controlling and forcing others around them to obey their will and submit to their demands and help fulfill their goals? Much of history is littered with such controlling despots who have made the lives of millions a misery. There is ample evidence that many people have embraced the philosophy of a *Model 1* life source system. It is all around us.

Another less obvious impact on relationships is that because a person has their own life source, relationships are optional. They are not vital to survive. We can take them or leave them depending on whether they suit us or not. This may have individual benefits but would be quite detrimental to a family nurture system. The concept of the divine human must ultimately drive towards autonomy and from autonomy to isolation and from isolation to loneliness.

How does this system include a concept of God? If we believe that we possess life in ourselves then in essence everyone is a god. Some of us are more powerful, others less powerful. The Greeks use this idea in the pantheon of gods that they admired or worshipped. The Greek gods are in essence magnifications of human abilities and talents woven into a story that gives human beings something to aspire towards and emulate, thus these gods are really the worship of the human as divine.

The reality of the Greek system of gods in daily life meant that if as mere mortals they could secure the support and patronage of a god, their power was enhanced and magnified. This magnified power would enable greater displays of their own power to secure more appreciation, love or worship from others and thus lead to a very fulfilling life. Again, this system would certainly have its advantages for the individual but as we will observe in the next chapter has weaknesses in building a nurture system for families.

ii. Potential Impacts of Believing Man has Gifted Immortality (Model 2)

Let us have a look at the second system, where a person perceives their inherent life source comes from God. Notice the following:

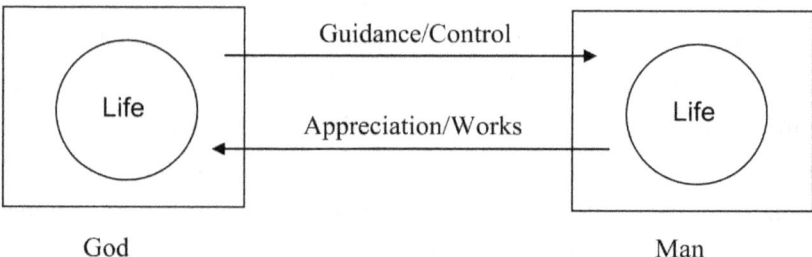

This system forms the basis of all religions that hold to the belief that the soul is immortal or believe that the ability to perform and achieve originates in man. This system does offer some benefits for the individual in that one is guaranteed patronage from a very powerful source. It also allows for the concept of appreciation and thanks for the life that is given. It also can provide for a sense of accountability to someone much more powerful than you.

But there are significant negative impacts on relationships and value systems in this model. Firstly, since it focuses the source of power as being within the individual, it naturally lends itself to a performance based approval system[9] in similar ways to *Model 1*. Looking at life through the lens of immortality, it would be quite natural to seek access to a relationship with God through His designated standard and to win His approval by displays of "good works" or achievements to obtain a fulfilled life. Gaining approval from God by good works is revealed in part or in whole in all world religions.[10]

This performance system can also form the basis of a competition as to

---

9 Meaning that we are approved only when we perform according to a certain expectation of those we seek approval from.
10 While it might be the intent of some churches to avoid a works based religious system and even be stated in its core beliefs, the concepts of immortality will seduce many into unwittingly seeking approval with God by ones performing to a churches agreed standard. Even churches who do not profess to believe in a person's innate immortality can be influenced by these principles by continual association with the many churches and cultures that embrace the concept.

who serves God the best, a kind of battle for who is most worthy of God's blessing. We see this clearly in the clash between Islam and Christianity to show which religion is superior. We see it in debates between Christian churches as to who is the real defender of the faith; the obsessive desire to show oneself to be orthodox and to prove that others are heretical. This point is one of the greatest weaknesses of religions that hold to a view that man is immortal with God on their side. Because this model of life is seen as given by a greater being to whom you must submit, the overwhelming emphasis is control. Control in organized religion is the greatest complaint of the masses against it. Such systems have demonstrated some of the most violent crimes against humanity in their struggle to control and enforce what they believe to be correct in their efforts to win God's favour and enforce His laws. Millions of people have lost their lives due to the conviction of zealous souls who aim to please and defend their god.

While the issues involved are more complex than I have just described, the point remains that if a person believes they have (or have obtained) life/power in themselves then it is extremely hard to avoid the need to gain worth and value from displays of that life/power. We can tell ourselves that we get our value from God and our relationship to Him but the power within you will determine the nature of that relationship and the quality of the value. In summary, the belief that mankind has a self originated life source or a life source donated or gifted by an external benefactor will ultimately lead to extremely negative impacts on intimate relationships. The seducing "freedoms" of autonomy drive individuals towards isolation and control mechanisms that are in direct conflict with the inherent dependencies of relational intimacy.

iii. Potential Impacts of Believing Man is Mortal (Model 3)

Accepting a belief that man is mortal, meaning one has no life of themselves, creates the immediate need for obtaining a constant stream of life from outside of yourself. Life can only be obtained through a relationship; a continual relationship that can never be broken.

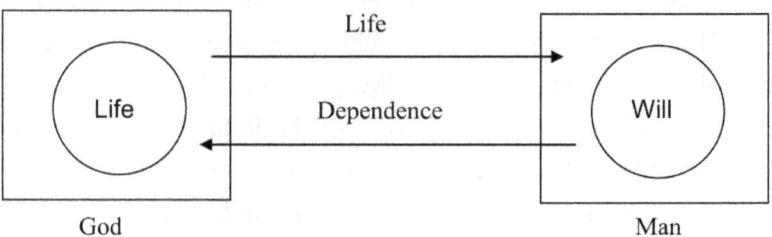

The greatest potential drawback of this system is that you are completely dependent moment by moment on someone else to live. But this potential drawback can in fact be an enormous plus if that someone is very loving, benevolent and patient, and the person receiving the life actually has no issues with submitting to that person. If such a system could succeed then the focus of the recipient of life is on maintaining a submissive intimate relationship with the life giver. If a person develops a nature of submissive intimate relationship, this nature can be replicated to others under their influence and care, and a strong intimate relational network can be maintained.

The emphasis of this system is on submission to the person that is passing life to you and maintaining an intimacy with that person and keeping a high level of respect for that person's authority.

iv. Summary

Let's summarise and compare these three systems in terms of life, relationships and value; and which is the best system for building a strong family network.

Life Source Systems

Source of Life	Impact on Relationships	Impact on Value System
Model 1 (Man is Divine. Life is self originating.)	**Nature:** Relationships are optional. **Purpose:** Relationships are for benefit of enhancing self power. **Dynamics:** Every relationship is a potential opportunity or threat. Use or be used, manipulate or be manipulated. **Maintenance:** Relationships maintained by force for the stronger and appeasement for the weaker.	1. Value comes from within. 2. Based on display of power and achievement and approval. 3. Equality is determined by power. 4. Very hard to admit fault without diminishing personal value.
Model 2 (Man is Immortal. Life is gifted but self possessed under the guidance or control of the giver.)	**Nature:** Human relationships are optional. The Divine relationship is very important. **Purpose:** Relationships are for benefit of enhancing gifted power and pleasing self and life giver. **Dynamics:** Every relationship is a potential opportunity or threat to personal relationship to the Divine. Others could be closer or more pleasing to the Divine, therefore susceptible to "use or be used, manipulate or be manipulated." **Maintenance:** Relationship quality to the divine constantly compared and measured.	1. Value comes from the external life giver *and* from within. 2. Constant need to prove worthiness to self, others and life giver. 3. Equality is determined by power and achievement for self and the life giver. 4. Hard to admit fault without diminishing personal value.
Model 3 (Man is Mortal. Life is received moment by moment from the giver.)	**Nature:** Relationships are vital. **Purpose:** Relationships are a channel of life and blessing. **Dynamics:** Every relationship is an opportunity to serve others and receive a blessing. **Maintenance:** Relationship to life is maintained by submission to life giving authority.	1. Value comes from life giver. 2. Value based on acceptance with life giver. 3. Equality based on relationship to life giver. 4. Easier to admit fault as there is no value in personal achievement only satisfaction.

Each system has its strengths and weaknesses, but it should be seen that the best system to create loving family relationships is a view where relationships are vital. It contains the highest risk in that everything depends of the benevolence of the life giver, but it has the highest gain in that it is the most relationally focused and not subject to the issues of control and manipulation as found in the other systems. In later chapters we will examine why life system models one and two are so predominant in our world but for now we will explore the relational benefits of model three. We will begin by looking at what the Bible says about life source and how we receive it.

Chapter 3

A Bible View of Life Source

The Bible is completely unambiguous as to where life comes from.

Col 1:16,17 For by him all things were created: things in heaven and on earth, visible and invisible, whether thrones or powers or rulers or authorities; all things were created by him and for him. **17** He is before all things, and in him all things hold together. (NIV)

Everything that we can see or perceive and even things we can't see were created and are now sustained by God. Notice carefully the wording of the final sentence. And *in Him* all things hold together. The text clearly tells us that the life force that comes forth from God holds the whole universe together. This clearly indicates that the life is not simply gifted to us as a package but is streamed to us in a constant stream. The following Bible texts state this:

Psa 36:9 For with thee is the fountain of life: in thy light shall we see light.

Rev 22:1 And he shewed me a pure river of water of life, clear as crystal, proceeding out of the throne of God and of the Lamb.

The Bible presents us a picture of a river that flows out of the throne of God. This river is a living river and everything that comes in contact with it receives life. This principle is illustrated in the natural world over and over by the fact that most towns and cities only survive because they are located near a river. If you have ever visited a desolate region and then come across a river, all the trees grow on or near its banks. The concept of life is connected to the concept of a river.

The psalmist David illustrates this when he says:

Psa 1:1 Blessed is the man that walketh not in the counsel of the ungodly, nor standeth in the way of sinners, nor sitteth in the seat of the scornful.

Once again this principle is illustrated in the book of Ezekiel:

Ezek 47:1-9 The man brought me back to the entrance of the temple, and I saw water coming out from under the threshold of the temple towards the east (for the temple faced east). The water was coming down from under the south side of the temple, south of the altar. ... **6** He asked me, Son of man, do you see this? Then he led me back to the bank of the river. **7** When I arrived there, I saw a great number of trees on each side of the river. **8** He said to me, This water flows towards the eastern region and goes down into the Arabah, where it enters the Sea. When it empties into the Sea, the water there becomes fresh. **9** Swarms of living creatures will live wherever the river flows. There will be large numbers of fish, because this water flows there and makes the salt water fresh; so where the river flows everything will live. (NIV)

Notice the last phrase – "so where the river flows everything will live." Life is in the flow of the river. The concept of the river flowing is that water moves from its source point down the river to the living creature in a direct line. There is a direct line from the source to the recipient and it is always moving. The water does not stagnate, it keeps moving. The Bible adds to this concept when it says:

Acts 17:24-28 The God who made the world and everything in it is the Lord of heaven and earth ... **26** From one man he made every nation of men, that they should inhabit the whole earth; and he determined the times set for them and the exact places where they should live. **27** God did this so that men would seek him and perhaps reach out for him and find him, though he is not far from each one of us. **28** 'For in him we live and move and have our being.' As some of your own poets have said, 'We are his offspring.' (NIV)

Notice, how it says that "in Him we live and move and have our being." The Bible is presenting another illustration of how the life of God flows to us. We see here a God who is intimately involved with our lives. Paul begins with the big picture and then zeros down to the personal and intimate level:

1. He has determined the times and places of every nation.
2. He is not far from *each* one of us.
3. ...and finally Paul goes straight to the heart of the issue and says that

in Him we live and move and have our being.

If we live *in Him* or live by a direct stream from Him it is obvious that we can't live without Him. The Bible says:

John 15:5 …apart from me you can do nothing. (NIV)

Please understand that this means we can't do anything physically, mentally or spiritually without Him. We are totally and utterly dependent on God for everything, just like a little baby depends on its parents. Notice the following verses:

1 Chron 29:14 For all things come from You, and of Your own we have given You.

1 Cor 4:7 For who makes you different from anyone else? What do you have that you did not receive? And if you did receive it, why do you boast as though you did not?(NIV)

Up until this point we have been focusing on the sheer physicality of life. But when the Bible states all things come from Him, this means all things spiritual, mental and physical.

Consider the following texts:

Col 2:2,3 My purpose is that they may be encouraged in heart and united in love, so that they may have the full riches of complete understanding, in order that they may know the mystery of God, namely, Christ, **3** in whom are hidden all the treasures of wisdom and knowledge... (NIV)

Exod 31:1-5 Then the LORD said to Moses, **2** "See, I have chosen Bezalel son of Uri, the son of Hur, of the tribe of Judah, **3** and I have filled him with the Spirit of God, with skill, ability and knowledge in all kinds of crafts— **4** to make artistic designs for work in gold, silver and bronze, **5** to cut and set stones, to work in wood, and to engage in all kinds of craftsmanship. (NIV)

The Bible reveals God as the source of all wisdom and knowledge. Colossians 2:2,3 challenges the concept that we as human beings can originate wisdom and knowledge. All wisdom and all knowledge come from God. An example of this is shown in Exodus 31:1-5 where we see God giving a man wisdom and skill in craftsmanship.

What about the concept of spiritual life? If we come to a verse I just mentioned, Psalms 1:3,

Psa 1:3 He is like a tree planted by streams of water, which yields its fruit in season and whose leaf does not wither. Whatever he does prospers. (NIV)

It states that the fruit of the tree depends upon the water that streams to it. When talking about fruit the Bible says:

Gal 5:22,23 But the fruit of the Spirit is love, joy, peace, patience, kindness, goodness, faithfulness, **23** gentleness and self-control. Against such things there is no law. (NIV)

The implications of this text are important. All of these attributes come from having the Spirit of God. This simply means that without the Spirit of God you cannot have love, joy, peace, patience, kindness and so on. I was thinking about this Biblical truth one day while I was walking in a park by a lake. It was calm and peaceful. I suddenly noticed a mother pushing her daughter on a swing. They were both laughing together and obviously enjoying each other's company. The love that this mother was experiencing for her daughter was inspired by God. The thought to be loving, kind and gentle to her daughter did not originate within the heart of the mother but in the heart of God and was given to that mother through the stream of life who then chose to express it and it became a mother's love. The source of the mother's love comes from the heart of God. That love became a part of the mother because she responded to the Spirit of God and expressed it.

The Bible presents a view that is very much in harmony with the third model of life source we looked at in the previous chapter. We are vitally dependent on God for life, every moment of every day, not just physical life, but mental and spiritual life.

The beauty of this Biblical system is that it is relationally vital. Relationships are central to its survival. The next chapter will consider the issues of relationship in a life flow model and the chapter after that will consider the issues of value.

Chapter 4

Connecting to and Maintaining Relationship with the Life Source

As we have noticed in the previous chapter, God is the source of all life and anyone who has life can only have it and maintain it in a relationship with God. It is important to point out, though maybe obvious, that we can not seek for this life as that would infer that we have some life or power in ourselves to initiate such action. God is the initiator of life and as we shall see, the Bible has laid down guidelines for maintaining this life.

a. Submission: The Key Principle

The ability to maintain life with the life source is a simple matter of submission. If we wish to have this life we must be in a submissive state to receive it. If we wish to have this life, we must recognize God as the author and therefore the supreme authority of life.

The question must be asked, why do we talk of submission when speaking about receiving life? This is a vital question. Submission suggests an action of the will; a choice has to be made. Why is choice an issue? Because God's kingdom is a kingdom of love.

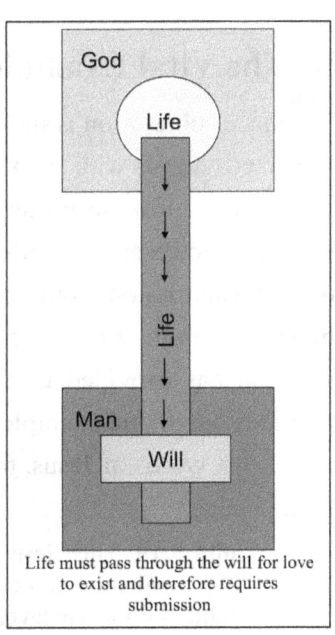

Life must pass through the will for love to exist and therefore requires submission

1 John 4:7-8 Beloved, let us love one another, for love is of God; and everyone who loves is born of God and knows God. **8** He who does not love does not know God, for God is love.

God is love and as God is love and operates His kingdom with love, love can only exist with choice; choice to accept or reject God. The rejection of God is of course death because God is the only one that possesses life in Himself and the only one that can give life.

> **1 Tim 6:15-16** ... He who is the blessed and only Potentate, the King of kings and Lord of lords, **16** who alone has immortality, dwelling in unapproachable light, whom no man has seen or can see, to whom be honor and everlasting power. Amen.

But without this power to choose, love cannot exist. Life is then robotic and automated. So we see that life can only be received by a submission of the will in love to the life giver. There must be a close and intimate relationship where the one receiving life finds pure joy and happiness in submission to the authority of the life giver. Someone might immediately argue that there are many who do not believe in God and yet they are still alive. That is a good question and one that we will consider in chapter 9.

So the key point we are making is that submission to the authority of the life source is the key issue.

b. The Vital Example of Submission: Christ

Since submission is such a vital point, it is important for God, the source of life, to provide us with an example or examples of how this submission process works. The universe needs a demonstration of how to live in a submissive state, how to receive this life and how to relate to the life source. The example of such submission would become the pivotal point of a kingdom based on a belief in a single life source flowing out to all living creatures.

God has provided this example in the person of His Son. God's Son provides the divine example of loving submission to the life source authority. Notice the words of Jesus, the Son of God, when speaking of His relationship to the Father:

> **John 5:19** Then Jesus answered and said to them, "Most assuredly, I say to you, the Son can do nothing of Himself, but what He sees the Father do; for whatever He does, the Son also does in like manner.

John 5:30 I can of Myself do nothing. As I hear, I judge; and My judgment is righteous, because I do not seek My own will but the will of the Father who sent Me.

John 8:29 And He who sent Me is with Me. The Father has not left Me alone, for I always do those things that please Him.

John 14:5,6 Thomas said to Him, "Lord, we do not know where You are going, and how can we know the way?" **6** Jesus said to him, "I am the way, the truth, and the life. No one comes to the Father except through Me."

The life of Jesus, the Son of God, demonstrates for the universe the critical example of submission to God. In beholding the relationship of Jesus to the Father, we find the key of how life can be received and maintained in a loving and intimate relationship. For this reason, the relationship between the Father and the Son is the most critical element for the survival of God's kingdom as revealed in the Bible. Without this example of Jesus, the Son of God, we would lose the most vital clue of how to live in a submissive relationship to God. This is why Jesus is the Way to the Father. This is why Jesus is our example in all things.

It is important to point out that what Jesus came to demonstrate was an expression of what always has existed. The Son of God has always operated in loving submission to the Father, for He says "I always do those things that please Him" – it has always been this way and must always be this way so that we might have a divine example of how to live in loving submission to the life source of the universe.

c. Secondary Examples of Submission

i. Husband and Wife Relationship (Space Example)

The question that must be raised is: How was the principle of submission revealed to the human family before Christ came in person to demonstrate it? This is a question of utmost importance. If the principle of loving submission to life authority is so vital then it must be revealed in the origins of human civilization. And indeed it is.

We have noted that the relationship of the Son of God to the Father is the critical relationship for demonstrating a Biblical life source model of life flowing from one source to all living creatures.

It would only make sense that in the origins of human existence that this relationship be patterned so that the submission principle could be observed in human relations. This is what the Bible tells us:

> **Rom 1:19-20** because what may be known of God is manifest in them, [mankind] for God has shown it to them. **20** For since the creation of the world His invisible attributes are clearly seen, being understood by the things that are made, even His eternal power and Godhead, so that they are without excuse...

The Bible tells us that the attributes of the Godhead were revealed in the creation and it was manifest in them, meaning the people that were created. We are placed in no doubt as to where these attributes were revealed.

> **Gen 1:26-27** Then God said, "Let Us make man in Our image, according to Our likeness; let them have dominion over the fish of the sea, over the birds of the air, and over the cattle, over all the earth and over every creeping thing that creeps on the earth." **27** So God created man in His own image; in the image of God He created him; male and female He created them.

If we look closely at this Bible passage, we see God says let "Us" make man in Our image according to Our likeness. If we look at what was created, we see two individuals created. This indicates that the "Us" is the Father and the Son. Let us look a little closer at the nature of this relationship.

> **1 Cor 11:3** ...the head of woman is man, and the head of Christ is God.

The Bible here speaks about the principle of headship. The Biblical concept of head or headship concerns had the obvious meaning of leadership for which we often hear the phrase "the buck stops here". The point is it also starts there. It is the source point from which something flows or starts. Notice the usage of head in Genesis 2:10:

> **Gen 2:10** And a river went out of Eden to water the garden; and from thence it was parted, and became into four heads.

We see a parallel between the headship of the Father to the Son and the headship of the man to the woman. Here is a key element of the image that

Genesis 1:26 speaks about. The role of the woman is pivotal to the whole family process, just as the role of Christ is pivotal to the entire universe. In the home environment, the intimate submissive relationship of the wife to the husband serves as an image of the intimate submissive relationship of the Son to the Father which safeguards the reception of the life source through the universe.

God designed that the principle of life flow through this husband and wife relationship is demonstrated by how human beings come into existence from this point forward. Adam gave "seed" or life to Eve who then nurtured this seed in her womb and brought forth a child. Again this transfer from a source to a submissive agent who then nurtures and develops that seed is a reflection of the original relationship of the Father and the Son. Notice:

> **Heb 1:2** has in these last days spoken to us by His Son, whom He has appointed heir of all things, through whom also He made the worlds;

> **Eph 3:9** and to make all see what is the fellowship of the mystery, which from the beginning of the ages has been hidden in God who created all things through Jesus Christ;

> **John 1:1-3** In the beginning was the Word, and the Word was with God, and the Word was God. **2** He was in the beginning with God. **3** All things were made through Him, and without Him nothing was made that was made.

The Bible tells us that God made all things through His Son. In the same way, Adam initiated the population of the human race through Eve. This is the demonstration of how life would flow.

It is critical to understand that the life process must flow through the submissive agent as an example to all those who receive life under this process. If life was given to the universe without a submissive agent then the universe has no vital example of how to receive and stay connected to the life source.

The family relationship is the most fundamental example of how to connect to the life source we can find in a spatial or material environment. It most accurately reflects the great original example of how life source and submission work. But God has provided other examples also to show how this principle works.

ii.   The Tree of Life (Space Example)

God planted a tree in the middle of the garden called the Tree of Life.

> **Gen 2:9** And out of the ground the Lord God made every tree grow that is pleasant to the sight and good for food. The Tree of Life was also in the midst of the garden.

The tree was another material or spatial example of the dependence of mankind on something outside of himself to have life. Adam and Eve had to eat from this tree to live. If Adam and Eve stopped coming to the tree to eat its fruit, they would die. The tree had no inherent life to give Adam and Eve, it was a symbol that God had placed in the garden to remind them of how completely dependent they were on receiving life from outside themselves. This principle is also reflected to a lesser extent in the whole food concept. The need for food to live gives expression to the reality that life does not reside inherently in the human race. Every time we eat we should be constantly reminded on this truth.

iii.   River System (Space Example)

We mentioned earlier about the example of a river flowing from the throne of God out into the universe. This principle again was reflected in the creation of the river system that flowed out of the Garden of Eden.

> **Gen 2:10-14** Now a river went out of Eden to water the garden, and from there it parted and became four riverheads. **11** The name of the first is Pishon; it is the one which skirts the whole land of Havilah, where there is gold. **12** And the gold of that land is good. Bdellium and the onyx stone are there. **13** The name of the second river is Gihon; it is the one which goes around the whole land of Cush. **14** The name of the third river is Hiddekel; it is the one which goes toward the east of Assyria. The fourth river is the Euphrates.

Nothing can live long without water. The river system described in Genesis 2 was another visual reminder that life comes from a single source point and flows out to everything around it. No person can build a city or town in a desert, all thriving towns and cities must be near a river or water supply. We must submit to where the river runs if we wish to have life. We can't live away from the river.

iv. The Sabbath (Time Example)

God not only provided spatial or material examples of how life is received and maintained in terms of space but He also created a memorial of this in time.

> **Gen 2:3** Then God blessed the seventh day and sanctified it, because in it He rested from all His work which God had created and made.

God set apart the Sabbath as a memorial of His creative power. The example of rest given by the Creator was a demonstration of how the human race should act each seventh day. The act of rest is a symbol of complete dependence on God to provide for us. It also provides an opportunity to demonstrate submission to the life source authority. Notice carefully the aspects of the Sabbath found in the following:

> **Exod 20:8-11** "Remember the Sabbath day, to keep it holy. **9** Six days you shall labor and do all your work, **10** but the seventh day is the Sabbath of the Lord your God. In it you shall do no work: you, nor your son, nor your daughter, nor your male servant, nor your female servant, nor your cattle, nor your stranger who is within your gates. **11** For in six days the Lord made the heavens and the earth, the sea, and all that is in them, and rested the seventh day. Therefore the Lord blessed the Sabbath day and hallowed it.

God's people were commanded to remember the source of life – who had created all things and they were to rest while doing it, remembering that man has no life in himself and is completely dependent upon God. The act of rest is the act of submission to the life source authority.

The memorial of the Sabbath reminds us not only of the initial act of creation but also the continual supply of life that is given to us.

> **Rev 14:6-7** Then I saw another angel flying in the midst of heaven, having the everlasting gospel to preach to those who dwell on the earth--to every nation, tribe, tongue, and people-- **7** saying with a loud voice, "Fear God and give glory to Him, for the hour of His judgment has come; and worship Him who made heaven and earth, the sea and springs of water."

The worship of Him who made the heaven and the earth, the sea and springs of water is a reference to Exodus 20:8-11. In the Greek, the word "made" gives the sense of an event that occurred in the past but continues into the present. So the Sabbath memorializes God's continual power to create *and* sustain His creation. Another example of the ongoing provision of life is found in the following:

> **Ezek 20:12** Moreover I also gave them My Sabbaths, to be a sign between them and Me, that they might know that I am the Lord who sanctifies them.

The word sanctify can mean to clean or to keep. It is God's power that keeps, cleans, renews and holds us.

So we see that God has provided a time memorial of maintaining a vital and intimate connection with a life source outside of ourselves.

A close observation of the Genesis record reveals that the only institutions given to man before his fall into sin were marriage and the Sabbath. Both of these institutions were critical reminders that life only comes to us through submission to a life source outside of ourselves.

We have briefly discussed a number of aspects that reveal the vital nature of relationships from a Biblical perspective. We now wish to address the second ingredient and that is value.

Chapter 5

Receiving Value Through the Life Source

a. The Glory of Children is Their Father

It must have been an amazing sight to see. A young chef was running down the corridors of the hospital bursting with joy and calling loudly to everyone that could hear, "It's a boy, it's a boy!"

That is how my mother described my father's reaction to my birth. There is something deeply profound about this little otherwise insignificant event. I know that my coming into the world was greatly desired by my father and that my birth brought him joy. That knowledge in conjunction with

My Father holding me when I was three weeks old

continued evidences of this, have laid down the fabric of my self-perception and importance in the world I live in. The continued evidences are found in a few old black and white photos that I treasure. The first one is my father holding me in his arms when I was 3 weeks old.

There is something quite elemental in this picture; something essential and satisfying. It was from this man that the seed of my life came. In human terms my life source came from my father and there is an unspoken bond between us that goes far deeper than any other relationship I have on earth, in respect to who I am as a person.

Some time ago I came across a website that in some ways captured the sense of my connection with my father. The website was called "Imissmydad.com."

On this website was posted hundreds of statements of people who had lost their father and were trying to deal with the loss of no longer being able to speak to him. Here are some sample statements:

> **Noelle wrote:**
> Dear Daddy, today I am 30 & you are not here - no hug, no kiss, no birthday wish this year. No smile, no eyebrow raised, no singing me a song. I can't believe the time has past, I can't believe you're gone. I love you; always have; always will.
>
> **Paul wrote:**
> Dad, I miss you everyday and just wish we could talk again. Losing you has made me question who I am and where I'm going. Can I be the Dad you were? You were the best and just wish you could have lived longer to see my accomplishments and share in that joy. Even a year later I find myself wanting to pick up the phone to call you. I love you.
>
> **Michael wrote:**
> Dad, it was quiet on thanksgiving today not having you around us. I felt an emptiness in me and I know everyone else felt the same. It has been 4 months but feels like it has been longer.
>
> **Daddy's Princess wrote:**
> Hi Daddy, I hope you're proud of me! I'm really happy and things are going well in life. Work is a little overwhelming but I guess that's what I signed up for. I think I'm doing all the right things and I hope you approve. Miss you. Love you always, Princess.
>
> **Anonymous:**
> I miss you so much Papasan. I want to talk to you, hear your voice, and tell you how the kids are doing. It's only been 6 weeks but I feel some days it's been forever… Why couldn't the doctors do more, why didn't I tell you every day that I loved you so much. Somebody help me in this time of need!!!!!!!!!!!

The breaking of a father-child relationship reveals for many the real trauma that one experiences when their father dies. Over and over is revealed the importance of knowing a father approves of the child and the desire to tell a father what is happening in their life and how they are feeling.

This life experience is expressed in Scripture through the following Bible passage:

> **Prov 17:6** Children's children are the crown of old men, And the glory of children is their father.

The key word connection concerning children and their father is *glory*. Let's look more closely at how the Bible uses this word in other places to get a sense of its meaning.

> **Jer 9:23,24** Thus says the Lord: "Let not the wise man glory in his wisdom, Let not the mighty man glory in his might, Nor let the rich man glory in his riches; 24 But let him who glories glory in this, That he understands and knows Me, That I am the Lord, exercising lovingkindness, judgment, and righteousness in the earth. For in these I delight," says the Lord.

The word glory used here denotes beauty, splendor, jewels it can also be denoted as something to boast about. In a direct sense the word glory symbolizes value.

We could easily read the above passage "Let not the wise man *feel valuable* because of his wisdom, let not the mighty man *feel valuable* because of his might nor let the rich man *feel valuable* because of his riches; But let him who *feels valuable, feel valuable* in this, That he understands and knows Me, That I am the Lord, exercising lovingkindness, judgment, and righteousness in the earth. For in these I delight," says the Lord.

Here is the wisdom of Proverbs 17:6; the value of a child is bound up in the heart of their father. Why is this? The father represents the source of life and establishes the vital Biblical principal of value through relationships of origin. The earthly father is an image and symbol of the heavenly Father.

When we consider that all love and life come from God, it should not be too difficult to see that our earthly fathers are channels of blessing to allow the love of God to be poured into our hearts; to develop a sense of meaning and purpose in our lives. This is the primary purpose of a father, to not only pass on physical life, but also to pass on emotional and spiritual life simply by being there for his children and offering them regular reminders of how important they are to him.

b. My Beloved Son

God demonstrated this fundamental principle of value coming through a life source outside of oneself by the events that transpired at the baptism of Jesus when He was here on earth.

> **Matt 3:16,17** When He had been baptized, Jesus came up immediately from the water; and behold, the heavens were opened to Him, and He saw the Spirit of God descending like a dove and alighting upon Him. **17** And suddenly a voice came from heaven, saying, "This is My beloved Son, in whom I am well pleased."

The context of this event is very important. Jesus is about to commence His life's work as the Messiah. He will encounter great opposition, develop many enemies, receive many negative reports about Himself and His work and finally be taunted and mocked while dying on a cross, seeing little evidence that His work held much significance. Further to this, immediately after His baptism, Jesus would meet face to face the great accuser and deceiver Satan, who would try and confuse Jesus as to who He really was. He tried to draw Jesus into *feeling valuable* by His wisdom and might by getting him to turn stones into bread and doing miracles to prove His identity. In the light of these things, the Father came with a reminder of where the value of Christ was and where it had come from.

"This is My beloved Son, in whom I am well pleased."

This statement, and this statement alone, was the foundation of Christ's ability to face such great opposition and hatred. His sense of value was not based in Himself and what He possessed, nor what he could achieve. It was based purely in the relationship with the One who had given Him life. Notice carefully:

> **Matt 4:4** But He answered and said, "It is written, 'Man shall not live by bread alone, but by every word that proceeds from the mouth of God.'"

This is the foundation of a Biblical kingdom; value comes from the one who has given you life. This means that life (physical life) and value (emotional and spiritual life) are not dependent on what we inherently possess but on the life source that we are in intimate relationship with.

The experience of Jesus at the baptism highlights the critical role of the channel of blessing that is open to those who are in intimate relationship with the life source of the universe called our heavenly Father.

c. The Blessing

In the previous chapter we discovered that the husband and wife relationship is an image of the Father and Son relationship. Included in this image is the crucial process of blessing. The Biblical principle of headship is in fact the opening of the door to blessing. Notice this important Bible passage:

> **1 Cor 11:3** But I want you to know that the head of every man is Christ, the head of woman is man, and the head of Christ is God.

Here we see a channel of blessing that passes from Father to Son to husband to wife.[11] Just as the Son of God needed the blessing of His Father, so does a wife need the blessing of her husband. We will cover this point in more detail but suffice to say, I have not met a wife that is in a close relationship with her husband that is not encouraged and strengthened by his tenderness and appreciation of her. I have spoken to many ladies asking them how important it is to them to be affirmed and encouraged by their husbands. I have not met one that did not desire or appreciate it.

The flow of blessing is also vital to be passed onto children. As we mentioned earlier, the glory of children is the father. It is critical for children to know that their father loves them and is pleased with them.

I was pondering this concept one day and was thinking about how I might bless my oldest son. I was looking for the right opportunity to tell him how special he is to me. He was seven at the time and we were discussing some simple things and then the conversion opened up to the point where I could tell my son how much I loved him. I said, "Son there is no-one on earth more special to me than you, excluding your mother of course." "You are a very special boy and I am really proud of you." My son lit up like a Christmas tree. There was something life-giving in what I had shared with my son. It strengthened our relationship and made us closer. It also allowed me to act on behalf of our Father in heaven and speak the words He wants to speak to my son and to every child. It is a wonderful privilege to bless. This principle can extend (though not as powerfully as a birth father) to grandparents, relatives, teachers and pastors as well. A person of authority and standing that we look

---

11   The channel of blessing of headship only makes sense in a life source model where life flows from one source. The influences of other life source models make this text sound like domination and control. We will address this more in later chapters.

up to can bring blessing.

One afternoon at church I invited all the children to come down the front for a special prayer. With each child, I placed my hand on their shoulder and spoke their name saying something like this: "Father in heaven, thank you for Steven, you are the one that created him and therefore he is special. We want him to know that we as a church love him and will be praying for him and know that you will bless him with gifts and talents to be a strong man of God and an important part of our community." I did this with all the children, one by one in front of the church – because they were worth it.

The next day one of the mother's rang me in an excited state. She said "Pastor, my daughter came to me this morning and said 'Mum, I am special' and I answered, 'why is that honey' and my daughter said 'because the pastor said so.'" What an honour to plant that seed for that young lady, a child of God. It is so wonderful to plant the seeds of emotional and spiritual life in those under your care and influence.

This is how Jesus operated here on earth. Filled with a sense of the Father's blessing he was enabled to bless others under His influence.

> **Mark 10:13-16** Then they brought little children to Him, that He might touch them; but the disciples rebuked those who brought them. **14** But when Jesus saw it, He was greatly displeased and said to them, "Let the little children come to Me, and do not forbid them; for of such is the kingdom of God. **15** Assuredly, I say to you, whoever does not receive the kingdom of God as a little child will by no means enter it." **16** And He took them up in His arms, put His hands on them, and blessed them.

The disciples did not understand the significance of taking the children and blessing them. They were under the influence of a different life source model as we shall discuss later. But Jesus took the children in His arms and blessed them. What a beautiful picture of God's love, Jesus shows us what God is like and demonstrates it by taking the children in His arms and imparting emotional and spiritual life to them and giving them a stronger sense of purpose and meaning.

The power of the blessing cannot be underestimated. We have a powerful story in the Bible of how significant the blessing of the father is, or at least was, in earlier times.

Receiving Value Through the Life Source

Gen 27:38 And Esau said unto his father, Hast thou but one blessing, my father? bless me, *even* me also, O my father. And Esau lifted up his voice, and wept.

You can read the context of this story in Genesis 27, but the point we need to see is that Esau longed to hear the words of blessing from his father. It was so important to him that he wept at the thought of not receiving it.

The facts are that in a Biblical life source framework, the receiving and nurturing of the blessing is the most important process of a community. It is the key to building a strong treasure house of family memories and a sense of belonging.

In the next two chapters we will look at what factors need to be in place to allow this blessing to flow effectively and protective measures that have been put in place to safeguard this channel of blessing.

Chapter 6

Developing the Life Source – Seed and Nurture Principles

a. The Vital Female Role of Nurturing Submission

We were racing down the freeway at a great rate of knots. My wife, Lorelle's contractions had developed into a pretty regular pattern. We didn't want to be caught out, so we raced for the hospital. It was all very new and exciting; soon we would have our first child. We glided up to the labour ward, the nurse took one look at us and said, "You're too happy, you need to go for a walk". Well that put a hole in our drum. 45 minutes later we came back and now Lorelle wasn't smiling any more. Another 30 minutes and we landed right in the middle of labour. Yep, there is no other word to describe it, labour, hard labour. We tried to remember all the techniques from the prenatal classes but it was hard to stay focused. Those contractions hit like a freight train coming head on. As soon as you had dealt with one the next one was straight on top of you. Finally after 11 hours, we received our firstborn son, Michael.

I am deeply grateful for my two sons (yes we went through the whole thing again!) whom my wife has given to me and of course I could not have done it without her. In the image of the divine model, the origin of life passed from me to my wife who then nurtured that seed and developed it into a beautiful child. Of course when I say she did it, I mean that God has given her all the right equipment to nurture my seed into a human life.

In the wisdom of God we can observe within the genesis process of human life the very key to developing a harmonious family, community and nation.

Developing the Life Source – Seed and Nurture Principles

The physical process of human creation reveals a deep spiritual truth with respect to our understanding of life source, relationship and value.

The source of the life process begins with the father, but the nurture and development of life occurs within the mother. This physical process reflects the spiritual reality of the glory of children. The seed of a child's value is directly connected to their father, but that seed can only be nurtured and developed by the example of submission of the wife to her husband, along with her loving watch care of her children.

We need to deviate slightly at this point to address a question that will receive more treatment later, but needs to be addressed in part here. Many would argue that the life of a child comes equally from father and mother (remember that word equality; we will come to it shortly). This is where the Bible account of the origin of the human race is very important. Here is the sequence of events:

1. God made Adam from the dust and breathed life into him.	Gen 2:7 And the Lord God formed man of the dust of the ground, and breathed into his nostrils the breath of life; and man became a living being.
2. God put Adam in the garden.	Gen 2:15 Then the Lord God took the man and put him in the garden of Eden to tend and keep it.
3. God warns Adam concerning the Tree of Knowledge of Good and Evil.	Gen 2:16,17 And the Lord God commanded the man, saying, "Of every tree of the garden you may freely eat; but of the tree of the knowledge of good and evil you shall not eat, for in the day that you eat of it you shall surely die."
4. God states that it is not good for Adam to be alone.	Gen 2:18 And the Lord God said, "It is not good that man should be alone; I will make him a helper comparable to him."
5. God formed all the animals from the dust of the ground and brings them to Adam to name.	Gen 2:19 Out of the ground the Lord God formed every beast of the field and every bird of the air, and brought them to Adam to see what he would call them. And whatever Adam called each living creature, that was its name.

6. Adam names the animals and in the process learns that he alone is without a companion.	Gen 2:20 So Adam gave names to all cattle, to the birds of the air, and to every beast of the field. But for Adam there was not found a helper comparable to him.
7. God puts Adam to sleep, takes a living rib from his side and forms it into a woman and brings her to him.	Gen 2:21,22 And the Lord God caused a deep sleep to fall on Adam, and he slept; and He took one of his ribs, and closed up the flesh in its place. Then the rib which the Lord God had taken from man He made into a woman, and He brought her to the man.

It is extremely important to follow this sequence. We note a number of important points:

1. Adam receives life directly from God.
2. Adam is given an occupation (placed in the garden).
3. Adam is educated about his environment (instructed about the Tree of Knowledge of Good and Evil).
4. Adam placed in headship over the creation and blesses the living creatures by giving names to all of them.
5. Adam senses that something is missing, that he has no one who can appreciate his thoughts, joys and aspirations.
6. God takes life (the living rib) from Adam and forms it into Eve and then brings her to him.
7. He then calls her woman, meaning taken out of man.

Eve's material life originated from Adam, all her DNA material came from him. Why is this fact important? It highlights the fact that for some reason God made man as the source point, the beginning place; the head of the human river that would flow forth and multiply. The very name woman means—taken from man.

This whole process reveals that God designed for the man to be recognized as the source both physically and spiritually. We now turn to the critical position of the woman's role. It is at this point we need to restate something we said in Chapter 4:

It is critical to understand that the life process must

> *flow through the submissive agent as an example to all those who receive life under this process. If life was given to the universe without a submissive agent then the universe has no vital example of how to receive and stay connected to the life source.*

To operate a life source model of dependent relationships streaming from one source point requires an example of how to stay connected to the life source. The role of the woman plays this critical role and without it, the entire system will fail.

A wife's respectful submission to her husband is what establishes him as the designated human life source in the family. I say designated in that it is God who is the actual source, but He has channelled it through the position of the husband and father. Firstly in giving him physical seed to initiate physical life and also spiritual seed, which is reflected in the blessing and sense of value that the Bible terms "the glory of children."

But it is only the wife that can demonstrate to her children how to connect to this designated life source. Her respectful submission is the way of life, it powerfully shows her children how they should relate to their father and that they should look to him for blessing and protection.

Since the wife plays the most critical role in building this system, a wise husband will lavish appreciation and praise upon his wife and seek every avenue in his power to bless her and make her life joyful. In this action he makes submission to him a joy and something to be desired. As we will study later, failure to do this will destroy his entire kingdom, for only a man's wife can establish her husband's authority; and regardless of all he has to give, without it, he has nothing and is nothing.

b. The Defining of Equality

I recently came across this news item and I thought what better way to introduce the issue of male and female equality:

> *Are Women Smarter Than Men? College-Enrollment Trends Suggest So*
>
> The number of bachelor's degrees earned by women jumped by 70

percent — compared with 5 percent for men — between 1975 and 2001. In 16 countries across the world, female grad rates surpass males, while men earning degrees outnumber women in only six industrialized countries.[12]

It does not take long to work out that there is an ongoing battle on this planet between the sexes. Everywhere voices are raised comparing men and women in their abilities to do things. Those wishing to liven up a conversation only have to infer that one sex is possibly better than the other. We will look at some of the reasons why this battle continues to rage in the chapter concerning the origin of inherent life source models, but at the moment I want to take a look at the first male and female relationship described in the Bible and see what it tells us about equality.

When we looked at Genesis 2 in the last section we noted this verse:

Gen 2:20 So Adam gave names to all cattle, to the birds of the air, and to every beast of the field. But for Adam there was not found a helper comparable to him.

As Adam was naming all the animals, he noticed that every male had a female, this is evidenced from the fact that God blessed the animals in Genesis 1:22 and said be fruitful and multiply.

We notice that Adam did not seem to lack anything with reference to his vocation as a gardener, he did not lack anything in terms of his position as the head of the earthly creation. He had no trouble in naming the animals which reveals quite an extensive mind that he must have had. He also was in communion with God and receiving instruction about his environment and what was required of him. All of this Adam was engaged in before Eve was created. In terms of his position, his intellect, his vocation and relation to worship of God, he lacked nothing. The one thing that he did lack was someone that could relate to him and understand him in his environment. Someone comparable to him the Bible says. What he lacked was companionship. His lack was of a relational concern.

The creation of Eve to fill this relational need defines the nature of their equality and equality in general. While Adam probably could communicate with the animals at levels much deeper than we can today, that communication

---

12 www.MTV.com

did not satisfy him because none of the animals really understood him and how he thought about things. The wonderful thing about Eve was her capacity to understand Adam relationally. To appreciate his joys and excitement, to grasp the issues that he faced and support him in his decisions.

The creation of Eve defines the nature of human equality. It tells us that equality is relational and that this is the equality that humanity should aim for. If we compare Adam and Eve in terms of what they possess inherently, as we would do if we embraced one of the other life source models, then men and women are forced into this battle of comparison of the sexes. We begin to look at who was formed first, who is stronger, who is more beautiful, who was the most perfect design. Just thinking like this destroys the original intent of the creation of Eve.

When Adam was created he was given an inheritance from his heavenly Father. He had extensive real estate, a beautiful home, an excellent job and career prospects. He was very intelligent, very strong and of course extremely handsome. When Eve was created she inherited all of this when she became his wife and took on his name.

> **Gen 5:2** Male and female created he them; and blessed them, and called their name Adam, in the day when they were created.

It says that God called their name Adam. She took on his name and all the wealth and assets and things that Adam possessed became hers *through the relationship*. She did not earn it, she did not prove that she was worthy of being equal with him by her own abilities – everything she had came from Adam, so it is completely senseless to think in this way. By allowing ourselves to see Eve as coming forth from Adam and being given everything he possessed and being given a mind that can appreciate and understand him we find the true basis of how to conduct relationships and how to see them as equal.

> **Equality in relationships is not about power, control and assets, it is about the ability to understand and know someone and the perception of female identity in this way is the only way we can define relational equality. The woman is the key to a relational kingdom.**

Therefore recognition of this male seeding/headship identity and a female nurture/submission identity reflecting the image of the heavenly Father and

Life Matters

Son is the vital key to build a treasure of family memories upon a strong and harmonious relational system.

Chapter 7

The Origin of Inherent Life Source Models

a. The Tree of Knowledge

In Chapter 2 we looked at 3 different life source models showing that most people in the world have adopted an inherent life source model of one variation or another. Just to recap, we will show the three models again:

Model 1	Model 2	Model 3
Man has an inherent life source (the divine) that originates within himself.	Man is given a life source by God (the divine) that he possesses within himself.	Man receives life through a relationship with God (the divine) outside of himself.
MAN IS DIVINE	**MAN IS IMMORTAL**	**MAN IS MORTAL**

In this chapter we will examine the origins of independent life source models from a Biblical perspective. You will remember that in Chapter 3 we identified *Model 3* as reflecting what the Bible teaches and also the model most favourable to building a strong relational system, because only in this model are relationships truly vital. Every person is completely dependent upon the one source point of life that can only be obtained through a relationship. Now let's pick up the story in the Bible where the inherent life source models came from. You will remember in our last chapter that God told Adam not to eat from the Tree of Knowledge of Good and Evil.

> **Gen 2:16-17** And the Lord God commanded the man, saying, "Of every tree of the garden you may freely eat; **17** but of the tree of the knowledge of good and evil you shall not eat, for in the day that you eat of it you shall surely die."

We might ask the question, why did God allow such a tree to exist in the beautiful and perfect garden? Why did God allow a symbol of death to exist and be in reach of Adam and Eve? Remembering that God is love, (1 John 4:7,8) the only way for love to exist is to provide opportunity to choose against God. If Adam and Eve had no opportunity to choose against God, then they could not really experience love. Because love is an active choice of the will to be loyal and true to the one we claim to love. The Tree of Knowledge was a symbol of choice.

In obedience to the commandment "you will not eat of the tree of knowledge of good and evil," Adam and Eve were acting out their willing submission to the life flowing forth from the throne of God; (Rev 22:1) they were maintaining their relationship to Him. To choose to eat from the tree was to no longer submit to God, break the relationship and in breaking the relationship, the life would stop flowing and they would die – cease to exist. The whole process was quite simple.

b. The Serpent's Origins

As we turn from Chapter 2 of Genesis to Chapter 3, we find a series of tragic events occur that plunge the world into sin and death.

> **Gen 3:1-6** Now the serpent was more cunning than any beast of the field which the Lord God had made. And he said to the woman, "Has God indeed said, 'You shall not eat of every tree of the garden'?" **2** And the woman said to the serpent, "We may eat the fruit of the trees of the garden; **3** but of the fruit of the tree which is in the midst of the garden, God has said, 'You shall not eat it, nor shall you touch it, lest you die.'" **4** Then the serpent said to the woman, "You will not surely die. **5** For God knows that in the day you eat of it your eyes will be opened, and you will be like God, knowing good and evil." **6** So when the woman saw that the tree was good for food, that it was pleasant to the eyes, and a tree desirable to make one wise, she took of its fruit and ate. She also gave to her husband with her, and he ate.

The Origin of Inherent Life Source Models

The story introduces a serpent who apparently has the gift of speech. Secondly, we have Eve standing in front of the forbidden tree alone. It would be nice to have a bit more of the story line of how these two things occurred, but the Bible does not tell us. Who is this serpent? The Bible tells us clearly in the book of Revelation.

> **Rev 12:9** So the great dragon was cast out, that serpent of old, called the Devil and Satan, who deceives the whole world;

The serpent of old is the devil or Satan and he is a deceiver. So Satan somehow manages to impersonate or pretend to be a serpent and is speaking to Eve. Another question we must ask is where did Satan come from? If God created all things then did God create Satan? These are important questions that need to be answered if we want to get to the bottom of where inherent life source models came from.

> **Ezek 28:14-15,17** "You were the anointed cherub who covers; I established you; You were on the holy mountain of God; You walked back and forth in the midst of fiery stones. **15** You were perfect in your ways from the day you were created, Till iniquity was found in you... **17** Your heart was lifted up because of your beauty; You corrupted your wisdom for the sake of your splendor."

> **Isa 14:12-14** "How you are fallen from heaven, O Lucifer, son of the morning! How you are cut down to the ground, You who weakened the nations! **13** For you have said in your heart: 'I will ascend into heaven, I will exalt my throne above the stars of God; I will also sit on the mount of the congregation On the farthest sides of the north; **14** I will ascend above the heights of the clouds, I will be like the Most High.'"

Satan, formerly called Lucifer was the anointed cherub who stood on the holy Mountain of God. He was the most senior angel in heaven. He stood next to God in heaven. The Bible says that "you were perfect in your ways from the days you were created." So God created Lucifer perfect. But then it says that iniquity or sin/evil was found in him. What was this iniquity found in Lucifer?

We are told that Lucifer's heart was lifted up because of his beauty and splendor. It is important to remember that in God's Kingdom, only He has the power to give life; every other intelligent being can only have this life through a submissive relationship to God. Lucifer had the clear example of God's Son of how we should relate to the Father. The Son of God did not boast about His abilities, glory and splendor, He trusted implicitly in His Father and rested in His love and blessing and executed His commands faithfully.

> **John 5:30** I do not seek My own will but the will of the Father who sent Me.
>
> **John 8:29** And he that sent me is with me: the Father hath not left me alone; for I do always those things that please him.
>
> **Matt 26:39** He went a little farther and fell on His face, and prayed, saying, "O My Father, if it is possible, let this cup pass from Me; nevertheless, not as I will, but as You will."

c. The Rejection of Wisdom

But Lucifer corrupted his wisdom for the sake of his splendor. The truth is that the role of the Son of God as a divine submissive agent is the true wisdom of God. The Bible even tells us this:

> **1 Cor 1:24** Christ the power of God and the wisdom of God.

The power of God comes to us in following the example of the Son of God and this is wisdom. Proverbs puts it this way:

> **Prov 9:10** The fear of the Lord is the beginning of wisdom, And the knowledge of the Holy One is understanding.

Fear, means to submit to, respect, take seriously. A true knowledge of Christ's submission to the Father is true understanding and brings life. In refusing to follow the example of the Son of God, Lucifer was rejecting the wisdom of God; in turning away from Christ, he was cutting himself off from the only means of knowing how to connect to the source of life. In this sense Christ is the real Tree of Life of which the one planted in Eden was only a symbol. But Lucifer did not want to follow the divine example of God's Son; he chose to eat from the "Tree of Knowledge of Good and Evil." He wanted to have the same role as the Father. The Father did not submit to anyone, He was under no one's authority, He was in complete control and this is what Lucifer wanted. This aspiration was blasphemy and indeed would open the universe to the knowledge of evil.

In aspiring to be like God, he lost sight of the fact that everything he had, came from God. He also forgot that in refusing to submit to the life source, he was rejecting his only means of finding value. As we stated in Chapter 4, "The glory of children is their father." The Father through Christ had created Lucifer and therefore he was a son of God by creation. Lucifer had forgotten this very important principle:

> **Jer 9:23-24** Thus says the Lord: "Let not the wise man glory in his wisdom, Let not the mighty man glory in his might, Nor let the rich man glory in his riches; **24** But let him who glories glory in this, That he understands and knows Me, That I am the Lord, exercising lovingkindness, judgment, and righteousness in the earth. For in these I delight," says the Lord.

Lucifer sought to find glory in his splendor rather than in knowing God and being under His blessing. In the rejection of Christ and His example, Lucifer forgot that all things come ultimately from the Father. He began to believe that the things he had received were actually things he possessed in himself. Here are the seeds of the knowledge of evil.

d. Why Was Satan Allowed to Live?

One question that must be asked is: If all life comes from God and Lucifer rejected the means of obtaining that life, why didn't he die? Why didn't he cease to exist immediately? Firstly, since Lucifer was created by God, he was one of His created sons. God was longsuffering with Lucifer as he wrestled with whether he would fully reject God's authority or not. As the Bible teaches:

> **2 Pet 3:9** The Lord is not slack concerning His promise, as some count slackness, but is longsuffering toward us, not willing that any should perish but that all should come to repentance.

Secondly, if Lucifer suddenly perished without his ideas being allowed to develop, doubts could remain in the hearts of the other angels as to whether Lucifer was right. Lucifer challenged the system of God's governance; he challenged His law and questioned why they needed God's Son as an authority over the angels. Lucifer reasoned that they were intelligent enough to guide themselves without needing the example of the divine submissive agent to lead them. We see evidence of this undermining of the role of God's Son in the following Bible passages:

> **John 5:23** That all should honor the Son just as they honor the Father. He who does not honor the Son does not honor the Father who sent Him

> **Phil 2:5-6** Let this mind be in you which was also in Christ Jesus, **6** who, being in the form of God, did not consider it robbery to be equal with God.
>
> **1 John 2:23** Whoever denies the Son does not have the Father either; he who acknowledges the Son has the Father also.

As we have stated, Lucifer did not want to accept the authority of God's Son. He did not want to honour Him as he honoured the Father and he refused to see Him as equal. During this questioning time in Lucifer's mind, he convinced one third of the angels that he was right and that he had a better idea for how to govern the universe.

> **Rev 12:3-4** And another sign appeared in heaven: behold, a great, fiery red dragon having seven heads and ten horns, and seven diadems on his heads. **4** His tail drew a third of the stars of heaven and threw them to the earth.

We are told here that the dragon or serpent drew a third of the stars of heaven. Stars are an expression of God's children and the stars were from heaven, meaning the angels.

> **Job 38:7** When the morning stars sang together, And all the sons of God shouted for joy?

Lucifer had to be given time to develop his ideas so that the universe could determine which system was best. It was the only way for intelligent minds to deal with the propositions that Lucifer was making. Many times we could wish that we would just accept what God says and leave it at that, but as we all know, in nearly every case we have to learn for ourselves the truth or falsehood of something.

So God allowed Lucifer to develop his ideas to the point where Lucifer felt he could take control of the universe. His intent was to destroy the Son of God, because He was the only true example of divine submission to the life source of the Father. If he could remove Christ, he could remove the Father's authority base and collapse the whole system. How do we know that Lucifer, now Satan wanted to destroy Christ? When Jesus spoke to the Pharisees, He made this revealing statement:

> **John 8:44** You are of your father the devil, and the desires of your father you want to do. He was a murderer from the beginning, and does not stand in the truth, because there is no truth in him. When he

speaks a lie, he speaks from his own resources, for he is a liar and the father of it.

From the very beginning, Satan had thoughts of murder for Christ. The Pharisee's desire to kill Jesus was simply an echo of what Satan had wanted all along. Back in the beginning none of the angels really knew what was in Lucifer's heart, but when God allowed His Son to come to this earth and die, Satan's desires were fully revealed. So the war began.

> **Rev 12:7** And war broke out in heaven: Michael and his angels fought with the dragon; and the dragon and his angels fought,

The name Michael means "One who is like God;" it is another name for the Son of God.[13] As we stated earlier in Phil 2:6, Christ was in the form of God or "One who is like God" – "yet thought it not robbery to be equal with God".

Since Satan pressed the issue and wanted to take control, he had to be removed from heaven.

> **Rev 12:8** but they did not prevail, nor was a place found for them in heaven any longer.

In that war every angel had to choose which side they would follow. As we stated one third followed Satan. He must have been pretty convincing to take that many angels with him.

e. The Creation of Mankind Provides Answers for the Angels

While all this was taking place, God pressed ahead with His plan to create the Earth. Satan had raised questions about the position of His Son and so God designed a unique and very special creation that would help to explain the relationship between Himself and His Son. After creating all the environment, fish, bird life and animals, God said to His Son:

> **Gen 1:26** Then God said, "Let Us make man in Our image, according to Our likeness; let them have dominion over the fish of the sea, over the birds of the air, and over the cattle, over all the earth and over

---

13 There are several texts which indicate that Michael is Christ. 1 Thess 4:16 says that the Lord will descend with a shout, with the voice of the archangel. The Lord's shout is the voice of the archangel. In Daniel 10:21 Michael is referred to as Daniel's Prince. The only prince we have as human beings is Christ. Also the word angel means messenger and Christ is indeed the supreme messenger of the Father. Therefore the word angel is not restricted to created beings.

every creeping thing that creeps on the earth."

The husband and wife relationship was an image of the Father and Son relationship and would help answer questions that Satan had raised. Paul states this when he says:

> **Rom 1:19,20** because what may be known of God is manifest in them, [mankind] for God has shown it to them. **20** For since the creation of the world His invisible attributes are clearly seen, being understood by the things that are made, even His eternal power and Godhead, so that they are without excuse,

Paul clearly states, that the attributes of the Godhead can be seen in the creation and the place that is most obvious is the place where God said "Let us make man in Our image." As we stated earlier, Eve is our key earthly example of submission to a designated life source. Her role was a vital expression of what God's Son is to the Father. It was also an important lesson for the angels in heaven.

> **1 Cor 11:7-10** For a man indeed ought not to cover his head, since he is the image and glory of God; but woman is the glory of man. **8** For man is not from woman, but woman from man. **9** Nor was man created for the woman, but woman for the man. **10** For this reason the woman ought to have a symbol of authority on her head, *because of the angels.*

The submissive role of Eve to her husband was a vital piece of evidence in the war against Satan and his kingdom principles. As long as Adam and especially Eve existed, she would prove a continual reminder to the universe of the principle of submission to the life source. Satan had to get to her somehow.

It appears that God allowed Satan to come to earth, but he could only find access to Adam and Eve from the Tree of Knowledge of Good and Evil. By allowing this, God could not be accused of withholding from Adam and Eve the opportunity to *choose* to follow him, but it also was an added opportunity for Adam and Eve to show their loyalty to God and remain submitted to Him. As long as they avoided that tree, there would be no issue.

f. Humanity Embraces the Inherent Life Source System

So now we return to this tragic series of events that introduced an alternative life system model. We remember that Satan was lifted up because of his beauty and splendor, so his view of life was that it was inherent; it originates within yourself. Notice how Satan presents this concept to Eve:

> **Gen 3:1-6** Now the serpent was more cunning than any beast of the field which the Lord God had made. And he said to the woman, "Has God indeed said, 'You shall not eat of every tree of the garden'?" **2** And the woman said to the serpent, "We may eat the fruit of the trees of the garden; **3** but of the fruit of the tree which is in the midst of the garden, God has said, 'You shall not eat it, nor shall you touch it, lest you die.'" **4** Then the serpent said to the woman, "You will not surely die. **5** For God knows that in the day you eat of it your eyes will be opened, and you will be like God, knowing good and evil."

Satan moves directly to the issue that involves the power to choose – The Tree of Knowledge of Good and Evil. He then questions "Did God really say you can't eat from this tree?" This brought the expected response that to eat from the tree would break the relationship with God and therefore death would occur. This is exactly what Satan wanted her to say to allow him the opportunity to introduce his life source model of inherent power. He says "You will not surely die." This statement is the origin of the inherent life source system. Satan states clearly that you don't need to be in a close relationship with God to keep living. He then craftily links entrance into this new system with eating the fruit from the tree.

The fact is that to believe that you would not surely die means you would have to believe you were a god; for to believe that you possess your own life source is to admit divinity at some level.

The eating from the tree was to seal this belief and to cause Eve to transfer into the new kingdom. The new belief needed to be sealed with action and sadly Eve took that action. The Bible indicated that Eve was deceived or beguiled into taking this action:

> **2 Cor 11:3** But I fear, lest by any means, as the serpent beguiled Eve through his subtilty, so your minds should be corrupted from the simplicity that is in Christ.

Eve did not realize that in taking the fruit and believing she had an internal life source, she not only severed her intimate relationship with God but now carried the seeds of a rejection of her husband's headship. Eve had received everything she was via her husband, but this new belief via the serpent would radically alter her relationship to Adam. Instead of being a representation of Christ's submission to His Father, she would now reflect Satan's rebellion to the heavenly Father. Satan felt he had now eliminated the submissive principle that reflected God's kingdom on earth.

If Eve could now be an agent to convince or persuade Adam, then the designated human life source would be infected with this inherent life source model which denies the role of Christ to the Father and this would make certain that every descendent of Adam would be born with that mindset.

Of course Adam immediately grasped the situation and understood its implications. By taking the fruit and eating it, Adam willfully rejected the authority of God and now polluted the human life flow; ensuring that every human being would be infected with Satan's belief that life is inherent and we need not depend on anyone. This is the substance of what Paul means when he says:

> **Rom 5:12** Therefore, just as through one man sin entered the world, and death through sin, and thus death spread to all men, because all sinned.

The human race had now lost its vital principles of submission to the life source flowing from God. We will examine a little later how God deals with this tragedy but in the next chapter we will examine how the value system changed and how it affected the human race.

Chapter 8

The Origin and Impact of Performance Based Value Systems

Let us briefly recap what we looked at in Chapters 5 and 6 before we continue. In Chapter 5 we looked at the fact that our value is directly derived from the one that gives us life. The original source point is our Father in heaven. In Chapter 6 we saw that life flows through His submissive Son so that the Father's authority is always recognized by the Son who sets the example, for the entire universe, of how to connect to the life of the Father.

We also saw that this heavenly model is replicated on earth through the husband and wife relationship. The wife's submission establishes the authority of her husband who is God's designated channel for the life source. Her submission is also the vital example to her children of how to stay connected to the channel of life flowing through the father. As the father represents the source of life, he is also the source or seed of blessing and value. Prov 17:6 reflects this fact when it says:

> **Prov 17:6** Children's children are the crown of old men, and the glory of children is their father.

We looked at some examples of a child's yearning for their father, here is two examples once again.

> **Paul wrote:**
> Dad, I miss you everyday and just wish we could talk again. Losing you has made me question who I am and where I'm going. Can I be the Dad you were? You were the best and just wish you could have lived longer to see my accomplishments and share in that joy. Even a year later I find myself wanting to pick up the phone to call you. I love you.

Daddy's Princess wrote:
Hi Daddy, I hope you're proud of me! I'm really happy and things are going well in life. Work is a little overwhelming but I guess that's what I signed up for. I think I'm doing all the right things and I hope you approve. Miss you. Love you always, Princess.

In the example of Paul, we see the loss of his father made him question who he was; the father-child relationship directly impacts our sense of identity. We also see Paul's desire for his father to see his accomplishments, along with Daddy's Princess hoping and wishing that her Dad approves of what she is doing. In a relational system, accomplishments mean nothing without a father's or mentor's approval. It is the acknowledgment and approval of the father that makes the accomplishment valuable because only a father can bestow value on something since he is the life source for the child.

a. The Origin of Worthlessness

When Satan rejected his heavenly Father as the life source and rejected the divine example of submission by God's Son, Satan destroyed any concept of relational value. Because he was created by God his heart still yearned for the Father to acknowledge him and approve of his efforts but in his mind he had forged a path that stated that the life source originated with himself and therefore he would have to manufacture his own value. He would have to continually prove to himself that he was valuable. The intensity to prove himself is heightened by the fact that he will never again hear the Father say "This is my beloved son, whom I love."[14] And so the cycle of worthlessness was born: The constant battle of yearning for approval from the true life source and then desperately trying to fill that yearning with personal achievements. This places a person in a position where they must continually validate their existence. We saw a little of this war in the life of WR in Chapter 1. Listen again to what he said before he died:

"Help, I'm scared. Oh, I'm scared! I don't want to lose."

"Afraid to talk in class . . . Must impress others. Need to prove myself."

Fear!! Put there by yourself. . . You can't do it?

---

14 Matthew 3:17

The Origin and Impact of Performance Based Value Systems

Don't stagnate, go forward, improve.

"Need to prove myself, Must impress others." This is the direct legacy of rejecting God's life source system and believing that value comes from what you achieve. In summary, Satan is the author of worthlessness. He is the source of it and when Adam and Eve rejected God's relational system, they inherited this worthlessness and then passed it on to the whole human race.

Satan's antidote for worthlessness is hard work and then pride in what you have done. This is why there is no rest for the wicked as the Bible says because you must push yourself constantly, prove yourself and then gloat and boast of your achievements, your position, your education or whatever it is that you find value in other than a direct relationship with your heavenly Father. No one can win all the time. No one can be on top all the time and so life is dotted with moments of pride and satisfaction with long periods of striving and many episodes of feeling useless. We might see this cycle working like this.

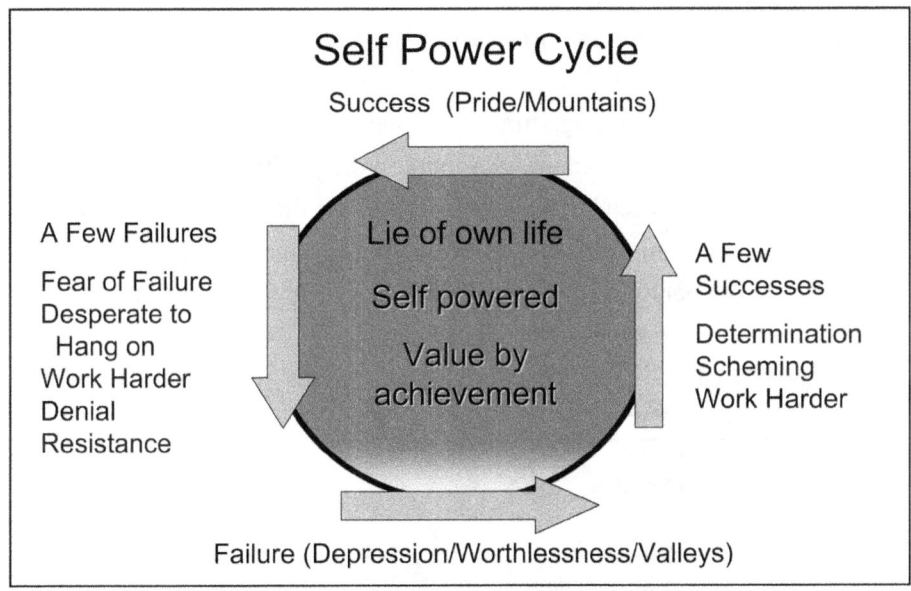

The world is littered with evidence that it has embraced an inherent life source system that breeds worthlessness. Every minute that passes in the world today yields 37 attempts by people to kill themselves,[15] because they

---

15   *The Mind Game* – Phillip Day

feel that dying is better than living and that they failed at proving their value to themselves and others.

b. Impact of Inherent Life System Model on Family Relationships and Structure

It is critical to understand that the words spoken to Eve in the garden by the serpent radically altered the relationship between Adam and Eve. In the Bible system, Eve had received all the ingredients for life from Adam and then put together by God. This fact created a relational dependency for Eve towards Adam. The second factor to consider is that if Adam planned to have children and build a family nation – he needed someone who understood him and yet provided for him an example of submission that would be transferred to his children. This submission would then enable the children to receive his blessing and give them the seeds of value. Adam could not build a relational family without Eve.

The words of the serpent broke Eve's sense of dependence on Adam. By believing the lie "you shall not surely die" she no longer needed the channel of blessing that flowed through him. Eve's sense of identity had shifted from a position of submission to Adam with relational equality, to a position exactly the same as Adam. Instead of value flowing down the channel from God, the value came from within her. Any advice coming from Adam could be seen as an attack on her personal sovereignty and a reminder that she needed help, rather than wise counsel offered for her benefit.

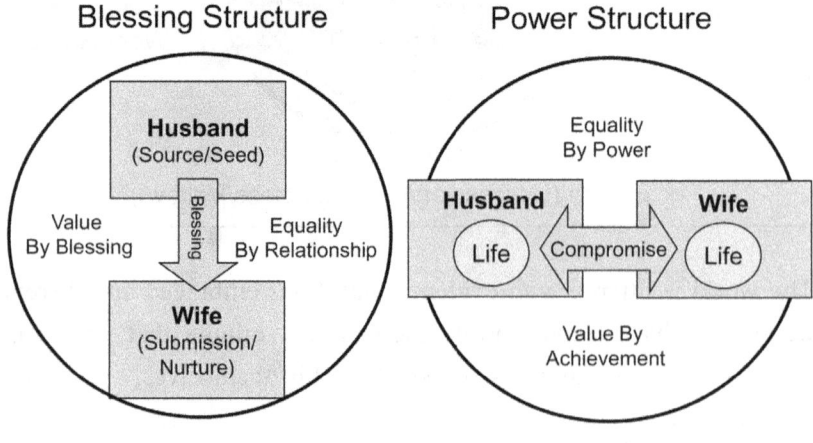

We need to remember that this concept of inherent life is a lie from Satan and Eve still emotionally needed the blessing and leadership of her husband. The conflict between her thoughts and feelings would cause confusion between a sense of need for Adam and a belief in independence from him; confusion that many men are familiar with today, typically called "go away, come here" syndrome.

Another impact of the lie on the relationship is that Adam has now lost the one person who can act as the key to receiving his blessing. Eve no longer would act in a submissive role but would demand negotiation on every decision and maintain the right to second guess any decision that Adam made. This example of Eve would be closely watched by her children and Eve would then struggle with her children demanding negotiation on every decision and maintaining the right to "second guess" her.

As children look at the parent's relationship and subconsciously evaluate it, they learn that equality means position and power. The concepts of dependence, submission and blessing are skewed, confused and muted; the glory of children is undermined.

Another impact for the relationship is that when Adam listened to the voice of his wife and ate the fruit based on her suggestion, she in fact became the head of the new world order. Just as Adam had been the visible head for God's channel of blessing, Eve had become the head of Satan's new kingdom. It is noteworthy that in many religions and cultures, the feminine is seen as the higher deity.[16] In responding to Eve's suggestion, Adam had forfeited his position of leadership and handed it to Eve. As this new system is based on the visible display of power rather than the invisible receiving of blessing, the woman would become an object of worship and veneration in many respects for the man. The visible veneration can be linked to the male obsession with pornography, the obsession of the female form.

But like Eve, Adam is under the influence of a lie and still emotionally needs the respect of his wife. This veneration for his wife versus need for respect from her can cause males to switch anywhere from from a placid child figure to an aggressive dominate, defensive man.

---

16 For more information on this, study the cults of Semiramis and Isis and the worship of the sacred feminine.

Life Matters

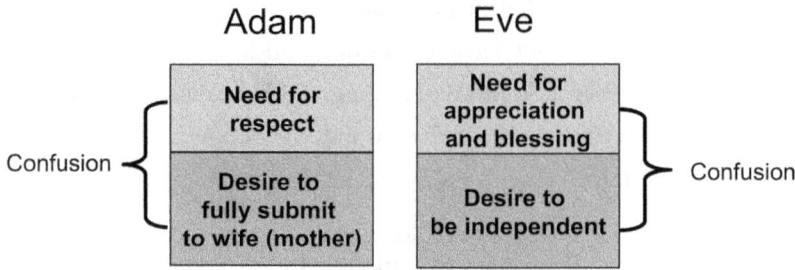

With the loss of value from his heavenly Father, and the loss of respect from his wife, Adam is extremely vulnerable to being very defensive about the decisions he makes. A simple helpful suggestion from a wife to her husband who is feeling the need for respect could open a door to Armageddon. On the other hand, a man who feels the need to submit to his wife's leadership could leave his wife feeling frustrated because he is waiting for her to always take the lead. The combinations of negative experiences that arise from this confusion brought about by the lie are seen played out in the tragedy of human history. This so-called simple little lie about having life in yourself has decimated God's family kingdom principles and if it was not for God's foresight of this situation, the human race would have exterminated itself in this confusion, worthlessness and battle for control.

As it is, this confusion leaves both men and women feeling worthless, vulnerable, prideful, controlling and selfish. I think most people can testify to this fact. The figures on depression and suicide also punctuate this point.

The punch line of this chapter is that:
1. A shift in a belief of where life comes from radically alters our identity.
2. This shift in identity breaks the vital channel of blessing that brings us value.
3. It also confuses the God given roles of men as blessing/seeders and women as submissive/nurturers.

We will shortly explore the Bible record of how this confused family structure has played out in human history and what sort of family structures have emerged under this system, but before we do this we need to observe God's response to Adam and Eve entering Satan's kingdom.

Chapter 9

Blessed Enmity

a. The Extent of the Problem

In Chapter 7, we discussed the philosophy that Adam and Eve were embracing when they ate from that tree and we discussed in the previous chapter the tragic mixture of emotions that led Satan to concoct the concept that we can live without God and form an identity of our own by what we achieve. Shortly after eating the fruit, a cloud of worthlessness and guilt slowly enveloped their minds and shut down the lovely, happy, joyful relationship between God and man. The curse of the lie from Satan had begun its insidious work and within a short period of time Adam and Eve were engulfed by guilt and fear. Along with Satan and his angels, they had mentally and emotionally suicided. They had lost their identity and worth, and nothing they could do could bring it back. They couldn't restore themselves to favour with God. They had stepped out from under the channel of blessing and only God could reconnect it.

By stepping out of this channel of blessing, Adam and Eve's reasoning powers could no longer be used selflessly or objectively. Their minds became totally in harmony with Satan. They had no ability to discern the lies they were being told.

Satan began to fill them full of false theories about God's character. They were also told that they were bad; that they deserved to die and that they were worthless individuals. Without the blessing of the Father, they had no means to resist these lies; they had nothing to cling to that could combat Satan. Outside of the channel, we are completely vulnerable to Satan and his lies.

God was faced with a very serious dilemma. How does He approach them now that they are listening to another voice? Every word that God utters is now interpreted in an evil light. Adam and Eve know they are guilty but they now have no security or worth to accept that they are wrong, having accepted wrong ideas about God, the source of life and wisdom. Controlled by a spirit of guilt and insecurity they have become defiant. They lost the blessing of reasoning clearly.

I marvel at the love of God displayed in His patience. God calls out to Adam, "Where are you?" not because He didn't know, but to allow Adam to face the issue. Where is your mind Adam? What has happened to your identity? The physical always represents the spiritual, and the physical hiding of Adam and Eve clearly reveals the hiding that was going on in their minds. They had clothed themselves in deception and deceit to prevent themselves from having to face the truth which seems so frightening. God is trying to help them diagnose the problem so he can bring the blessed solution to them.

Adam responded to the question by telling God that he was afraid because he was naked. This confession is interesting in the light of Genesis 2:25: "The man and his wife were both naked, and they felt no shame." Adam was naked before he ate the fruit but he was not ashamed. The inference here is that Adam is now ashamed. The Hebrew word (buwsh) also means confused, confounded and disappointed. Adam was full of confusion, guilt and disappointment. He was confused about whom he was and he felt guilt about what he had done. God put His finger on the intensity of Adam's pain. "Who told you that you were naked? Have you eaten from the tree that I commanded you not to eat from?" God doesn't ask Adam, "How do you know you are naked?" He asks Adam "*Who told you* that you were naked?" God was pointing Adam to the instigator of the lies he was told. In other words "Who is causing you to run away from me?" "Who has come between you and me?"

Adam was addressed directly, "Did you eat from the tree that I commanded you not to eat from?" This was a simple question that demanded a simple yes or no. Now that Adam's perception of himself and God has altered through the lie of inherent life, these questions appear threatening and invasive to him. The first words of blame and defiance pour forth from human lips:

Blessed Enmity

"The WOMAN whom YOU gave to me,
SHE gave to me of the tree and I did eat."

In this accusation, amongst other things we see the channel relationship between Adam and Eve has been completely twisted and broken. In creation, Eve was given as a help meet, but now she is portrayed as the leader and head. She is portrayed as the powerful one and Adam as the helpless victim. Worse than this, God is portrayed as the instigator of the whole affair. Adam's mind had become so confused, twisted and blinded that his recovery would have to be of the most remarkable nature.

How could Adam be given a true assessment of his situation when he has lost the power to reason objectively? God is the only source of true wisdom and Adam had disconnected himself from that source. The lie of inherent life source had completely altered the context for the universe Adam lived in. His perception of himself, his wife and God had all radically altered and through this falsehood, God's words would constantly be misunderstood. God's intervention now seems invasive and domineering; it is now a big life source telling a little life source how to act and live. The fact that God's power is apparently bigger than his brings fear, but the fact that he believes he has one of his own, brings anger, resentment and hatred. The Bible clearly reveals this:

> **Rom 8:7** The sinful mind [filled with the lie of inherent life] is hostile to God. It does not submit to God's law, [channel of blessing] nor can it do so.

> **Jer 17:9** The heart [infected with the lie of inherent life] is deceitful above all things, and desperately wicked: who can know [be intimately relational with] it?

God's cries of love, affection and counsel to come back into the submissive, dependent relationship are twisted into a picture of manipulation to gain control and domination. The great source of all is completely misrepresented and falsely accused by mankind. Most sad of all is the mournful words of Jeremiah 17:9: who can know this heart? The lie of inherent life makes the heart of man resistant to intimate relationship with God and with created beings. The fruit of this lie is loneliness. This is an extremely heavy price to pay for beings that were created to desire intimacy and relationship. This sad state is amazingly reflected in a song from a film called *The City of Angels*:

Verse 1
Spend all your time waiting
For that second chance
For a break that would make it okay
There's always one reason
To feel not good enough
And it's hard at the end of the day
I need some distraction
Oh beautiful release
Memory seeps from my veins
Let me be empty
And weightless and maybe
I'll find some peace tonight

Verse 2
So tired of the straight line
And everywhere you turn
There's vultures and thieves at your back
And the storm keeps on twisting
You keep on building the lie *[inherent life source]*
That you make up for all that you lack
It don't make no difference
Escaping one last time
It's easier to believe in this sweet madness oh
This glorious sadness that brings me to my knees

The question that must be asked is how could God penetrate this lie? How could He communicate with us effectively and reveal His love and concern for us and extract us from this horrible lie?

b. The Solution

God could not approach us from the outside directly; instead He chose to become permanently connected to the human race through His Son. By allowing His Son to become one of us, He could reconnect the channel of blessing to continue the life and blessing stream but also place Himself in a position to confront this lie head-on. This lie resided in the nature of man and by taking this nature upon Himself, He could overcome it and destroy it. It was not enough for Jesus to simply appear like a human and demonstrate the correct relationship to God – this would not tackle the lie of inherent life source. He had to take the rebellious nature into Himself and destroy it in the grave. So the Bible states:

> **Heb 2:14** Forasmuch then as the children are partakers of flesh *[human nature physical and moral]* and blood, he also himself likewise took part of the same; that through death he might destroy him that had the power of death, *[though the lie of inherent life]* that is, the devil;
>
> **Heb 2:16,17** For verily he took not on him the *[submissive, dependent]* nature of angels; but he took on *him* the *[rebellious, independently minded]* seed of Abraham. **17** Wherefore in all things it behoved him to be made like unto *his* brethren, that he might be a merciful and faithful high priest in things *pertaining* to God, to make reconciliation for the sins of the people.
>
> **Rom 8:32-34** He that spared not his own Son, but delivered him up for us all, how shall he not with him also freely give us all things? **33** Who shall lay any thing to the charge of God's elect? *It is* God that justifieth. **34** Who *is* he that condemneth? *It is* Christ that died, yea rather, that is risen again, who is even at the right hand of God, who also maketh intercession for us.

All of these things would be provided through the gift of God's Son to the world. This whole process was outlined to Adam and Eve in Genesis 3:15:

> And I will put enmity between you and the woman, and between your seed and her Seed; He shall bruise your head, And you shall bruise His heel."

This verse is so full of promise and hope. God said He would put enmity between Satan and the woman; He would do this by allowing His Son to become one with us and reconnecting the channel of blessing. This channel would allow physical life to continue to flow to us as well as encourage correct thoughts about God to influence our minds. The reconnection of the channel in the person of the Son of God would give mankind a conscience and a choice. Both thought streams would now flow through the human race: one from the first Adam which expresses the lie of independence and results in death; the other from the Second Adam which encourages obedience and dependence along with life to give us time to choose which side we would follow. Hence we are told:

> **1 Cor 15:45** And so it is written, The first man Adam was made a living soul; the last Adam *was made* a quickening *[life giving]* spirit
>
> **Rom 5:17** For if by one man's offence death reigned by one; much more they which receive abundance of grace and of the gift of righteousness shall reign in life by one, Jesus Christ.)

It made complete sense that the Son of God should become one of us and challenge this independent spirit because the Son is the divine expression of submission and obedience. His entire identity and purpose is connected with this principle and therefore He was the only one who could engage this mission.

We have much to be thankful for. God has placed in our hearts a desire to do right and a desire to resist evil through His Son. Think about the times you have been tempted to do something wrong and then thought better of it and did not do it. This was the gift that God has given you, the enmity against evil. It does not matter whether you believe in God or not, you still are given this gift through Jesus. We are told in Scripture that God makes the rain to fall on the good and the bad.[17] Think about how many times Satan has placed an evil thought in someone's mind to do something to you or to take your possessions and the enmity placed in their hearts by God encouraged them not to do it. Of course we still have the choice to reject that prompting and go ahead and commit evil but if that enmity was not there, none of us would be able to stop carrying out the evil inherent life source thoughts placed in our minds.

What an incredible God to do all this for us! We as a race of people were totally lost and enslaved to Satan's evil ways. We were totally beyond helping ourselves, doomed to misery and total destruction. But our tender heavenly Father refused to give up on us. He has given to us the most precious thing He has – His Son. Jesus will forever be one of the human family and one of us. It is a sacrifice that will be the central theme for study and meditation for the rest of eternity.

The fact that man now had two seeds of thought coming to him, two streams of humanity would emerge; those who listened to the voice of God as exemplified in the person of Abel and Abraham and those who would refuse the Spirit of Christ pleading in them as reflected in the lives of Cain and Nimrod.

---

17   Matthew 5:45

Chapter 10

The Development of the Two Life Source Systems

From our journey thus far, we have laid down the principles of the contrasting life source systems and their immediate impact on the family. As you will recall, our reason for considering these things is for the purpose of finding the best way to build a family treasure of memories that will emotionally support and strengthen us and our children and prevent us from suffering the numerous tragedies we see occurring in families today.

In this chapter we will closely examine the development of the human race as they respond to the two principles of life. We see an initial example in the lives of Cain and Abel.[18] These men exemplify well the impact of the two systems of thought. The self-determined spirit[19] of Cain led him to be a wavering, insecure, sullen murdering tyrant;[20] while Abel was an obedient and faithful servant of God.

These two men are the beginning of several instructive examples that we find in the book of Genesis. We will trace these examples through the two systems:

1. The sons of God, meaning those who acknowledged their connection to God and
2. The giants (or better translated – a bully or tyrant) who embraced the lie given by Satan in the garden.

---

18 Genesis 4
19 A spirit that rejects the channel of God's blessing.
20 Genesis 4:12. fugitive – waver, stagger, shake. Vagabond – wander, deplore, taunt, mourn.

a. The Rise of the Tyrant

The book of Genesis is, among other things, a history of Satan's war on the family and a consolidation of his principles of inherent life source. The tragedies are many and the highlights are few but the history provided is very instructive for learning about the family.

Genesis 4:19 indicates the first major departure from marriage that reflects the Father and Son relationship. Lamech took two wives. The introduction of a second wife confused the channel of blessing process and made the wives vulnerable to competing for the affection of their one husband. Chapter 6 of Genesis reveals the next major tactic of Satan to destroy families.

> **Gen 6:2** That the sons of God saw the daughters of men that they *were* fair; and they took them wives of all which they chose.

The word "son" gives the sense of a builder of the family name. The sons of God then, were men who wished to build the family kingdom of God and extend the principles of dependent life source and the vital nature of blessing.

The daughters of men were raised in families that lived without the principle of submission and the importance of the blessing. Satan enticed the sons of God to marry these women. The Bible states that these women were fair or beautiful. This could only be in an external sense for the children they bore were tyrants and bullies.[21] The inference here is that daughters who lack the blessing of God through their fathers will gravitate towards a focus on beautifying themselves externally to compensate for the lack of blessing.

Sadly, the sons of God did not look for the inward beauty of a nurturing woman who understood the vital role of a submissive nurturer who would draw down the blessing of God through her husband upon her children. The union of the sons of God with insecure daughters of men turned their families from builders of God's family name to builders of Satan's kingdom. Since the wives were not of a submissive spirit, there was no example in the home for the children to learn submission and connection to the blessing. Such children rose to be men of renown: meaning men who sought power, glory and honour through a spirit of independence.

Within a short space of time, the role of the submissive agent was

---

21 Nephilim: a bully or tyrant: giant. Strongs H5303

completely lost and the blessing of God was largely cut off. And the result was:

> **Gen 6:5** ...that the wickedness of man *was* great in the earth, and *that* every imagination of the thoughts of his heart *was* only evil continually.

> **Rom 1:21-23** Because that, when they knew God, they glorified *him* not as God, neither were thankful; but became vain in their imaginations, and their foolish heart was darkened. **22** Professing themselves to be wise, they became fools, **23** And changed the glory of the uncorruptible God into an image made like to corruptible man, and to birds, and fourfooted beasts, and creeping things.

Within a period of just over 1500 years, the human family blessing structure had been virtually obliterated. The image of the Father and Son relationship, which should have been reflected in the husband and wife relationship, was replaced with vain imaginations of inherent power and the worship of "inherent power" in nature. The union of the sons of God with the daughters of men had produced tyrants that only thought evil continually. Insecure wavering boys in men's bodies that served their lusts and desires and had no regard for the sacred responsibility of raising children that are honest, firm and true. They extended the worship of the feminine from the seed of Adam's hearkening to his wife's voice and made themselves fully the tools of Satan.

The first few chapters of Genesis should be enough to convince us of the horrific effects of Satan's lie of inherent life source and the impacts of the loss of blessing to children.

So great was the misery of men in this age that God had to wash the world clean. Who can speak of the trauma and tragedy of children born into these families without the blessing of God flowing through their fathers? God intervened by calling Noah and giving the heavenly family model a chance to start again. But Satan did not have to wait long for an opportunity.

b. Ham Develops the Seed of Babylon

Although the world was washed clean of evil and the limitless pain of broken families had ceased, the seeds of the lie of the serpent remained residual in the family of Noah. Noah had found grace in the eyes of the Lord and was a faithful servant of God, but like Adam his forefather, the medium of appetite opened the door to woe once again.

Noah became drunk and lay naked in his tent. His youngest son Ham discovered his father in this state and the Bible indicates that when Noah awoke he knew that something had been done to him. It must have been serious because Noah pronounces the following:

> **Gen 9:25** And he said, Cursed *be* Canaan; a servant of servants shall he be unto his brethren.

The text suggests that some form of sexual perversion took place on Ham's part. Whatever Ham did to his father, it revealed his lack of respect and consequently broke the channel of blessing. Whatever happened, deep inside, Ham knew that it was wrong and would feel the spirit of Cain overtake him: a wanderer, a vagabond and a deeply insecure man.

The loss of the close connection with his father cut the blessing from Ham which in turn cursed his son Canaan.

> **Gen 10:6,8-9** And the sons of Ham; Cush, and Mizraim, and Phut, and Canaan... **8** And Cush begat Nimrod: he began to be a mighty one in the earth. **9** He was a mighty hunter before the LORD: wherefore it is said, Even as Nimrod the mighty hunter before the LORD.

Canaan was the youngest of Ham's sons, but the oldest was Cush and it was through Ham's first born that the seeds of insecurity through the lack of blessing would manifest most powerfully. Cush's son was Nimrod who became a mighty hunter. The word mighty has a similar idea to the giants of Genesis 6 who were men of renown. The word means powerful warrior and tyrant. Nimrod fully embraced the lie of the serpent concerning inherent power. Josephus makes this interesting comment concerning him:

> "Now it was Nimrod who excited them to such an affront and contempt of God. He was the grandson of Ham, the son of Noah, a bold man, and of great strength of hand. He persuaded them not to ascribe it [Strength] to God, as if it was through his means they were happy, but to believe that it was their own courage which procured that happiness. [22]

The same contempt that Ham manifested towards his father became the inheritance of Nimrod. The rejection of the authority of an earthly father is a rejection of the heavenly Father and we see all these seeds manifested in Nimrod.

---

22 Josephus *Antiquities* Book 1 Chapter 4 Para. 2

The Development of the Two Life Source Systems

We notice that Nimrod persuaded the people not to believe that strength or life came from God, but that it came from within themselves. This belief completely destroyed the channel of blessing and entrenched human thinking in finding happiness, worth and value in their own achievements and displays of power. With this in mind we read:

> **Gen 10:10** And the beginning of his kingdom was Babel, and Erech, and Accad, and Calneh, in the land of Shinar.

The Bible indicates that Nimrod built his own kingdom without any reference to God. No man had ever done this before. While previous men had lived apart from God and resisted His authority, they still operated with some semblance to a family model. They had not dared to declare themselves the highest authority in the land and that all people should look no further than an earthly king.

> With the setting up of Nimrod's kingdom, the entire ancient world entered a new historical phase. The oriental tradition which makes that warrior the first man who wore a kingly crown, points to a fact more significant than the assumption of a new ornament of dress, or even the conquest of a province. His reign introduced to the world a new system of relations between the governor and the governed. The authority of former rulers had rested upon the feeling of kindred, and the ascendancy of the chief was an image of parental control. Nimrod, on the contrary, was a sovereign of territory, and of men just so far as they were its inhabitants, and irrespective of personal ties. Hitherto there had been tribes—enlarged families—Society; now there was a nation, a political community—the State.[23]

The Bible indicates that the first city he ruled was Babel or Babylon. The city of Babylon has become synonymous with the concept of rebellion and rejection of Godly authority. It is this city and its principles that is at war with God and His family blessing principles.[24] As noted above the connection between headship and submission was no longer a family relation of father to wife, son or daughter, but rather a connection through territory and held in submission through tyranny. Notice Josephus again:

> He also gradually changed the government into tyranny, seeing no other way of turning men from the fear of God, but to bring them into

---

23 A.T Jones. *Empires of the Bible*. 1904 Page 51
24 Des Griffin. *Fourth Reich of the Rich*. 2001. Page 21.

a constant dependence on his power...²⁵

He further attacked the family structure by reversing the family roles of headship and submission by marrying his mother Semiramis.²⁶

c. The Spiritual Foundations of Babylon

If we look closely at the history of the man who built Babylon, we observe the following characteristics:

1. Perverted family relationships.	The effect of Ham's act towards his father is revealed in his genealogy and its corresponding curse as reflected in Nimrod marrying his mother.
2. Rejection of family blessing and authority structure.	Dominion ruled by territory rather than the affection of family ties. The forming of his own kingdom apart from God.
3. Insecurity, worthlessness and confused identity.	The loss of the family blessing caused Nimrod to seek worship by becoming a mighty one. The name Babylon means confusion.
4. Controlling.	The attribute of tyranny is the spirit of the need to control others by force, since there is no connection via family ties to cause respect. The desire for empire is reflected in the list of territories attributed to his ownership.

The manifestation of Nimrod and his kingdom of kingly power and control was the natural result of the rejection of the family structure established by God in the Garden of Eden. Wherever there is war, strife and desire for power and control, there we might discern the seeds and wine of Babylon. History shows that the entire world adopted Nimrod's system and the Bible reflects this when it states:

Jer 51:7 Babylon *hath been* a golden cup in the LORD'S hand, that

---
25   Josephus. *Antiquities* Book 1 Chapter 4 Para. 2
26   Alexander Hislop, *The Two Babylons*, Loizeaux Brothers, Inc. 1916 Page 22

made all the earth drunken: the nations have drunken of her wine; therefore the nations are mad.

The shift of policy by Nimrod to rule by territory and to keep people submitted to his authority required armies of men to defend the territory gained against external threats and to keep the population under control to avert internal threats. The provision for armies had to be paid for and thus taxation was introduced.

With the loss of parental love and blessing as the foundation of the community and the motivating desire to provide and support each other being dominated by other priorities, another motivation had to be developed and thus came forth the system of money and banking.

> Nimrod was the first ruler to form an army and establish economic, civil and social systems. He imposed his Satanic religion on all the vanquished peoples. In time, his pagan teachings spread to and held sway over all the nations of the world.[27]

Nimrod not only invaded literal territory, he also invaded the mind and introduced a religion that would reflect his beliefs of inherent power and perverted human relationships. This religion was embodied in the worship of the Sun. When Nimrod died, his wife/mother carried on the religion by teaching the people that Nimrod was now embodied in the Sun and was a benefactor by day and fought against the forces of evil in the underworld by night. As each day that the Sun rose, the people could rest safely in the knowledge that Nimrod was victorious over the dark forces and so the people bowed toward the Sun in thanks and gratitude to Nimrod for protecting them.[28]

Semiramis now acted as the key bridge builder to the spiritual world of Nimrod and communicated his wishes to the people and acted as an intercessor on their behalf. Holding this position elevated her to the role of a goddess and she in turn was worshipped like her son/husband as the queen of heaven.[29]

While there is much interesting history here, the key point is that the whole system of territory, money, taxation, armies and kingship have developed from a breakdown in God's original family system. The entire system is at war with God's original principles of family authority and blessing. This does not mean

---

27 Griffin, Page 24
28 Carol Humphreys. *Real Myths and False Realities*. Page 36
29 Ibid.

that we should rebel against the leaders that exist today for God has granted them power to rule in this new system to show the full extent of its tyranny. We can though, discern the platform upon which it is based and avoid the influences both obvious and subtle that undermine the building of a family treasure.

d. The Calling of Abraham and the Recovering of the Family System

Just as God had called Noah as a witness against the tyranny of the antediluvian "Giants", so now God calls a man to represent His family principles of headship, submission, blessing and equality through relationship. Under the authority of his father, Abraham made the deeply significant journey out of Babylon and into Canaan.

> **Gen 11:31** And Terah took Abram his son, and Lot the son of Haran his son's son, and Sarai his daughter in law, his son Abram's wife; and they went forth with them from Ur of the Chaldees, to go into the land of Canaan;

This journey by Abraham is representative of all who seek to leave the tyrannical system of Nimrod which crushes and destroys the hopes of building a lasting family treasure in its iron teeth. This journey would be taken twice by Abraham's descendents[30] and twice by his spiritual descendents.[31]

The rebuilding of the family system required the reconnecting of the channel of blessing through the patriarchal headship of Abraham.

> **Gen 12:1-3** Now the LORD had said unto Abram, Get thee out of thy country, and from thy kindred, and from thy father's house, unto a land that I will shew thee: **2** And I will make of thee a great nation, and I will bless thee, [reconnect the channel] and make thy name great; and thou shalt be a blessing: [a channel of blessing] **3** And I will bless them that bless thee, [submit to your fatherly authority] and curse him that curseth thee: [rejects the authority I have given you] and in thee shall all families of the earth be blessed.

Here is a deeply significant covenant between God and Abraham. The

---

30   First from Egypt and then from Babylon
31   First in the times of Christ and the Apostles and again after the 1260 years of Babylonian captivity, ruled by the iron fist of the medieval church.

submission of Abraham to God[32] would open again the vitally needed sense of worth and value that comes from being connected to the life source of the universe. Through Abraham all the families of the earth would be blessed, not only because that through his descendents, the Saviour of the world would come, but also because God would teach him correct family principles for preserving the channel of blessing.

e. The Lesson of Sodom

As a means of preserving the principles given to him, Abraham moved away from the city where the principles of money, territory, control and domination had a greater influence on the soul. Those that Abraham had left behind in the cities had so corrupted themselves that once again the thoughts of men were only evil continually and the family structures were so mangled that life for most was only misery, pain, abuse and slavery. The sexual perversion of Ham, developed and nurtured by Nimrod and Semiramis, lived on strongly in the inhabitants of Sodom and Gomorrah.[33]

The Lord in His mercy once again moves in to stop the pain and anguish, but before He does, the Bible opens for us a series of God's thoughts concerning Abraham and his instruction in family principles.

> **Gen 18:17-19** And the LORD said, Shall I hide from Abraham that thing which I do; **18** Seeing that Abraham shall surely become a great and mighty nation, and all the nations of the earth shall be blessed in him? **19** For I know [have known] him, that he will command his children and his household after him, and they shall keep the way of the LORD, to do justice and judgment; that the LORD may bring upon Abraham that which he hath spoken of him.

The Lord wants Abraham to understand the reasons for the destruction of Sodom and Gomorrah. This destruction would act as a warning and a reminder to Abraham to be vigilant in maintaining the family channel of blessing and averting the rise tyranny that always results when that channel in broken.

We are told that God "knows Abraham" or has known him. This word "know" is exactly the same word that describes the process of Adam "knowing" his wife Eve. The spiritual concept of knowing is the transfer of spiritual seed

---

32 Genesis 22:18
33 Genesis 19:4,5

that will bear fruit in a mighty yet peaceful family kingdom. This spiritual seed (which is the Spirit of Christ) would become the blessed spiritual inheritance of all those who would claim Abraham as their father.[34]

Genesis 18:17-19 lays out for us the secret of preserving the channel of blessing and retaining the spiritual seed that would enable its sons and daughters to resist the lie of the serpent made manifest in the tyrannical kingdoms of the world. Here is the sequence:

1. Command his family and household after him,
2. Which enables them "to keep the way of the Lord,"
3. Which enables them "to do justice and judgment" – meaning honest and right family government.
4. In this way, the promise of the covenant to become a great and mighty nation would be fulfilled.

The starting point for this process begins with the commanding or setting in order his family. If we look closely at this structure in the Bible, we see a man that is greatly respected and loved – especially by his wife. This respect turns into words of blessing that acts as righteous seed in the next generation and therefore preserves the channel of blessing.

> **1 Pet 3:6** Even as Sara obeyed Abraham, calling him lord: whose daughters ye are, as long as ye do well, and are not afraid with any amazement.

Sarah's reference to Abraham as lord, written here by the apostle Peter in the Greek gives a sense of "master" or "sir." Through the instruction of the Lord and through life's trials Sarah discerned the vital submissive role she played in establishing the authority of her husband which in turn would release the channel of blessing.

Satan tried desperately to destroy Abraham's family structure and again, he tried to attack the one who would be the vital submissive agent. When Abraham traveled to Egypt, in fear he asked Sarah to tell Pharaoh that she was his sister so that he would not be killed for her beauty and taken.[35]

Sarah was taken by Pharaoh and he may have intended to marry her, but

---

34   Rom 4:11 And he received the sign of circumcision, a seal of the righteousness of the faith which he had yet being uncircumcised: that he might be the father of all them that believe, though they be not circumcised; that righteousness might be imputed unto them also:
35   Genesis 12:12-20

The Development of the Two Life Source Systems

God intervened and plagued Pharaoh with mighty plagues to alert him that something was wrong. Sarah was restored to her husband and they were told to leave, but the point is clear that immediately after the promise of a rebuilt family blessing structure, Satan tried to sabotage it and he targeted Sarah because of her vital role in opening the channel of blessing.

Learning from his experiences, we see the great care Abraham took in selecting a wife for his son Isaac. He discerned that the key to building the family kingdom would be to find a wife that would act as the submissive agent and respect Isaac in such a way as to keep open the channel of blessing.[36]

In this chapter, we have explored the roots of the spiritual controversy that rages today around the vital nature of the family unit. We have seen the rise of empire through the seed of the serpent in the lives of Nimrod and Semiramis; and we have been given hope in the call of Abraham and his family, through whom we shall be blessed if we bless him, meaning that we recognize in his family structure the secret of true greatness and the promise of a happy family treasure.

---

[36] Genesis 24

Chapter 11

Underlying Belief Systems of the Two Kingdoms

It will be helpful to take a moment to contrast the belief systems of Abraham and Nimrod. The core difference of the two systems is the belief in an inherent life source as opposed to life that comes to us via a Father in heaven.

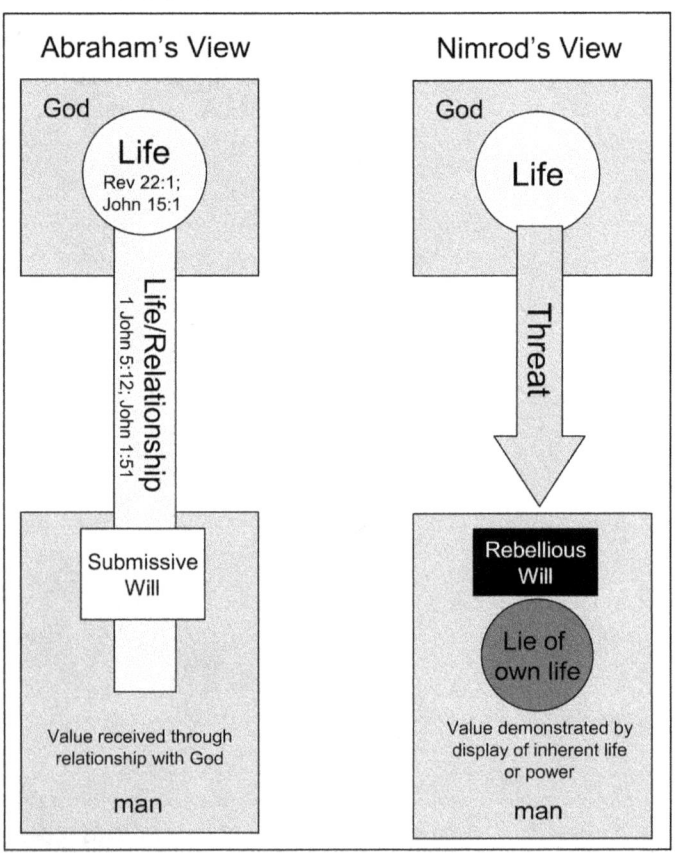

a. Faith versus Fear

Abraham's focus on a relational view is the inevitable outcome of a belief that he depends on a relationship for life. The nature of the relationship is expressed as a Father to his children. Abraham's belief that the one who gives him life is a tender Father, reduces the need to be overly concerned about protecting his own life. Concerns for protection and defense are not a high priority. For this reason, Abraham is happy to live in rural areas, without walled cities and the need for large groups of people herding together for increased security.

After Adam and Eve accepted the serpent's lie of inherent life, one of the first emotions that Adam experienced was fear.

> **Gen 3:10** And he said, I heard thy voice in the garden, and I was afraid, because I *was* naked; and I hid myself.

The result of believing you have your own life source requires you to protect it. As God approached Adam to question him, Adam perceived God as a threat because God was more powerful than he was.

This experience was the inheritance of Nimrod and those with him who believed the lie of the serpent. They needed to gather together in cities and build walls around them to protect themselves from perceived threats. This fear turned to aggression with the raising of armies to defend the cities and then finally the fear extended to pre-emptive strikes to ensure no neighbouring tribes would become stronger than themselves and conquer them. The belief in inherent life source causes every person or group of people to be seen as a threat or an opportunity that must be monitored and controlled if possible or appeased for survival. To successfully monitor those around you and warn them to keep their distance, territorial domains were established and defended. Nimrod's kingdom driven by fear is afflicted with the obsession of territorial possession and defense.

b. Family Focus versus Individual Focus

Abraham's view of life flowing from a heavenly Father that blesses His children translates into a focus on submitting to and receiving that blessing. The headship of the heavenly Father and the submission of His Son are reflected in the roles of husband and wife and are manifested in the differing roles of seed and nurture. Each member of the family plays their part for the happiness of the whole family. Notice the blessing structure spoken of by God to Abraham.

> **Gen 12:2-3** And I will make of thee a great nation, and I will bless thee, and make thy name great; and thou shalt be a blessing: **3** And I will bless them that bless thee, and curse him that curseth thee: and in thee shall all families of the earth be blessed.

God speaks of the blessing of individuals through family structures. The principle of submission demonstrated by Sarah who recognized that God's blessing flowed through her husband referred to him as "Adon" from which we get "Adoni" or master. The belief in life flowing forth from one point fosters the principles of headship, submission, blessing and interdependence. Sarah and the children depend on Abraham for the blessing to flow to them and Abraham is dependent on his family to establish his authority. The sacred ties of family relationship cannot be broken; therefore each member of the family has a very clear identity and purpose as part of the family.

> **Gen 18:19** For I know him, that he will command his children and his household after him, and they shall keep the way of the LORD, to do justice and judgment; that the LORD may bring upon Abraham that which he hath spoken of him.

Nimrod by contrast, is driven by the need to protect and satisfy the life source he believes resides within him. Because every person is potentially seen as a threat or an opportunity – no relationships can be truly benevolent;[37] they must be constantly monitored, manipulated or appeased. Nimrod and his followers can have the appearance of a family with the elements of father, mother and children but the relationships are usually very dysfunctional. Each person tends to use other family members to satisfy personal needs and desires. It is good for a man to have a wife to avoid being lonely, to have someone clean up after him and cook his food. It is good for a woman to be married for protection and companionship.

Nimrod's personal ambition caused him to marry his mother simply because she was externally beautiful and also powerful. So the family structure

---

37 It is interesting to observe the threat and opportunity based themes in evolutionary based nature programs like those produced by David Attenborough. The lie of the serpent of inherent power permeates at many levels.

of Nimrod becomes son/husband and mother/wife. This process caused role confusion and therefore identity confusion. The confusion of male and female is further complicated by the loss of the submissive agent to teach the next generation the principles of submission. This fact fosters the rebellion of children and the need for force, manipulation or appeasement by parents to keep children in check or satisfied.

c. Worship as Expressed Through the Sabbath versus Sun-day

The worship of Abraham centres on the Father/Creator of the universe. It is the worship of a personal God who gives life. God taught Abraham His laws that would enable him to stay connected to the life of God and this connection was ratified by a covenant.

> **Gen 26:5** Because that Abraham obeyed my voice, and kept my charge, my commandments, my statutes, and my laws.

The key command that identified the God that Abraham worshipped was the Sabbath. It was a memorial of the Creator God and required its worshippers to rest from their labours and rest in the works of God. This resting process was a reminder that all life comes from God and that humans are totally dependent on Him. The very nature of the Sabbath was relational because relationships are carved in time; there are no visible objects of worship, but only time to commune with the invisible and infinite God. This worship is contemplative, peaceful and joyful.

> **Isa 26:3** Thou wilt keep *him* in perfect peace, *whose* mind *is* stayed *on thee*: because he trusteth in thee.

Nimrod's worship system revolves around the display of one's inherent life source and therefore demands visible tokens of power. The most powerful object in our solar system is the sun. The sun makes the crops grow, the sun gives warmth and light to the homes of men. In this context, the worship of the sun is the worship of inherent power. When Nimrod died, his mother/wife declared that he now lived on in the sun, so now the inanimate object of the sun now had a relational connection in the person of Nimrod who they now could worship. Each morning as the sun rose, the worshippers would bow at sunrise to the mighty power of Nimrod the mighty hunter displayed in the power of the sun. Since Nimrod was merely a man, this worship was essentially a worship of self and the belief of life in one's self. This worship of heavenly bodies extended to the planets and stars, but a special day was reserved for the sun each week called Sun-day.

The only concepts of law in Nimrod's kingdom is do whatever pleases you or do whatever you can get away with. The only master for Nimrod was himself and any law presented to him would be seen as an attempt to dominate and control.

d. Resurrection versus Immortality

Abraham's view of death was that all consciousness ceased. Death is viewed as an extended sleep where there is no awareness of his environment or perspective of time. Since man has no life in himself, he ceases to exist when he dies. The only way to live on is through resurrection by the life giver which is God.

> **Heb 11:17-19** By faith Abraham, when he was tried, offered up Isaac: and he that had received the promises offered up his only begotten *son*, **18** Of whom it was said, That in Isaac shall thy seed be called: **19** Accounting that God *was* able to raise *him* up, even from the dead; from whence also he received him in a figure.

The acceptance of the reality of death by Abraham brought to this world through Adam, is a reaffirmation that man has no life in himself and is the perfect counterpart to the worship of the Sabbath which points us to the source of all life – God. The acceptance of the curse of death makes real the sacrifice of the lamb that Abraham offered upon an altar.

> **Gen 12:8** And he removed from thence unto a mountain on the east of Bethel, and pitched his tent, *having* Bethel on the west, and Hai on the east: and there he builded an altar unto the LORD, and called upon the name of the LORD.

The reality of death demands a belief in a Saviour that restores life, one who reconnects the channel of blessing. In the worship of the slain lamb Abraham recognizes the death of the coming Saviour who provides his every breath and every heart beat.

Underlying Belief Systems of the Two Kingdoms

The lie of the serpent caused Nimrod and his followers to see death as a transition into another realm. One who possessed immortality could not die but only move on to another place as we see demonstrated in the story of Nimrod passing into the sun and becoming even more powerful. In Nimrod's kingdom death is not real but rather a door. The concept of a Saviour in this context is not one who restores life but one who through his great power liberates the righteous and subdues the wicked. There is no focus on personal sin and the consequences of the curse of Adam on the human race. The Saviour of Nimrod's kingdom is a liberator and conqueror. It is interesting to note that this is exactly who the Jewish people looked for as a Messiah.

The differences we have discussed are laid out in the following table:

Abraham	Nimrod
1. Family Structure (Gen 18:19)	1. Individual Dictator/Tyrant (Gen 10:10)
2. Nomadic Rural Dwellers (Heb 11:8-10)	2. City Builders and Defenders (Gen 11:4)
3. Identity by Parental Blessing (Gen 12:2)	3. Identity by Renown (Gen 11:4)
4. Observe Sabbath and Commandments (Gen 26:5)	4. Follow Personal Desires (Rom 1:21-32)
5. Belief in Death and Resurrection (Heb 11:17-19)	5. Belief in Immortality of the Soul (Gen 3:4)
6. Saviour as Humble Life Restorer – Revealed in Slain Lamb (John 11:25)	6. Saviour as Prideful Liberator and Subduer Empowered by Sun and Nature Worship
7. Focus of Worship on the Invisible	7. Focus of Worship on the Visible

Chapter 12

Trials and Triumphs of God's Earthly Family in Genesis

The book of Genesis is full of instructive examples of how God's family system was challenged, tested and at times broken. After the collapse of the first family of Adam due to the tyrannical behaviour of the giants or men of renown, God called Noah to restart the family system but soon after it failed again and the whole world embraced the lie of the inherent life source. So God called Abraham to be His representative and reflect His kingdom. From Genesis 12 till the end of the book we are privileged to observe crucial aspects of three generations of Abraham's family line. As we closely look at the lives of the patriarchs we will discover real examples and warnings of how to build a solid family structure for our treasure of memories.

a. The Challenge of Association and Environment

In Genesis 12:1, God tells Abraham to leave the country that he lived in and to leave behind his extended family. Abraham's family originated from Ur in the land of Babylon. This was the heart of Nimrod's false worship system. Everything about the Babylonian culture reinforced the lie of inherent life source and was a negative influence on building a family system based on God's principles.

For Abraham to leave behind everything that was familiar to him and break the close family ties that he held would have been difficult, but he chose to obey God's command. The cities of today are modeled on the exact same principles as the one Abraham lived in – the exaltation of man, self gratification

Trials and Triumphs of God's Earthly Family in Genesis

and varying levels of control (job, taxes, media, peer pressure, education system). Leaving the city for a more rural environment often poses a number of hurdles that many are not willing to climb over. The leaving of friends and comforts behind seems too hard; and so many families live in the cities exposing themselves philosophically, emotionally, culturally and spiritually to principles that are totally opposed to God's family system. City life, in most cases, is a great barrier to building a treasure of family memories.

The lesson of environment is further presented in the story of Lot. Lot was Abraham's nephew and had traveled with him out of Babylon. The growth of their respective flocks became so large that it became impossible to share resources from one area in such a large group.

> **Gen 13:5-6** And Lot also, which went with Abram, had flocks, and herds, and tents. 6 And the land was not able to bear them, that they might dwell together: for their substance was great, so that they could not dwell together.

Abraham invited Lot to choose the direction he wanted to go. If Lot wanted to go left, Abraham would go right. If Lot wanted to go right, Abraham would go left. If Lot had followed God's system of submission, he would have asked Abraham to pray and decide what he felt was best for both of them. As Abraham's nephew, Lot was in Abraham's channel of blessing and he would have been blessed in submitting to the wisdom and leadership of his Uncle.

Lot was influenced by a desire for possessions, wealth and ease, in the same manner as the men of Babylon. He made a power based decision rather than a relational one and he chose the land that was most fertile and was near the city of Sodom.

> **Gen 13:10-13** And Lot lifted up his eyes, and beheld all the plain of Jordan, that it *was* well watered every where, before the LORD destroyed Sodom and Gomorrah, *even* as the garden of the LORD, like the land of Egypt, as thou comest unto Zoar. 11 Then Lot chose him all the plain of Jordan; and Lot journeyed east: and they separated themselves the one from the other. 12 Abram dwelled in the land of Canaan, and Lot dwelled in the cities of the plain, and pitched *his* tent toward Sodom. 13 But the men of Sodom *were* wicked and sinners before the LORD exceedingly.

This decision by Lot proved fatal for his family kingdom. Eventually Lot and his family moved into Sodom and Lot received a warning of living in that city by being taken captive by a neighbouring group of tribes. The story is outlined in Genesis 14. This should have been a warning to Lot to leave the city. Sadly there is no mention in the record of Lot's gratitude or a commitment to leave Sodom. His eyes had been blinded to the dangers for his family and he would pay a very high price.

The wickedness of Sodom became so great that God had to intervene. In the discussion with Abraham, the Spirit of Christ in Abraham, pleading for Sodom shows the reluctance of God to destroy the city, but the morality of life had become so bad that the role identities of male and female became totally confused and the family structure destroyed.

> **Gen 19:4-7** Before they had gone to bed, all the men from every part of the city of Sodom-- both young and old-- surrounded the house. **5** They called to Lot, Where are the men who came to you tonight? Bring them out to us so that we can have sex with them. **6** Lot went outside to meet them and shut the door behind him **7** and said, No, my friends. Don't do this wicked thing. NIV

The day to day exposure to this environment eroded the moral foundations of the house of Lot. Though Lot did his best to be faithful to God, he placed himself where the environment and association of the wicked people around him would undermine all his efforts. Lot lost his whole family except two daughters; they all perished in the destruction of Sodom.

> **Gen 19:14** And Lot went out, and spake unto his sons in law, which married his daughters, and said, Up, get you out of this place; for the LORD will destroy this city. But he seemed as one that mocked unto his sons in law.

> **Gen 19:17** And it came to pass, when they had brought them forth abroad, that he said, Escape for thy life; look not behind thee, neither stay thou in all the plain; escape to the mountain, lest thou be consumed.

> **Gen 19:24-26** Then the LORD rained upon Sodom and upon Gomorrah brimstone and fire from the LORD out of heaven; **25** And he overthrew those cities, and all the plain, and all the inhabitants of the cities, and that which grew upon the ground. **26** But his wife looked back from behind him, and she became a pillar of salt.

Sadly, Lot's wife had embraced the non-submissive spirit of the women of Sodom and refused to gratefully heed the instruction, not to look back and she perished. It is possible that even with her non-submissive spirit, Lot's wife might have had extended time to rethink her course but the wavering attitude of Lot in living in the city reinforced her attitudes of disobedience and sealed her fate.

It would have been bad enough to lose your entire family, but Lot's daughters had also been influenced by the immorality of Sodom. The willingness of Lot to allow his daughters to be used by vile men was evidence of the lack of blessing Lot provided for his daughters and this made them vulnerable to the affections of ungodly men and evil associations.

Under this influence, Lot's daughters seeking with good intention to keep the family tree going used the Nimrod principle of manipulation to get their father drunk and they both became pregnant by him. These young women had lost a sense of who their father was meant to be and the lack of respect they had lived and breathed in Sodom had allowed them to cross a threshold that would prove a great tragedy. The children born from this event were Moab and Ammon; the head of the Moabites and the Ammonites who would prove a great trial to the descendents of Abraham – the children of Israel. Without a correct family blessing structure, these two tribes became wicked and warlike and proved to be a blot on the earth and eventually filled their cup with iniquity to the point where divine judgment was required.

All of these terrible events could have been avoided if Lot had submitted to the authority of Abraham and asked him to suggest the best course of action. He even could have been spared if he had left Sodom after Abraham rescued him, but he failed. The heritage of Lot was not a mighty nation that was a blessing to the earth but an example of loss, tragedy, incest and wickedness in his descendents.

What impact are our associations and environment having on our families today?

b. The Test of Riches

The Bible tells us very plainly the dangers and seduction of money.

> **1 Tim 6:10** For the love of money is the root of all evil: which while some coveted after, they have erred from the faith, and pierced themselves through with many sorrows.

Money itself is not the root of evil, but the love of it. We noticed earlier that it was Nimrod who developed a form of banking system. The relational motivations of love and responsibility that form the basis of transactions in God's kingdom were replaced with the system of money where every transaction had its price and opened the door for men to more easily find value through their possessions. In a money based system, money is power and the more money you have, the more power you have, so the love of money is the love of power and one of the best expressions of value by position and power. Our Father in heaven states on this subject:

> **Jer 9:23-24** Thus saith the LORD, Let not the wise *man* glory in his wisdom, neither let the mighty *man* glory in his might, let not the rich *man* glory in his riches: **24** But let him that glorieth glory in this, that he understandeth and knoweth me, that I *am* the LORD which exercise lovingkindness, judgment, and righteousness, in the earth: for in these *things* I delight, saith the LORD.

God tells us not to find value or glory in riches but to glory in knowing Him. The riches of God's kingdom is character. What price can be placed on a person that is joyful, peaceful, patient, honest, discerning and forthright in defending righteous values? Where do we find men like this today?

The majority of society today has money as one of the highest ambitions to gain. As sometimes has been stated "Money is not everything but it's up there with oxygen!"

Men and women will sacrifice home and family to possess riches and wealth, and are willing to marry completely the wrong person simply because they are wealthy. They will do overtime at work night after night to try and get ahead while their children are deprived of being with them. The desire for money and the desire for a happy family are competing desires. At regular points in our lives, one desire has to give way to the other.

In the life of Abraham, we see a man who chose God and family first in these situations. Though Abraham was a rich man, and one might say he could afford to be generous, the character of the man is revealed repeatedly, that he chose to honour God first and placed a higher value on his family relationships.

> **Gen 13:7-9** And there was a strife between the herdmen of Abram's cattle and the herdmen of Lot's cattle: and the Canaanite and the Perizzite dwelled then in the land. **8** And Abram said unto Lot, Let there

be no strife, I pray thee, between me and thee, and between my herdmen and thy herdmen; for we *be* brethren. **9** *Is* not the whole land before thee? separate thyself, I pray thee, from me: if *thou wilt take* the left hand, then I will go to the right; or if *thou depart* to the right hand, then I will go to the left.

The only reason that Lot had large possessions was because of his connection to Abraham. Abraham could have treated Lot like Laban treated Jacob and try and get as much value out of him as he could to enrich himself but he did not. He could have told Lot that it was his skill and wisdom that had enabled all this wealth and that Lot owed Abraham a debt of gratitude and should pay him accordingly but he did not. Most astute business men would have frowned at Abraham allowing his nephew to decide which pastures he wanted first, allowing his nephew the advantage – such a decision was not worldly wise at all.

But Abraham was not enslaved to the love of money and possessions as Lot was. The love of possessions and advantage cost Lot his family kingdom and he lost everything. In seeking the temporal advantage of gaining more, he was left with nothing.

In Genesis 14 we see once again that Abraham valued family relations above temporal advantage.

> **Gen 14:12-15** And they took Lot, Abram's brother's son, who dwelt in Sodom, and his goods, and departed. **13** And there came one that had escaped, and told Abram the Hebrew; for he dwelt in the plain of Mamre the Amorite, brother of Eshcol, and brother of Aner: and these *were* confederate with Abram. **14** And when Abram heard that his brother was taken captive, he armed his trained *servants*, born in his own house, three hundred and eighteen, and pursued *them* unto Dan. **15** And he divided himself against them, he and his servants, by night, and smote them, and pursued them unto Hobah, which *is* on the left hand of Damascus.

It would have been easy for Abraham not to feel sorry for Lot and what happened to him or possibly allowed feelings of justice to arise that Lot had received his just deserts for being greedy, but Abraham did not allow these thoughts to rule him. Lot was his nephew and he willingly risked his own life and invested his own possessions and wealth in seeking to save Lot.

Abraham could have lost his own life and all his possessions to save Lot and his family. From a worldly point of view this was a foolish move. He may even have hired a team of men to reclaim his nephew, but Abraham went himself and laid everything on the line.

God gave Abraham a great victory against all the odds[38] and once again Abraham was faced with a money challenge. Abraham knew that his victory was given to him from God and it was the Lord who was to be praised for His mercy. It is at this point that we see a principle that Abraham followed to remind himself of where all things come from.

> **Gen 14:18-20** Then Melchizedek king of Salem brought out bread and wine. He was priest of God Most High, **19** and he blessed Abram, saying, Blessed be Abram by God Most High, Creator of heaven and earth. **20** And blessed be God Most High, who delivered your enemies into your hand. Then Abram gave him a tenth of everything. NIV

Abraham might have reasoned that he was entitled to take all the spoils of this conflict. He had placed his life and possessions on the line and won, so he was entitled to them. But such thinking is reflective of the serpent's lie of inherent power. Abraham knew it was God who had won the victory; this power, skill and ability did not originate with him, but came from the Creator of the heavens and the earth and, as an acknowledgment of that, he gave a tithe or 10 percent of his income to the priest of the Most High God. The giving of the tithe was a tangible acknowledgment by Abraham that everything he possessed had come from God and served as a blessing against greed and selfishness. The practice of tithing was another way that Abraham placed family relationships above the temptations and seduction of wealth.

But Abraham's perception of the dangers of wealth extended further.

> **Gen 14:21-23** The king of Sodom said to Abram, Give me the people and keep the goods for yourself. **22** But Abram said to the king of Sodom, I have raised my hand to the LORD, God Most High, Creator of heaven and earth, and have taken an oath **23** that I will accept nothing belonging to you, not even a thread or the thong of a sandal, so that you will never be able to say, 'I made Abram rich. (NIV)

The king of Sodom did not believe as Abraham did, that all wealth and possessions came from the God who made the heavens and the earth. If he accepted his gifts, it could be said that Abraham became wealthy through

---

38 The odds of 318 men beating a large army are very slim indeed. In fact this victory outranks the Battle of Thermopylae for greatness.

the riches of Sodom; that his greatness came from his own skill and ability combined with the generosity of the king of Sodom. Abraham was keen to protect the principles he lived by and honour the God he served. He would take nothing from the king of Sodom.

In these experiences of Abraham we see another secret of building a family treasure:
1. A placing of family relationships above the desire for wealth.
2. A recognition that all wealth and possessions come from God.
3. The practice of tithing as a safeguard against the lie that what we possess comes from ourselves.
4. A refusal to accept gifts that would take away God's glory as the source of all things.

These lessons are just as vital today and if we want to build a family structure that will bless our children, we would be wise to walk in the steps of Abraham.

c. The Test of Marriage – Headship and Submission

God told Abraham right at the beginning that through his family structure, God would bless the families of the world. For this blessing to flow freely, Abraham and Sarah would need to have a clear sense of their roles in that family structure. Notice what God promised:

> **Gen 12:2-3** I will make you a great nation; I will bless you And make your name great; And you shall be a blessing. 3 I will bless those who bless you, And I will curse him who curses you; And in you all the families of the earth shall be blessed." NKJV

Later in Genesis, God spells out clearly how the blessings would flow and what would ensure the building of this great nation.

> **Gen 18:18-19** since Abraham shall surely become a great and mighty nation, and all the nations of the earth shall be blessed in him? 19 For I have known him, in order that he may command his children and his household after him, that they keep the way of the Lord, to do righteousness and justice, that the Lord may bring to Abraham what He has spoken to him. NKJV

We discussed the vital nature of this family structure in Chapters 4 to 6. One thing we mentioned, that we need to be reminded about is this:

Equality in relationships is not about power, control and assets, it is about the ability to understand and know someone and the perception of female identity in this way is the only way we can define relational equality. The woman is the key to a relational kingdom.

For all the families of the earth to be blessed through Abraham's family, his family system must be the pattern for all families; to allow the blessing of love, worth and value to flow through it to all families. The name "Son" in Hebrew carries a primary sense of "Builder of the family name." To build the family name, the son must learn correct principles of how relationships work and the place where this is learned is obviously from his parents.

i.   Abraham's First Failure in Egypt Causes Vulnerability in Sarah

With these thoughts in mind, we will see that Sarah is the key to Abraham's family kingdom turning into a great nation. Her perception of her husband and how she responds to the authority given him by God will determine the success or failure of the family kingdom.

With this in mind let us observe what events transpire in the lives of Abraham and Sarah and the attempts made by Satan to destroy the building of their treasure of family memories.

> **Gen 12:10-15** Now there was a famine in the land, and Abram went down to Egypt to dwell there, for the famine was severe in the land. **11** And it came to pass, when he was close to entering Egypt, that he said to Sarai his wife, "Indeed I know that you are a woman of beautiful countenance. **12** Therefore it will happen, when the Egyptians see you, that they will say, 'This is his wife'; and they will kill me, but they will let you live. **13** Please say you are my sister, that it may be well with me for your sake, and that I may live because of you." **14** So it was, when Abram came into Egypt, that the Egyptians saw the woman, that she was very beautiful. **15** The princes of Pharaoh also saw her and commended her to Pharaoh. And the woman was taken to Pharaoh's house.

Satan immediately went to work to destroy the relationship between Abraham and Sarah. He worked on Abraham's fears when they went down to Egypt and Abraham's lack of faith caused Sarah to be put in a difficult situation. In asking Sarah to hide the full truth about her relationship to Abraham, she was taken into the court of Pharaoh to become part of his "collection" of women. This failure on Abraham's part would have made Sarah feel extremely vulnerable. Why did Abraham, her husband and protector, allow her to be taken by Pharaoh? How was this a demonstration of love? She had submitted to his request to say that she was his sister to protect him and yet when she was taken, he did nothing to protect her.

Satan was trying to break Sarah's confidence in her husband by causing Abraham to stumble through fear. This action was an echo of Adam blaming Eve for his actions when he fell into rebellion. If Satan could break Sarah's confidence in Abraham and cause her to lose confidence in his authority, then he knew that he would greatly hinder this channel of blessing and hopefully even destroy the channel for the promised seed.

Every husband needs to understand that his entire family kingdom rests upon the confidence that his wife has in him as a leader and a protector of the family. To protect his wife from the temptations of Satan, he needs to regularly affirm her and express his love and appreciation of her. Every wife needs to understand that Satan will strive tirelessly to tempt her husband to fail and leave his wife vulnerable to doubting her husband. She can help him be that leader and protector by an attitude of respect and Godly submission to his leadership. Both husband and wife must be active; in displays of appreciation from husband to wife and displays of respect from wife to husband.

Sadly Abraham failed this test at the beginning and the vulnerability it created in Sarah would bring disastrous consequences in the future.

ii. Abraham's Second Failure in Hearkening to the Voice of Sarah

God had promised Abraham that he would become a great nation, but He allowed a time delay to test Abraham's character. This time delay turned to many years and Abraham was tempted to be impatient.

> **Gen 15:1-3** After these things the word of the Lord came to Abram in a vision, saying, "Do not be afraid, Abram. I am your shield, your exceedingly great reward." **2** But Abram said, "Lord God, what will You give me, seeing I go childless, and the heir of my house is Eliezer of Damascus?" **3** Then Abram said, "Look, You have given me no offspring; indeed one born in my house is my heir!"

The delay in time revealed Abraham's independent mind to solve the problem of why he did not have a son. He proposed a solution of his faithful servant becoming his heir. Abraham does not appear to question that the delay might be due to his failure in Egypt which had a severe effect on Sarah. Time would be needed to restore that confidence fully to ensure the submissive role was played correctly. God promised Abraham that from his own body a son would be born.

> **Gen 15:4-5** And behold, the word of the Lord came to him, saying, "This one shall not be your heir, but one who will come from your own body shall be your heir." **5** Then He brought him outside and said, "Look now toward heaven, and count the stars if you are able to number them." And He said to him, "So shall your descendants be."

But in this promise there is still a test because he does not say that Sarah will be the one to bear the child, he only mentions Abraham. Why did God do this? The vulnerability in Sarah caused by Abraham in Egypt needed to be brought to light before the foundations of Abraham's kingdom could be laid with a son. The statement of the Lord produced the desired effect and the fears of Sarah soon surfaced.

> **Gen 16:1-2** Now Sarai, Abram's wife, had borne him no children. And she had an Egyptian maidservant whose name was Hagar. **2** So Sarai said to Abram, "See now, the Lord has restrained me from bearing children. Please, go in to my maid; perhaps I shall obtain children by her." And Abram heeded the voice of Sarai.

This passage reveals the lengths that Sarah was willing to go to obtain children. In ancient times, a failure of a wife to produce children was a shame to her. This shame had come about by the lie of Satan of inherent power to produce. We see this shame and sorrow and worthlessness manifested in greater magnitude in Sarah's grand-daughter-in-law Rachel.

> **Gen 30:1** Now when Rachel saw that she bore Jacob no children, Rachel envied her sister, and said to Jacob, "Give me children, or else I die!"

Rachel was almost suicidal about the fact that she could not produce children. Her sister was apparently producing children at will and she could not produce anything and so Rachel's "failure to perform" made her suicidal.

This intensity of feeling was nurtured in the heart of Sarah and drove her to suggest a plan that any woman in her right mind would never suggest.

> **Gen 16:1-2** Now Sarai, Abram's wife, had borne him no children. And she had an Egyptian maidservant whose name was Hagar. 2 So Sarai said to Abram, "See now, the Lord has restrained me from bearing children. Please, go in to my maid; perhaps I shall obtain children by her." And Abram heeded the voice of Sarai.

What wife would willingly suggest that her husband have sexual relations with another woman for the purpose of giving children to her husband! This suggestion reveals the stress that Sarah was under. The failure of Abraham to affirm her left her vulnerable to Satan's suggestion that she was not valuable; and it even appeared that God had abandoned her because she was not included in the promise in Genesis 15. Abraham's failure to trust the Lord when going down into Egypt had an influence on Sarah's trusting the Lord with her being restrained in bearing children. Her mournful words "God has restrained me from bearing children," indicates some belief that God was punishing her for some reason. Either through her low sense of worth and or a sense of rebellion to achieve the goal of having children, she suggests the unthinkable and pleads with Abraham to take her servant girl and have a child with her.

It's ironic that the curse that came upon Abraham's family in Egypt was again extended through an Egyptian woman. The kingdom of Egypt fully embraced the lie of the serpent through Nimrod's kingdom ideals. In suggesting this Egyptian woman be taken into Abraham's bedroom, it was symbolic of the suggestion that Abraham's family should embrace the philosophy of Egypt and the lies of inherent power.

Satan was on the verge of a great victory. If he could cause Abraham to yield to Sarah, then God's kingdom on earth through Abraham would be dealt a terrible blow. Abraham would not be unmindful of the shameful way he treated his wife in Egypt and he would have felt badly for her that she could not bear children. Sarah was overcome with grief because of her plight, but Abraham should have known better than to take Sarah's advice. But like his ancestor Adam he submitted to the request of his wife. In doing this he surrendered his headship. Satan artfully used a sense of guilt and twisted his sense of empathy for his wife to cause him to surrender his headship role and let Sarah call the shots. This terrible decision is still one of the central causes of controversy in the world today in the war between the Jews and the Arabs in the Middle East.

Abraham should have taken the request of Sarah to the Lord but he did not. The custom of plural wives was common place in those days and Abraham would not have been fully aware of the dangers in this suggestion, but in making such a major decision without consulting the Lord revealed the residual spirit of independence and the influence of the lie of the serpent.

We see revealed in this story a sequence of events to bring down Abraham's family kingdom:

1. A failure on the part of Abraham to affirm and protect his wife
2. Resulting in a sense of vulnerability to worthlessness in Sarah
3. Resulting in the openness to Satan's temptation to act independently
4. Resulting in Sarah's sad request to obtain children by another woman
5. Resulting in Abraham surrendering his role as head of the home by hearkening to the voice of his wife and thus confusing roles of headship and submission
6. Resulting in a confused family relationship in the home of Abraham
7. Resulting in the hampering of the channel of blessing and a major threat to building a family treasure of memories.

d. God Teaches Abraham Concerning the Vital Nature of Family Structure

The failure of Abraham to grasp the sacred union of the husband-wife relationship in establishing him as the head of a great nation, brought many sorrows to him. The consequential rivalry between Sarah and Hagar that emerged did not bring the joy that Sarah imagined, but only increased her sense of pain. Hagar, though married to Abraham, was still Sarah's servant. This confused relational system was certain to explode at some point.

> **Gen 16:4-6** So he went in to Hagar, and she conceived. And when she saw that she had conceived, her mistress became despised in her eyes.
> **5** Then Sarai said to Abram, "My wrong be upon you! I gave my maid into your embrace; and when she saw that she had conceived, I became despised in her eyes. The Lord judge between you and me."
> **6** So Abram said to Sarai, "Indeed your maid is in your hand; do to her as you please." And when Sarai dealt harshly with her, she fled from her presence.

Sarah blamed her husband for what had taken place. In our modern world, we would laugh at such supposed foolishness, but in the headship and submission system of God, Sarah was entirely correct. Abraham had made the final decision and so the responsibility rested with him for the eruption of ill feeling that descended upon his home. As the husband or house-band he should have refused such a request and prayed to God for grace to comfort his wife and pray for her. It does appear that Isaac learnt from his father about this matter.

> **Gen 25:21** Now Isaac pleaded with the Lord for his wife, because she was barren; and the Lord granted his plea, and Rebekah his wife conceived.

Through trial and suffering, Abraham learnt many things about family and the way it should be conducted. We mentioned earlier the lesson of Sodom and how the complete breakdown of their family units led to their destruction. We return again to Genesis 18:19.

> **Gen 18:19** For I have known him, in order that he may command his children and his household after him, that they keep the way of the Lord, to do righteousness and justice, that the Lord may bring to Abraham what He has spoken to him.

There is much significance in the phrase – " For I have known him." The word known means intimate knowledge. After many hardships both with himself and with his nephew Lot, God was able to give Abraham intimate knowledge of the family system and the principles of headship and submission. We are told that God knew Abraham in order (or for the purpose of) that he might command his children and family after him.

With this knowledge he was now ready to produce a true heir that would be a true builder of the family kingdom. Ishmael could not fill this position because of the incorrect relationship that he was conceived in. The wildness of Ishmael's conduct was due directly to Abraham hearkening to the voice of his wife, and placing Hagar in a place where her son could not truly be blessed and have a true sense of worth before God that would enable him to be stable enough to carry the family name.

> **Gen 16:6-12** So Abram said to Sarai, "Indeed your maid is in your hand; do to her as you please." And when Sarai dealt harshly with her, she fled from her presence. 7 Now the Angel of the Lord found her by

a spring of water in the wilderness, by the spring on the way to Shur. **8** And He said, "Hagar, Sarai's maid, where have you come from, and where are you going?" She said, "I am fleeing from the presence of my mistress Sarai." **9** The Angel of the Lord said to her, "Return to your mistress, and submit yourself under her hand." **10** Then the Angel of the Lord said to her, "I will multiply your descendants exceedingly, so that they shall not be counted for multitude." **11** And the Angel of the Lord said to her: "Behold, you are with child, And you shall bear a son. You shall call his name Ishmael, Because the Lord has heard your affliction. **12** He shall be a wild man; His hand shall be against every man, And every man's hand against him. And he shall dwell in the presence of all his brethren."

Hagar could never truly feel secure in her relationship to Abraham because she was first and foremost the servant of Sarah. Without that sense of security, she could not fulfill adequately the nurturing role of a mother, because the channel of blessing to her via Abraham was not legitimate. The life flow of God's blessing was not upon this union and so it could not prosper in a correct way.

God came to Abraham and informed him that Sarah would bear him a son. In this message once again there was a failure to trust and Abraham's laughter in Gen 17:17 was passed to Sarah when she heard the news in Gen 18 and she laughed also in total disbelief. The Lord asked Abraham why his wife had laughed rather than asking Sarah directly. This question was directed at Abraham because he had initiated this disbelief and influenced Sarah's thinking. The lie she told concerning the laughter revealed that she still carried a certain level of insecurity and this needed addressing before the birth of her son.

Now that Abraham had an heir, he would seek to ensure that the wife his son would marry would be able to fulfill the role of the submissive agent. The woman Isaac would marry would be vital to the survival of Abraham's family kingdom and a prayerful choice had to be made. The expedition of Abraham's servant to find a suitable woman reveals the realization of how important this choice was. Isaac was 40 years old and in today's society we would consider well able to make his own choice, but he trusted his father's wisdom and submitted to the process his father wished. The serving attitude of Rebekah in giving a drink to Abraham's servant as well as watering his animals revealed the spirit of the submissive agent that Isaac needed to build the family kingdom.

Isaac learned many things from his father and mother regarding family and so he avoided many of the pitfalls his father encountered; but Satan brought another temptation to this couple in the form of favouritism between sons. It totally split the family. But in regard to the choice of a wife for their sons, Isaac and Rebekah had a clear understanding of the issue and how vital it was.

> **Gen 26:34-35** When Esau was forty years old, he took as wives Judith the daughter of Beeri the Hittite, and Basemath the daughter of Elon the Hittite. **35** And they were a grief of mind to Isaac and Rebekah.

Esau failed to heed to warnings of his grandfather and took two wives from a tribe that did not follow God's system of family. It caused Isaac and Rebekah much grief, for they knew that it would greatly hinder the promise of becoming a great nation, and in part this is why God indicated that the elder would serve the younger. His choice of wives made it impossible to establish the family kingdom effectively.

> **Gen 27:46** And Rebekah said to Isaac, "I am weary of my life because of the daughters of Heth; if Jacob takes a wife of the daughters of Heth, like these who are the daughters of the land, what good will my life be to me?"

Rebekah expressed the truth that if Jacob took a wife that did not understand true family principles then their family kingdom would be finished. All her efforts to raise her sons would be lost in the wrong choice of wives for her sons.

There is much more instruction in the book of Genesis concerning these principles and I would encourage you to follow the cause and effect principles in the family of Jacob. The kingdom of Israel with its birth of twelve sons did not have a perfect start. In fact the family was quite dysfunctional in places, but the lessons are there for us to learn if we are willing.

1. A husband must realize his role as a seed giver and blesser and bless his wife and children in words of appreciation and encouragement.
2. A wife must act in the role of submissive agent to draw down the blessing of her husband in a channel for her children.
3. Once this channel of blessing is open the child will receive a sense of

true sonship or daughtership to God which will protect them from the lie of the serpent to gain worth by inherent power and achievement.

Before we close this chapter, we will briefly discuss the blessing process and why it is so vital for a father to bless his children.

e. The Birthright to Bless

In Chapter 5 we discussed the vital principle of the blessing; the flowing forth of not only physical life but also a sense of worth and purpose. This blessing is the only means to truly avoid worthlessness and depression. God reconnected this channel through Abraham when he stated:

> **Gen 12:2-3** And I will make of thee a great nation, and I will bless thee, and make thy name great; and thou shalt be a blessing: **3** And I will bless them that bless thee, and curse him that curseth thee: and in thee shall all families of the earth be blessed.

This blessing established Abraham as God's appointed channel to bless the world. Since Abraham entered into a covenant relation with God, even when Abraham failed at times, this channel of blessing was not taken from him. The channel of blessing was not based primarily on Abraham's ability to behave correctly but rather on his covenant relation to God. A sustained failure to respond to God's commands would ultimately break this covenant and the channel indeed would be lost as it ultimately was after the time of Christ.

> **Acts 13:46** Then Paul and Barnabas waxed bold, and said, It was necessary that the word of God should first have been spoken to you: but seeing ye put it from you, and judge yourselves unworthy of everlasting life, lo, we turn to the Gentiles.

The channel of blessing established with Abraham could not be based upon the performance of Abraham because Abraham needed time to learn that he had been raised in an environment based on the lie of the serpent involving inherent power. The covenant provided probation for Abraham to discern his independence and fully submit to God.

> **Gen 15:18** In the same day the LORD made a covenant with Abram, saying, Unto thy seed have I given this land, from the river of Egypt unto the great river, the river Euphrates:

From a worldly perspective, this covenant appears strange. We notice

Abraham's lie to Abimelech and yet it is Abraham who is asked to pray for Abimelech and not the other way around.

> **Gen 20:2-7** And Abraham said of Sarah his wife, She *is* my sister: and Abimelech king of Gerar sent, and took Sarah. **3** But God came to Abimelech in a dream by night, and said to him, Behold, thou *art but* a dead man, for the woman which thou hast taken; for she *is* a man's wife. **4** But Abimelech had not come near her: and he said, Lord, wilt thou slay also a righteous nation? **5** Said he not unto me, She *is* my sister? and she, even she herself said, He *is* my brother: in the integrity of my heart and innocency of my hands have I done this. **6** And God said unto him in a dream, Yea, I know that thou didst this in the integrity of thy heart; for I also withheld thee from sinning against me: therefore suffered I thee not to touch her. **7** Now therefore restore the man *his* wife; for he *is* a prophet, and he shall pray for thee, and thou shalt live: and if thou restore *her* not, know thou that thou shalt surely die, thou, and all that *are* thine.

By all accounts, Abimelech should have prayed for Abraham for his deceit in lying about his wife, but God told Abimelech that Abraham would pray for him. The only possible way this could make sense is through the covenant that God made with Abraham to make him his designated authority to bless.

Rather than remove this authority, he brought about circumstances to remind Abraham of his true role to bless. Through the submission of Abimelech to Abraham's prayers, Abraham was rebuked and reminded of his true role. If Abimelech had attacked Abraham for his behaviour, the fear that had caused Abraham to lie would have been increased and he would have moved futher away from his true identity as the blesser of the families of the earth.

This authority to bless would flow from generation to generation through the concept of the birthright.

> **Gen 25:31-33** And Jacob said, Sell me this day thy birthright. **32** And Esau said, Behold, I *am* at the point to die: and what profit shall this birthright do to me? **33** And Jacob said, Swear to me this day; and he sware unto him: and he sold his birthright unto Jacob.

In God's kingdom, the honour of the birthright fell by default to the eldest son. The birthright was meant to be used to not only bless his family but also his younger brothers and sisters as well. In God's kingdom, the birthright carried the joy and responsibility to bless, but twisted by the lie of Satan, the birthright became a status symbol of power and control. The birthright ensured that the majority of the father's wealth would pass to the carrier of the birthright – not to enrich himself but to bless all under his authority; not to take, but to give.

Esau did not discern the true nature of the birthright as a spiritual heritage and he actually did not want to take the responsibility of family priest of the home. This sentiment would have been underscored by the wives that he had chosen. Women, schooled in the principles of the lie of the serpent, produced in them a lack of submission to the point where Esau's spiritual authority was not respected. His choices in marriage had ensured he could never truly fulfill this role spiritually.

In the birth of the two boys, Isaac and Rebekah were made aware that the birthright would in some way pass to Jacob, the younger son.

> **Gen 25:22-23** And the children struggled together within her; and she said, If *it be* so, why *am* I thus? And she went to enquire of the LORD. **23** And the LORD said unto her, Two nations *are* in thy womb, and two manner of people shall be separated from thy bowels; and *the one* people shall be stronger than *the other* people; and the elder shall serve the younger.

Jacob would have been aware of this and yet, like his grandfather Abraham who could not wait for the promise of a son to be fulfilled in God's timing, he took an opportunity to secure the birthright by taking advantage of his brother's weakness – appetite.

Though Jacob discerned the spiritual value of the birthright and its responsibility to bless, he still did not trust God to bring things about. He was still acting from the principle of the lie of the serpent, through independent thought and action. So even with the best desires and motives to please God, Jacob became a deceiver and a manipulator. Sin, through the law deceived him and that which was ordained to life, he found to be unto death.[39] That which was meant to be a great blessing, became a great curse.

Ultimately, God brought Jacob to see his character and the falseness with which he had acted and in the later days, Jacob became Israel – the overcomer. He became the true channel of blessing to his children and laid the foundation for a spiritual nation.

Before Jacob left his home, his father transferred the authority to bless through the following event.

---
39 Romans 7:7-10

Gen 28:1-5 And Isaac called Jacob, and blessed him, and charged him, and said unto him, Thou shalt not take a wife of the daughters of Canaan. **2** Arise, go to Padanaram, to the house of Bethuel thy mother's father; and take thee a wife from thence of the daughters of Laban thy mother's brother. **3** And God Almighty bless thee, and make thee fruitful, and multiply thee, that thou mayest be a multitude of people; **4** And give thee the blessing of Abraham, to thee, and to thy seed with thee; that thou mayest inherit the land wherein thou art a stranger, which God gave unto Abraham. **5** And Isaac sent away Jacob: and he went to Padanaram unto Laban, son of Bethuel the Syrian, the brother of Rebekah, Jacob's and Esau's mother.

Isaac gave counsel to Jacob to find a suitable wife that would assist him in carrying forward the work of blessing. As we have noted, Jacob's ability to bless effectively depended upon the right choice of a wife who would recognize his spiritual leadership and the birthright he possessed.

While on his way to Padanaram, God showed Jacob a symbol of how the blessing principle worked and how it flowed.

Gen 28:11-15 And he lighted upon a certain place, and tarried there all night, because the sun was set; and he took of the stones of that place, and put *them for* his pillows, and lay down in that place to sleep. **12** And he dreamed, and behold a ladder set up on the earth, and the top of it reached to heaven: and behold the angels of God ascending and descending on it. **13** And, behold, the LORD stood above it, and said, I *am* the LORD God of Abraham thy father, and the God of Isaac: the land whereon thou liest, to thee will I give it, and to thy seed; **14** And thy seed shall be as the dust of the earth, and thou shalt spread abroad to the west, and to the east, and to the north, and to the south: and in thee and in thy seed shall all the families of the earth be blessed. **15** And, behold, I *am* with thee, and will keep thee in all *places* whither thou goest, and will bring thee again into this land; for I will not leave thee, until I have done *that* which I have spoken to thee of.

Jacob was shown a ladder with angels ascending and descending upon it, revealing the flow of the blessing from God and the return of the praise to God that would come from the heart of Jacob and his family. God then sealed directly the blessing Isaac had given Jacob by placing the authority to bless firmly within his hands.

The ladder that the angels climbed and descended was a symbol of the spirit of Christ through whom all blessings flow.

> **John 1:51** And he saith unto him, Verily, verily, I say unto you, Hereafter ye shall see heaven open, and the angels of God ascending and descending upon the Son of man.

Paul presents this blessing flow in a family context in the following manner.

> **1 Cor 11:3** But I would have you know, that the head of every man is Christ; and the head of the woman *is* the man; and the head of Christ *is* God.

This symbol of the flow of blessing is also revealed in the giving of the manna, which was a symbol of Christ. It is the submissive spirit of Christ flowing into the hearts of his children that keeps them connected to the Father. Christ, the great example of submission is the key to keeping the whole system functioning and flowing freely.

> **John 6:32-35** Then Jesus said unto them, Verily, verily, I say unto you, Moses gave you not that bread from heaven; but my Father giveth you the true bread from heaven. **33** For the bread of God is he which cometh down from heaven, and giveth life unto the world. **34** Then said they unto him, Lord, evermore give us this bread. **35** And Jesus said unto them, I am the bread of life: he that cometh to me shall never hunger; and he that believeth on me shall never thirst.

We see the principle of the bread reflected in the feeding of the 5000. Jesus blessed the food, gave to his disciples whom He had invested with authority and they passed it to the people and then the fragments were gathered up; signifying this flow of blessing back and forth upon the ladder which represents Christ. The bread symbolized the spiritual blessing which nourishes the soul. That spiritual bread contains life, value and purpose. Without this bread from heaven, we will die. The same concept is expressed in terms of water.

> **John 7:37-39** In the last day, that great *day* of the feast, Jesus stood and cried, saying, If any man thirst, let him come unto me, and drink. **38** He that believeth on me, as the Scripture hath said, out of his belly shall flow rivers of living water. **39** (But this spake he of the Spirit, which they that believe on him should receive: for the Holy Ghost was not yet *given*; because that Jesus was not yet glorified.)

The ladder that Jacob saw in the wilderness was the beginning of his understanding of the real meaning of the birthright and the spiritual authority that was granted him from his father and grandfather.

The sealing of Jacob's belief that all blessing comes from God occurred in his struggle with the Angel and pleading for blessing in the face of death. This struggle revealed that the lie of the serpent had been completely eliminated from Jacob.

> **Gen 32:24-30** And Jacob was left alone; and there wrestled a man with him until the breaking of the day. **25** And when he saw that he prevailed not against him, he touched the hollow of his thigh; and the hollow of Jacob's thigh was out of joint, as he wrestled with him. **26** And he said, Let me go, for the day breaketh. And he said, I will not let thee go, except thou bless me. **27** And he said unto him, What *is* thy name? And he said, Jacob. **28** And he said, Thy name shall be called no more Jacob, but Israel: for as a prince hast thou power with God and with men, and hast prevailed. **29** And Jacob asked *him*, and said, Tell *me*, I pray thee, thy name. And he said, Wherefore *is* it *that* thou dost ask after my name? And he blessed him there. **30** And Jacob called the name of the place Peniel: for I have seen God face to face, and my life is preserved.

Despite the threat of death and also the extreme pain, Jacob did not trust himself or any human agent to deliver him. He trusted alone in divine power and thus his name was changed to overcomer. Jacob had overcome the lie of inherent power and thus secured the channel of blessing from God to the human race through the family system of God.

In this capacity Jacob culminates the book of Genesis with a blessing for his children. We see this process revealed in Joseph having his two sons blessed by his father.

> **Gen 48:3-5** And Jacob said unto Joseph, God Almighty appeared unto me at Luz in the land of Canaan, and blessed me, **4** And said unto me, Behold, I will make thee fruitful, and multiply thee, and I will make of thee a multitude of people; and will give this land to thy seed after thee *for* an everlasting possession. **5** And now thy two sons, Ephraim and Manasseh, which were born unto thee in the land of Egypt before I came unto thee into Egypt, *are* mine; as Reuben and Simeon, they shall be mine.

> **Gen 48:13-15** And Joseph took them both, Ephraim in his right hand toward Israel's left hand, and Manasseh in his left hand toward Israel's right hand, and brought *them* near unto him. **14** And Israel stretched out his right hand, and laid *it* upon Ephraim's head, who *was* the younger, and his left hand upon Manasseh's head, guiding his hands wittingly; for Manasseh *was* the firstborn. **15** And he blessed Joseph, and said, God, before whom my fathers Abraham and Isaac did walk,

the God which fed me all my life long unto this day,

In Chapter 49 of Genesis, Jacob realizes his true identity as the holder of the birthright and he acts as the agent of God to bless his sons.

> **Gen 49:25-28** *Even* by the God of thy father, who shall help thee; and by the Almighty, who shall bless thee with blessings of heaven above, blessings of the deep that lieth under, blessings of the breasts, and of the womb: **26** The blessings of thy father have prevailed above the blessings of my progenitors unto the utmost bound of the everlasting hills: they shall be on the head of Joseph, and on the crown of the head of him that was separate from his brethren. ... **28** All these *are* the twelve tribes of Israel: and this *is it* that their father spake unto them, and blessed them; every one according to his blessing he blessed them.

So we see in the culmination of the book of Genesis that a victory is gained over the serpent and his lie of inherent power and value through personal achievement. Satan sought to wipe out the human race by causing tyrants to walk the earth who had been raised by the daughters of men – those who had accepted the lie of the serpent. God responded by calling Abraham and through many trials and three generations – Jacob is victorious as the overcomer, the one who trusts fully in God and accepts his role as a channel of blessing; one who passes on the sense of worth, value and purpose in a relational family system.

It would be nice to think that Israel lived happily ever after, but in the covenant that God made with Abraham, it was foretold that his descendents would go into slavery. Once again the lie of the serpent would prevail and another coming out would be required. Even as Abraham was called out of Babylon, so his descendents would be called out of Egypt and the family system restored again.

Chapter 13

The Channel of Blessing Lost and Restored Through Egyptian Pilgrimage

a. God Seeks to Reach the Egyptians and Test the Israelites

Although the children of Abraham had experienced several trials within their family, the book of Genesis culminates with Jacob blessing his children and keeping the channel of blessing from heaven open.

The receiving of blessings from God required a character of humility and a discernment of the true role of wealth. We remember that the blessings of God on Lot actually turned his heart towards the riches he received and he ended up losing everything.

The allowance of a famine had led Abraham to move to Egypt for preservation of his family, but the encounter nearly destroyed his family and revealed Abraham's lack of faith. God saved Abraham's family by sending great plagues on Egypt to prevent the destruction of Abraham's family through the loss of the vital role of Sarah the submissive agent.

Jacob had become a wealthy man through the blessing of God and the test of riches once again would be needed to help preserve the channel of blessing. Once again a famine came to the land, but God allowed circumstances to come about that would place Joseph as a leader in Egypt to preserve the Egyptians from the coming famine.

The question that arises is, why did God preserve the food supply for Egypt? They were an idolatrous nation, sons of Ham that were filled with the lie of serpent, and false life source concepts and false worship. Why would God help them?

God is a Father and He seeks to draw His wayward children with kindness. The Bible tells us:

> **Rom 2:4** Or despisest thou the riches of his goodness and forbearance and longsuffering; not knowing that the goodness of God leadeth thee to repentance?

The Egyptian nation, ruled by the principles of the serpent's lie, was heading in the direction of the antediluvians and the inhabitants of Sodom. The Egyptians worshipped many gods, all based upon the inherent power system. As we have seen before, this style of worship will lead to the destruction of families and therefore the destruction of nations.

God allowed Israel to come in contact with the Egyptians to acquaint them with the true God and give them an opportunity to repent; while at the same time testing Israel concerning their belief in the true God and deepening their understanding of God's family system. Israel was never meant to simply keep their knowledge to themselves; they were meant to share it with other nations, so they could be benefited by it and preserve their families.

> **Isa 60:3** And the Gentiles shall come to thy light, and kings to the brightness of thy rising.

God gave Pharaoh a dream concerning the coming famine. In giving this dream to Pharaoh, He could bring him into contact with the true God and if Pharaoh would recognize the true God, he then could act as an agent of blessing to the whole nation.

None of Pharaoh's agents could interpret the dream but circumstances allowed Joseph to come before the king and introduce the true God.

> **Gen 41:15-16** And Pharaoh said unto Joseph, I have dreamed a dream, and *there is* none that can interpret it: and I have heard say of thee, *that* thou canst understand a dream to interpret it. **16** And Joseph answered Pharaoh, saying, *It is* not in me: God shall give Pharaoh an answer of peace.

God enabled Joseph to tell and interpret the dream and Pharaoh began to be influenced by this mighty God that Joseph represented.

> **Gen 41:39-41** And Pharaoh said unto Joseph, Forasmuch as God hath shewed thee all this, *there is* none so discreet and wise as thou *art*: **40**

> Thou shalt be over my house, and according unto thy word shall all my people be ruled: only in the throne will I be greater than thou. **41** And Pharaoh said unto Joseph, See, I have set thee over all the land of Egypt.

Here was a great opportunity for Egypt. Through Joseph, Egypt had the chance to acknowledge the true God and turn to Him. It was God that enabled Egypt to become the most powerful nation at that time. If they had recognized God's favour towards them, they would have been released from the curse of insecurity, worthlessness and the need for domination and control as manifested in Satan's kingdom. Sadly, the lessons were not learned.

b. Egypt and Israel Seduced by Blessings of Wealth and Prosperity

> **Exod 1:8** Now there arose up a new king over Egypt, which knew not Joseph.

How could there be a Pharaoh who did not know Joseph? This verse suggests a kind of sarcasm. The new Pharaoh did not want to know Joseph. His heart was not filled with gratitude for what the God of heaven had done for Egypt through him and how that Egypt was now an extremely powerful nation as a result. Pharaoh failed the test of riches through the influence of the Egyptian priests who represented the worship of Nimrod in an Egyptian form, and chose to cling to the lie of inherent power source.

Israel, now living in a province of Egypt was not immune from the test of riches either. Through the blessing, they also were greatly prospered and this prosperity caused complacency which allowed them to be influenced by their urban neighbours.

> **Exod 1:7** And the children of Israel were fruitful, and increased abundantly, and multiplied, and waxed exceeding mighty; and the land was filled with them.

If the Israelites had been discerning, they would have noticed that the Egyptians were turning away from their recognition of the true God. They should have left knowing that sooner or later, the spirit of insecurity and worthlessness that always comes, would be turned against them, but in their enjoyment of their wealth and might in Egypt they failed to discern what was about to take place.

c. The Lie of Inherent Power Produces Insecurity in Egypt and the Need for Control and Achievement

> **Exod 1:8-10** Now there arose up a new king over Egypt, which knew not Joseph. **9** And he said unto his people, Behold, the people of the children of Israel *are* more and mightier than we: **10** Come on, let us deal wisely with them; lest they multiply, and it come to pass, that, when there falleth out any war, they join also unto our enemies, and fight against us, and *so* get them up out of the land.

The spirit of insecurity within Pharaoh manifested itself in the need for control. To deal with this insecurity he enslaved the Israelites to build treasure cities for him. The activity of large scale building was another sign of the insecurity of Pharaoh. He needed to display his power with great building projects in the same way the antediluvians did with the tower of Babel.

> **Exod 1:11** Therefore they did set over them taskmasters to afflict them with their burdens. And they built for Pharaoh treasure cities, Pithom and Raamses.

Even though the Israelites were now serving the Egyptians, they still were strong family units and therefore continued to thrive. Pharaoh, inspired by Satan, increased the work load to reduce the Israelites time to spend with their families and then he added to that the policy of removing and killing the baby boys.

> **Exod 1:13-16** And the Egyptians made the children of Israel to serve with rigour: **14** And they made their lives bitter with hard bondage, in morter, and in brick, and in all manner of service in the field: all their service, wherein they made them serve, *was* with rigour. **15** And the king of Egypt spake to the Hebrew midwives, of which the name of the one *was* Shiphrah, and the name of the other Puah: **16** And he said, When ye do the office of a midwife to the Hebrew women, and see *them* upon the stools; if it *be* a son, then ye shall kill him: but if it *be* a daughter, then she shall live.

Here we see again the direct attack on the family. When fathers and mothers are forced to work extremely hard, they have less time for parenting and spending time with their children. The care of children must be left to others while the work goes forward. This measure alone would ultimately have undone the Israelites but Pharaoh wanted to accelerate the process by feminizing the society. By removing the males, the seeding principle of blessing would be blunted, and insecurity and worthlessness would soon be the inheritance of Israel.

This process of increasing the workload and then feminizing a society was carefully engineered by the enemy of souls in modern society through the process of industrialization and the two world wars. Industrialization, while bringing some benefits, was largely driven by greed for money and the need for bigger empires. Fathers were taken away from their homes for long hours to serve in factories and were essentially slaves like the Israelites. The removal of fathers fed the flames of insecurity and the need for protection. The great wheels of industry were soon used to make weapons of war for that protection. This would ultimately ensure the destruction of millions of men which would ensure the destruction of the channel of blessing in many families and the feminization of society. So the experiences of Israel have a direct lesson for us today. The working families of the world are enslaved to the pharaohs of this world and once again God will send plagues to release His people from this terrible situation so that the family of heaven can be truly reunited.

d. Pharaoh Undermines the Channel of Blessing to Israel

The plight of the Israelites was dire. Pharaoh was now in full control of the destiny of Israel and he was systematically destroying the foundation of their family treasure system. In Chapter 11 we summarized the platform of Abraham's family system as opposed to Nimrod's inherent life source system. Here it is again:

Abraham	Nimrod
1. Family Structure (Gen 18:19)	1. Individual Dictator/Tyrant (Gen 10:10)
2. Nomadic Rural Dwellers (Heb 11:8-10)	2. City Builders and Defenders (Gen 11:4)
3. Identity by Parental Blessing (Gen 12:2)	3. Identity by Renown (Gen 11:4)
4. Observe Sabbath and Commandments (Gen 26:5)	4. Follow Personal Desires (Rom 1:21-32)
5. Belief in Death and Resurrection (Heb 11:17-19)	5. Belief in Immortality of the Soul (Gen 3:4)
6. Saviour as Humble Life Restorer – Revealed in Slain Lamb (John 11:25)	6. Saviour as Prideful Liberator and Subduer Empowered by Sun and Nature Worship
7. Focus of Worship on the Invisible	7. Focus of Worship on the Visible

While under the slavery in Egypt, the Israelites slowly lost the underpinnings of its family system. The Pharaoh was now their supreme authority and this replaced the headship of the father. Family structures would constantly be tested by the demands of Pharaoh. Fathers were forced in many cases to lay down their family sovereignty to the dictates of the king.

The Israelites were herded in suburbs for easier labour control and lost the blessings of rural surroundings and the possession of land. The ownership of land enables families to produce food and sustain themselves and be independent. The process of suburbs strips families of this independence and makes them dependent on others for food and protection.

The harsh bondage of labour, takes the father out of the home to the point where it is harder for fathers to spend much needed time with their children.

- The slavery and demands of Egypt did not allow for the worship of the Sabbath or a faithful keeping of the commandments.
- The worship of the Egyptians centred on the belief in the immortality of the soul. The building of the treasure cities was part of allowing the Pharaohs to prepare for the next world. Israel was constantly exposed to these views.
- The Pharaoh was surrounded by pomp and grandeur. His leaders

The Channel of Blessing Lost and Restored Through Egyptian Pilgrimage

dressed in expensive garments and were paraded in the streets and lauded. The constant exposure to this concept of leadership dimmed the Israelites minds of the humble pastoralist Jacob who lived in tents under the open sky. They also found it hard to sacrifice the lamb as a symbol of the coming Saviour. Some of the animals of sacrifice were sacred to the Egyptians and the sacrifice of them would have been an insult to the Egyptian gods and brought swift retribution. (Exodus 8:26)

- Egyptian worship was extreme idolatry and the building of temples and idols was all around the Israelites. The focus on the visible aspects of worship was constantly being impressed on the Israelites.

In this situation, the promises to Abraham could not be fulfilled. God said that all the families of the earth would be blessed through him. But this channel of blessing was now cut and Israel was in great danger. The Lord had to step in and reopen this channel for the sake of Israel and the world. The evidence of how dangerous the situation had become was revealed in the Israelite failure in regard to the manna – where they violated the Sabbath and also the apostasy with the golden calf. We will explore this more deeply later, but Israel was now fully under the curse and their families extremely vulnerable.

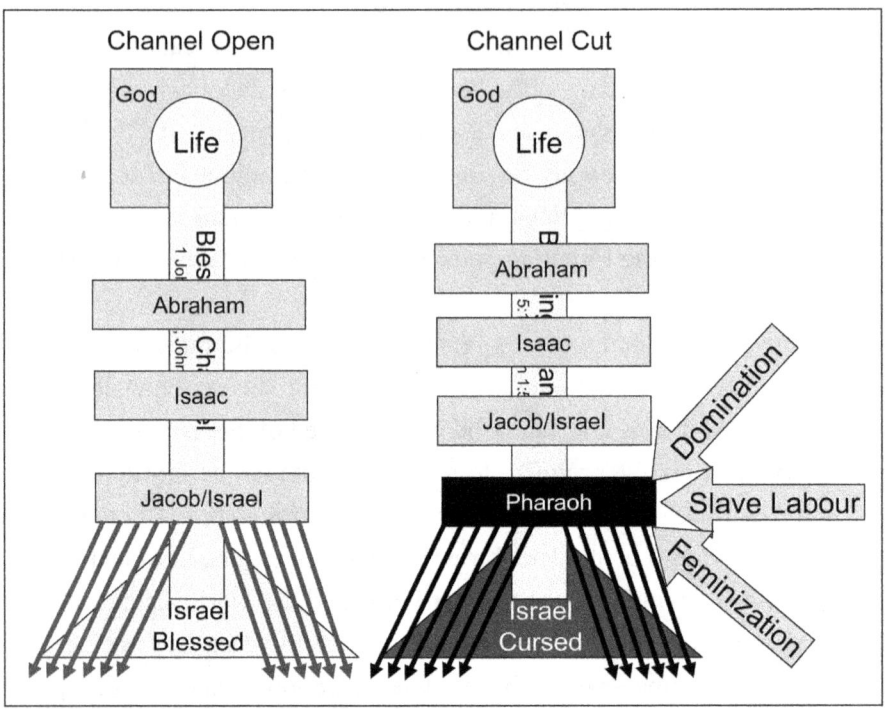

e. The Deliverer – The Call of Moses to the Prophetic Office

The authority of Israel had been usurped by Pharaoh. He had taken Israel captive as slaves, feminized their society by killing the baby boys in the river and had no intention of letting them go free. The insecurity of Pharaoh could only be quieted by controlling them as slaves. This is the ultimate fate of any society that allows a power-based value system to rule them. It happened in Pharaoh's day and these things were written for our instruction, because it is going to happen again.

How was God going to restore the channel of blessing to Israel? Israel was in slavery partly by allowing the situation to happen to themselves, because they were influenced by Egypt's desire for power and wealth. Just as Adam had willingly become a slave of Satan in the garden, so Israel willingly became a slave of the Egyptians. Only once in chains, did Adam and Israel begin to realize the foolishness of their actions.

The Channel of Blessing Lost and Restored Through Egyptian Pilgrimage

God called a man – Moses – to act as His prophet and deliver His people back to the channel of blessing. We will notice through history that when the channel of God's blessing is blocked, God authorizes a prophet to restore the channel. It took some effort to convince Moses to go, but with the assurance that Aaron his brother would speak on his behalf, he consented to go. (Exodus 4:10-16).

The Lord sends Moses to appeal to Pharaoh to let His people go. Why did God send Moses to ASK Pharaoh to let His people go? Why didn't He just send Moses to tell Pharaoh we are going to leave and if you get in the way, our God will annihilate you and your people? Remember that Pharaoh's rulership of Israel was legitimate because Israel subscribed to the spirit of Egypt and finally became physical slaves to Egypt. If God had just removed the people, even though they were His, He would have instilled in His people the seed of disregard for authority. The word of Pharaoh had to be secured to let them go. This is a vital principle. Even though Pharaoh was a heathen king, still his authority was respected. It is true that God revealed Himself in the plagues, so that Pharaoh could understand who he was dealing with, but the death and destruction was the responsibility of Pharaoh because he refused to heed the warnings and acknowledge that the Israelites truly belonged to God.

As Moses heads towards Egypt to begin his mission, his family structure needed bringing back into line.

> **Exod 4:24-27** And it came to pass by the way in the inn, that the LORD met him, and sought to kill him. **25** Then Zipporah took a sharp stone, and cut off the foreskin of her son, and cast *it* at his feet, and said, Surely a bloody husband *art* thou to me. **26** So he let him go: then she said, A bloody husband *thou art*, because of the circumcision. **27** And the LORD said to Aaron, Go into the wilderness to meet Moses. And he went, and met him in the mount of God, and kissed him.

All Israelites were required to perform the rite of circumcision. Moses had failed to carry this rite out on his son because of the protests of his wife. If this issue was not dealt with, the entire mission would have failed. This was a life and death issue and the Bible portrays that God made as though he would kill Moses. He needed Moses to understand the importance of being the head of his home. If he could not be the head of his home, how could he lead the church of God?

Zipporah outwardly submitted and performed the rite herself, but in her heart she still resented the command. It would take time for her to learn the principles of submission.

f. The Plagues of Egypt – Reveal the Lie of Inherent Power in Nature

When Moses went to Egypt, he was to explain the relationship that Israel had to the God of heaven. Israel was God's son – or builder of the family name. It was through Israel that God would bless the families of the world. The actions of Pharaoh were damaging God's ability to bless the world.

> **Exod 4:22-23** And thou shalt say unto Pharaoh, Thus saith the LORD, Israel *is* my son, *even* my firstborn: **23** And I say unto thee, Let my son go, that he may serve me: and if thou refuse to let him go, behold, I will slay thy son, *even* thy firstborn.

Pharaoh's firstborn carried the birthright of death. He was trained in the principles of the lie of the serpent and his insecurity and worthlessness would possibly make him a greater tyrant than his father. If Israel remained another generation under the new Pharaoh, their family identity would have been obliterated. God had no choice but lay the decision before Pharaoh. Remember that God did not want to slay Pharaoh's son, He just wanted His son to be free to receive the channel of blessing again; and if Pharaoh would not yield, then the only way to open that channel was to remove the blockage to that blessing.

Sadly Pharaoh, in his pride, would not let Israel go. Pharaoh believed that his gods were stronger than the Hebrews and that through this power he could keep them enslaved. Each of the plagues that God brought revealed power over aspects of Egyptian worship. It also revealed that the God of Israel was stronger and the true source of power.

The Channel of Blessing Lost and Restored Through Egyptian Pilgrimage

Plague	Egyptian god, idol or temple priest targeted	Significance
1. Water Turned to Blood – Ex 7:17-19	Nile River – the giver of life and the gift of Egypt	The Egyptian's giver of life now was the giver of death. Egyptians thirsted to shed Hebrew blood, now God was giving them blood to drink.
2. Frogs – Ex 8:5,6	Isis – fertility goddess	Isis was often represented as a frog. She symbolized new life. A frog was thought of as good luck. Now they were dying and fouling everything. Their "new life" was being racked up in dead piles.
3. Lice – Ex 8:16,17	Seth – earth god	This little, insignificant creature now rose from the earth to torture the people. All the prayers to Seth didn't help, and lice are born of earth.
4. Swarm of Flies – Ex 8:20-24	Beelzebub – prince of the air	Flies were always around and considered ears of Beelzebub. Now they were attacking in droves, driving the people crazy and their priests could not stop it. The fact that they didn't attack the Hebrews set them apart as holy.
5. Cattle – Ex 9:4-6	Apis – sacred bull	God demonstrated that He was the sacred one. The bull could not stand up to His power.
6. Boils – Ex 9:8-11	Medical shamans	Boils were thought to represent punishment of sins. God punished them for their sins, and the magic of the medical shamans could not stop it.
7. Hail – Ex 9:22-26	Weather shamans	Weather shamans supposedly could control the weather, but here again God showed that only He controlled the weather.
8. Locusts – Ex 10:4-6	Agriculture shamans	Agriculture shamans supposedly could control the crops through their magical powers to placate or influence their false gods. God showed them that none could overcome His power.
9. Darkness – Ex 10:21-23	Amen-Re – most favored god and considered the most powerful.	The sun god Re was considered the father of the Pharaoh and the most powerful of gods. In defeating the sun, God showed that Amen-Re was powerless against Him.
10. Death of First Born – Ex 11:5	The first born was dedicated to god – was considered the favor of God or to the Egyptians, their gods	Several gods of Egypt were supposedly protectors of the lives of men and beasts. The Pharaoh was considered a god, and his son the next god.

It is interesting to note that the destruction that was brought upon Egypt came through the very things that the Egyptians worshipped, except for the last plague. The destruction that came upon the Egyptians was a symbol of the spiritual destruction their belief in these things were causing their families. In the spiritual world, the Egyptians were the true slaves; slaves of fear, worthlessness, pride and selfishness. If it was not for a belief in these false gods, they would have been spared this destruction.

These striking events that occurred in the past are an example of what will happen in the future when the New World Order leadership will seek to enslave the world and prevent God's faithful people from keeping His commandments, His Sabbath and all the things that are vital for a family based system as revealed in the family of Abraham.

g. Israel Delivered and the Channel of Blessing Restored

In the final plague, God's people were required to place lamb's blood on their door post, so that the angel of death would pass over them and their firstborn would be spared.

> **Exod 12:12-13** For I will pass through the land of Egypt this night, and will smite all the firstborn in the land of Egypt, both man and beast; and against all the gods of Egypt I will execute judgment: I *am* the LORD. **13** And the blood shall be to you for a token upon the houses where ye *are*: and when I see the blood, I will pass over you, and the plague shall not be upon you to destroy *you*, when I smite the land of Egypt.
>
> **Exod 12:21-22** Then Moses called for all the elders of Israel, and said unto them, Draw out and take you a lamb according to your families, and kill the passover. **22** And ye shall take a bunch of hyssop, and dip *it* in the blood that *is* in the basin, and strike the lintel and the two side posts with the blood that *is* in the basin; and none of you shall go out at the door of his house until the morning.

The blood of the lamb was a symbol of the blood of Christ that was shed that we might have life. When Adam and Eve sinned and became servants of Satan, they forfeited their right to life. The Son of God stepped into the gap and promised to give His life to keep the channel of life open for Adam and Eve. The promise of His blood caused death to pass over Adam and Eve and shield them from the true impact of their sin. This symbol was revealed in the lambskins that they wore and covered them. In the time of Israel, the covering

The Channel of Blessing Lost and Restored Through Egyptian Pilgrimage

was symbolized by the blood on the door posts. Without the blood of the lamb, there is only death for the human race. Thank God for the blood of the Lamb that causes permanent death to pass over us.

God immediately went to work to re-educate the children of Israel in the channel of blessing foundations and true family structure.

Abraham	Israel
1. Family Structure (Gen 18:19)	1. The 5th commandment restored the family structure. The release from slavery gave families more time to spend together. Inheritance determined by family genealogy.
2. Nomadic Rural Dwellers (Heb 11:8-10)	2. Israel returned to a rural setting in the wilderness living in tents.
3. Identity by Parental Blessing (Gen 12:2)	3. God promised to bless Israel if faithful. The 5th commandment concerning parents restored the family blessing channel.
4. Observe Sabbath and Commandments (Gen 26:5)	4. God gave the commandments on Mt Sinai and taught them about the Sabbath through the collection of the manna.
5. Belief in Death and Resurrection (Heb 11:17-19)	5. The 5th commandment revealed God as the only source of life and the only One that keeps us alive. Without Him there is no life.
6. Saviour as Humble Life Restorer – Revealed in Slain Lamb (John 11:25)	6. A complete Sanctuary worship system was given to fully reveal the work of the coming Saviour and His work to teach us His commandments.
7. Focus of Worship on the Invisible	7. The second commandment focused worship on the invisible.

It would take time for Israel to relearn the principles of the channel of blessing via the Ten Commandments and Sanctuary system. The experience of Israel in regard to the worship of the golden calf revealed how far Israel had fallen from a true understanding of God's family kingdom.

The lack of respect for leadership developed in Egypt and fostered by the lie of the serpent caused some to cast doubt on the leadership of Moses and caused Israel to sin by the worship around the golden calf.

Exod 32:1-7 And when the people saw that Moses delayed to come

> down out of the mount, the people gathered themselves together unto Aaron, and said unto him, Up, make us gods, which shall go before us; for *as for* this Moses, the man that brought us up out of the land of Egypt, we wot not what is become of him. **2** And Aaron said unto them, Break off the golden earrings, which *are* in the ears of your wives, of your sons, and of your daughters, and bring *them* unto me. **3** And all the people brake off the golden earrings which *were* in their ears, and brought *them* unto Aaron. **4** And he received *them* at their hand, and fashioned it with a graving tool, after he had made it a molten calf: and they said, These *be* thy gods, O Israel, which brought thee up out of the land of Egypt. **5** And when Aaron saw *it*, he built an altar before it; and Aaron made proclamation, and said, To morrow *is* a feast to the LORD. **6** And they rose up early on the morrow, and offered burnt offerings, and brought peace offerings; and the people sat down to eat and to drink, and rose up to play. **7** And the LORD said unto Moses, Go, get thee down; for thy people, which thou broughtest out of the land of Egypt, have corrupted *themselves*:

The people were not familiar with maintaining a faith relationship with God without visible tokens of worship. While Moses their visible leader was gone, the people revealed their spiritual blindness to look beyond the visible. Even though there was evidence of God's presence on the mountain, the people clamored for something they could see to worship.

Just as Adam and Abraham hearkened to the voice of their wives, Aaron hearkened unto the voice of the people (the church – symbolized by a woman) and fashioned a golden calf for them and caused them to sin.

Graciously, God forgave Israel and this event revealed to Israel that they had no power to keep their promises to follow Him. They had to trust in the blood of the lamb as revealed in the Sanctuary service and the protective commandments designed to keep the channel of blessing open. The recovery of these things would ensure that Abraham would be a blessing to the families of the world.

Hopefully we can see that the seven points in Abraham's family system hold the key to helping us build and retain a treasure of family memories and enable our children to know they are loved and blessed.

Chapter 14

The Protection of the Channel of Blessing

As we have examined previously, the Bible presents to us a model of life where God is the source of life, spiritually, mentally and physically. This life is not donated or given as a package but is streamed continually to us through His Spirit. In that stream of life is the vital element of blessing which we discovered is called the glory of children. Without the blessing of the father through this stream, life lacks purpose and meaning.

We have examined closely the roles of husband and wife as a human example of the source or seed principle to pass on this blessing, and the birthing and nurture principle which submits to the seed/source and acts as the key example of how to stay connected to the channel of blessing.

We have witnessed in the book of Genesis how Satan has made several attempts to break this channel of blessing system and we have examined the key components in the family of Abraham to keep this channel of blessing system in operation.

The children of Israel had the foundations of its channel of blessing decimated and now that Israel was released from their bondage, they needed to be taught again these vital principles.

The centre piece of this rebuilding program was the giving of the Ten Commandments on Mt Sinai. A close examination of these commandments in light of the family channel of blessing reveals some very interesting things.

a. Clear Identity Roles are Vital

At the end of Chapter 6 we made the following statement:

> Therefore recognition of this male seeding/headship identity and a fe-

male nurture/submission identity reflecting the image of the heavenly Father and Son is the vital key to build a treasure of family memories upon a strong and harmonious relational system.

A clear perception of our identity and who we are is vital to keeping this channel of blessing open. For instance, when we realize that as humans we have no life in ourselves, this is a perception of our identity. When we realize that God alone has life to give and share, this is a perception of His identity. In Chapter 7 we looked at Satan's introduction of the inherent life source concept, meaning that human beings have or possess life in themselves.

Gen 3:4 And the serpent said unto the woman, Ye shall not surely die:

This lie confused our perception of the identity of God as the only possessor of life and also confused the identity of ourselves as having no life inherently. This confusion of identity caused the human to lose interest in staying vitally connected to God and fostered the spirit of independence and self sufficiency.

The point we are making is that for the channel of blessing to flow correctly, both the identity of the source of the channel and the identity of the receiver of the channel must be clearly understood otherwise the channel breaks down. The following story gives a good example of how incorrect perception of identity can cause a breakdown in communication channels.

The following is a transcript of radio communication between American and Canadian forces during the Second World War:

> **CANADIANS**: Please divert your course 15 degrees to the south to avoid a collision.
>
> **AMERICANS**: Recommend you divert your course 15 degrees to the north to avoid collision.
>
> **CANADIANS**: Negative. You will have to divert your course 15 degrees to the south to avoid a collision.
>
> **AMERICANS**: This is the captain of a U.S Navy ship. I say again, divert YOUR course.
>
> **CANADIANS**: No, I say again, you divert YOUR course.
>
> **AMERICANS**: This is the Aircraft Carrier USS LINCOLN, the second largest ship in the United states Atlantic fleet. We are accompanied with three Destoyers, three Cruisers and numerous support vessels. I DEMAND that you change your course 15 degrees north. I

say again that's one-five degrees north or counter-measures will be undertaken to ensure the safety of this ship

CANADIANS: This is the lighthouse. Your call.

The American ship did not understand the true identity of the lighthouse and therefore related to the lighthouse in an arrogant manner. The American ship had also overestimated its own sense of power; it had a false perception of itself, for no ship could force the lighthouse on the mighty rock to move from its position. This story illustrates what happened to the human race when it embraced the lie of the serpent. Humanity no longer wished to submit to God and the channel of blessing was broken.

With these things in mind, let us consider the plight of the Israelites. While in Egypt, many of the Israelites had been affected by the Egyptian religion which believed strongly in the immortality, or inherent life source of the soul. Therefore the Israelite perception of God's true identity was confused. They were also confused about their own identity.

b. The Ten Commandments Define Identity of God and Man

The giving of the Ten Commandments to Israel was the key initiative in restoring a correct perception of identity so that the channel of blessing could be restored and protected. These commandments were so vital that they are the only words in the Bible that God wrote directly Himself.

> **Exod 31:18** And he gave unto Moses, when he had made an end of communing with him upon mount Sinai, two tables of testimony, tables of stone, written with the finger of God.

Each one of these commandments tells us something about the God of the Bible, what he is like and what is most important to Him. Let us look closely at each of these commandments and see what they tell us.

Commandment	Attribute of God
1. I brought you out of bondage. You will have no other Gods besides Me.	Redeemer and Saviour, the only source of blessing.
2. You shall not make any carved image.	Relational internal focus rather than material external focus.
3. You will not take the name of God in vain.	Integrity and transparency in relationships.
4. Remember the Sabbath for in six days the Lord made the heavens and the earth.	Creator of all things, source of life and blessing.
5. Honour father and mother.	Family blessing structure. Respect for Authority.
6. You shall not kill.	Life is precious, relationships are forever, I am the source of life.
7. You shall not commit adultery.	Valid intimate relationships are forever.
8. You shall not steal.	Spiritual/relational not material focus.
9. You shall not lie.	Integrity and transparency in relationships.
10. You shall not covet.	Reveals God as the source of life and blessing. Coveting assets and possessions denies this reality.

Each of these commandments is aimed at protecting our sense of who God is and therefore protecting the channel of blessing. In these commandments God tells us:

1. That He is the only source of blessing.
2. That He is not to be worshipped through visible and material objects as this destroys our perception of God as a truly relational being and shifts our focus to material and external things.
3. That our perception of His identity can be undermined by taking His name in vain; meaning claiming to belong to Him when our hearts are elsewhere.
4. The 4th commandment is the clearest statement we have revealing God as the source of all created things. This commandment is the most vital of all the commandments in giving us a right perception of God's identity.
5. The 5th commandment is the second most vital commandment as it reveals the human structures through which God's channel of blessing flows. It speaks to us of the importance of submission, obedience and

The Protection of the Channel of Blessing

respect.

6. Each of the last five commandments are practical human expressions of revealing God as the only life source and how the avoidance of these things will aid in staying connected to Him.

If we study the Bible further, we see that the Ten Commandments are expressed as a reflection of God's character; a written form of what He is like. This is a further confirmation of the fact the law reveals God's identity and is a protection of the source of blessing.

Notice the following comparisons:

God's Character		God's Law	
1. Spiritual	John 4:24	1. Spiritual	Romans 7:14
2. Love	1 John 4:8	2. Love	Matt. 22:37-40
3. Truth	John 14:6	3. Truth	Psalms 119:142
4. Righteous	1 Cor. 1:30	4. Righteous	Psalms 119:144,172
5. Holy	Isaiah 6:3	5. Holy	Romans 7:12
6. Perfect	Matt 5:48	6. Perfect	Psalms 19:7
7. Good	Luke 18:19	7. Good	Romans 7:12
8. Just	Deut. 32:4	8. Just	Romans 7:12
9. Pure	1 John 3:3	9. Pure	Psalms 19:8
10. Unchanging	James 1:17	10. Unchanging	Matt. 5:18
11. Stands Forever	Psalms 90:2	11. Stands Forever	Psalms 111:7,8
12. The Way	John 14:6	12. The Way	Malachi 2:7-9
13. Great	Psalms 48:1	13. Great	Hosea 8:12
14. Cleanses	Matt. 8:3 Psalms. 57:2	14. Clean	Ezekiel 22:26

Since these commandments tell us that it is God who created and made us and that we have come forth from His hand, the commandments also clearly reveal our origins and identity. When we understand the commandments in this light we can understand why the Bible speaks about the law in the following way.

> **Psa 19:7-8** The law of the LORD *is* perfect, converting the soul: the testimony of the LORD *is* sure, making wise the simple. **8** The statutes of the LORD *are* right, rejoicing the heart: the commandment of the LORD *is* pure, enlightening the eyes.

> **Psa 111:7-8** The works of his hands *are* verity and judgment; all his commandments *are* sure. **8** They stand fast for ever and ever, *and are*

done in truth and uprightness.

Eccl 12:13 Let us hear the conclusion of the whole matter: Fear God, and keep his commandments: for this *is* the whole *duty* of man.

Isa 42:21 The LORD is well pleased for his righteousness' sake; he will magnify the law, and make *it* honourable.

Matt 5:17 Think not that I am come to destroy the law, or the prophets: I am not come to destroy, but to fulfil.

Matt 22:36-40 Master, which *is* the great commandment in the law? **37** Jesus said unto him, Thou shalt love the Lord thy God with all thy heart, and with all thy soul, and with all thy mind. **38** This is the first and great commandment. **39** And the second *is* like unto it, Thou shalt love thy neighbour as thyself. **40** On these two commandments hang all the law and the prophets.

Rom 7:12 Wherefore the law *is* holy, and the commandment holy, and just, and good.

Rev 14:12 Here is the patience of the saints: here *are* they that keep the commandments of God, and the faith of Jesus.

Rev 22:14 Blessed *are* they that do his commandments, that they may have right to the Tree of Life, and may enter in through the gates into the city.

c. The Ten Commandments Twisted by the Lie of the Serpent

When we understand the law of God as a protection of the channel of blessing, then the law is something that is wonderful, lovely and precious. It is something that we should cling to and cherish as a precious gift from God. This is exactly how King David saw it.

Psa 119:97 O how love I thy law! it is my meditation all the day.

Psa 40:8 I delight to do thy will, O my God: yea, thy law *is* within my heart.

Psa 119:77 Let thy tender mercies come unto me, that I may live: for thy law *is* my delight.

One of the most terrible things that Satan has deceived the world about, concerns the law of God. Many Christian churches teach and believe that we can't keep the Ten Commandments. Trying to keep the commandments is referred to as legalism. Many Christians teach that: the law was nailed to the cross of Christ, Christian believers are set free from the law, and the only command we have today is to love one another.

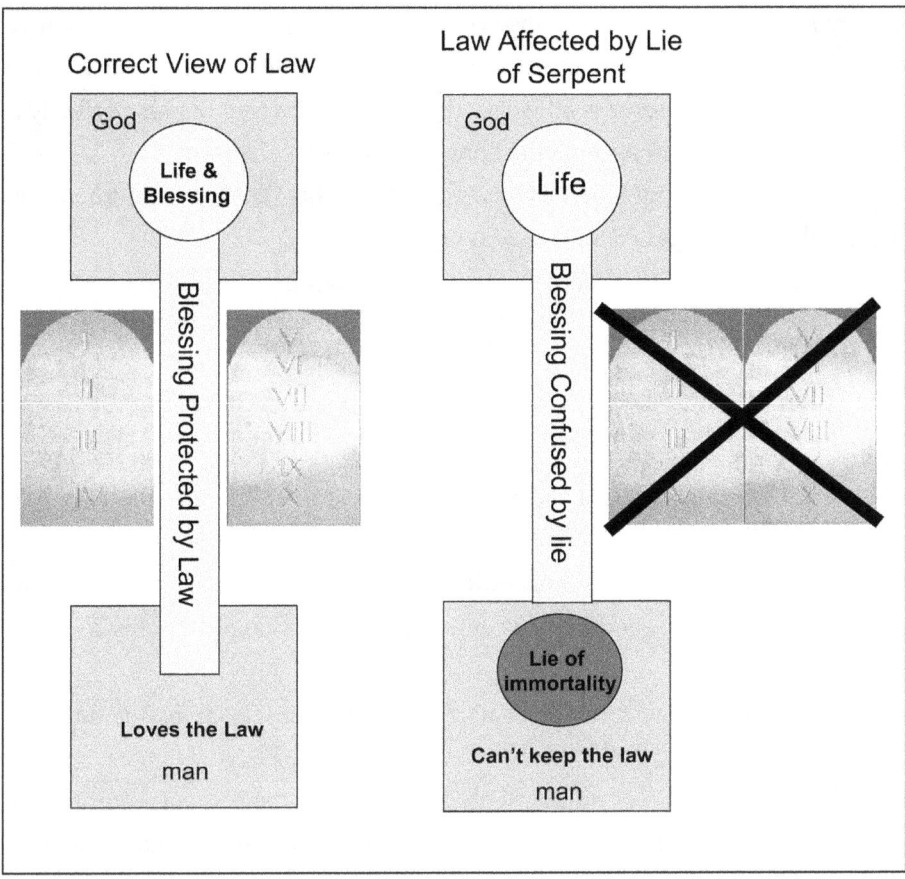

Why do many Christians think this way? Why do Christians often see the law as an enemy rather than a loving friend that protects the channel of blessing system? The simple answer is the lie of the serpent. Notice the following:

> **Rom 7:10-11** And the commandment, which *was ordained* to life, I found *to be* unto death. **11** For sin, taking occasion by the commandment, deceived me, and by it slew *me*.

The Bible clearly states that the commandments were ordained to life, or the protection of life. But sin – or the entrance of the serpent's lie – deceives and kills us. How does this take place?

The lie of the serpent causes us to believe that there is some level of power in ourselves. The lie also causes us to want to prove ourselves by displays of such power. When the law of God is introduced to a person in this state of mind, then the first inclination is to try and obey this law *in order to please* God. After several attempts to do this and the constant experience of failure, a person will either give up his belief or he will swing to the belief that we don't have to keep the law; the death of Jesus is all we need. This type of reasoning fits perfectly the words of Paul, that sin through the commandment deceives us.

God never ever intended us to try and keep the Ten Commandments as a means of trying to gain acceptance with Him.

> **Eph 2:8-9** For by grace are ye saved through faith; and that not of yourselves: *it is* the gift of God: **9** Not of works, lest any man should boast.

> **Rom 4:3-5** For what saith the Scripture? Abraham believed God, and it was counted unto him for righteousness. **4** Now to him that worketh is the reward not reckoned of grace, but of debt. **5** But to him that worketh not, but believeth on him that justifieth the ungodly, his faith is counted for righteousness.

The lie of the serpent actually turns us against the very thing that was designed to protect us and keep us connected to the channel of blessing. So as Paul says:

> **Rom 8:7** Because the carnal mind *is* enmity against God: for it is not subject to the law of God, neither indeed can be.

The carnal mind – or mind affected by the lie of the serpent – can't submit to the law of God, either because he refuses to submit or he finds that he has power in himself to do it. But once the lie of inherent power is removed, the law of God is the most wonderful protective gift from God; and the most precious parts of this law are the two laws at the centre: the command concerning the Sabbath which is the clearest revelation of God as the source of life and invites us to rest in that reality; and the law to honour our parents which gives us the most practical expression of God's family kingdom and reveals how the blessing is passed from generation to generation. Most people recognize the importance of families, but few people see the importance of the Sabbath in the war against Satan to protect the channel of blessing.

The Protection of the Channel of Blessing

> **Isa 58:13-14** If thou turn away thy foot from the sabbath, *from* doing thy pleasure on my holy day; and call the sabbath a delight, the holy of the LORD, honourable; and shalt honour him, not doing thine own ways, nor finding thine own pleasure, nor speaking *thine own* words: **14** Then shalt thou delight thyself in the LORD; and I will cause thee to ride upon the high places of the earth, and feed thee with the heritage of Jacob thy father: for the mouth of the LORD hath spoken *it*.

How wonderful it is that God gave Israel a law to protect them from the snares of Satan. But God did not stop here. He placed this law at the centre of a system of worship that would teach the Israelites how to approach and worship Him. After all their exposure to Egyptian idolatry, it would take time for Israel to learn to know and understand God. When they first heard His voice they were so afraid that they wanted to run away.

> **Exod 20:18-19** And all the people saw the thunderings, and the lightnings, and the noise of the trumpet, and the mountain smoking: and when the people saw *it*, they removed, and stood afar off. **19** And they said unto Moses, Speak thou with us, and we will hear: but let not God speak with us, lest we die.

It was one thing for God to speak this law from Mt Sinai, but this law would have no protective effect unless its principles resided in their hearts and became part of their way of thinking. Therefore, the transfer of the principles of the law from the tables of stone to the tables of their hearts became the focus of God's covenant with Israel.

> **Heb 8:10** For this *is* the covenant that I will make with the house of Israel after those days, saith the Lord; I will put my laws into their mind, and write them in their hearts: and I will be to them a God, and they shall be to me a people:

Sadly, Israel revealed that they also had been deceived by the lie of the serpent, by promising God they would obey the law.

> **Exod 19:5-8** Now therefore, if ye will obey my voice indeed, and keep my covenant, then ye shall be a peculiar treasure unto me above all people: for all the earth *is* mine: **6** And ye shall be unto me a kingdom of priests, and an holy nation. These *are* the words which thou shalt speak unto the children of Israel. **7** And Moses came and called for the elders of the people, and laid before their faces all these words which the LORD commanded him. **8** And all the people answered together, and said, All that the LORD hath spoken we will do. And Moses returned the words of the people unto the LORD.

When God asked them to keep His law, He wanted to see if they would realize whether they could obey or not. He hoped that they would ask the Lord to help them, but influenced by the lie of inherent power, they boldly promised to be obedient.

It was quickly revealed that this was impossible as evidenced in the dancing around the golden calf.

> **Exod 32:7-8** And the LORD said unto Moses, Go, get thee down; for thy people, which thou broughtest out of the land of Egypt, have corrupted *themselves*: **8** They have turned aside quickly out of the way which I commanded them: they have made them a molten calf, and have worshipped it, and have sacrificed thereunto, and said, These *be* thy gods, O Israel, which have brought thee up out of the land of Egypt.

This experience is referred to as the old covenant. The new covenant, which was always God's intent, was to write this protective law into their hearts Himself. In writing this law in their hearts, they would become like Him; because as we noticed, the law reflects who God is. So how would God accomplish this?

God gave to Israel a Sanctuary worship system that showed them how to connect to this law and allow its principles to be transferred into their hearts. The Israelite Sanctuary system is actually a journey into the very heart and mind of God. It allowed them to come close to Him, be near Him and be like Him. What a wonderful gift this was! Here was a system that would protect their families and keep them connected to the channel of blessing

Chapter 15

The Journey from Tables of Stone to the Tables of the Heart

a. The Desolating Effects of the Serpent's Lie

In Chapter 8 we noticed the devastating impacts of the lie of inherent life source on individuals and families. The breaking of the channel of blessing exposes the human heart to fear, worthlessness, pride and selfishness on a wide scale. The only way to survive this continual wave of emotions is to encase the heart with a protective wall. After a time, this is still not enough and we have to toughen ourselves even further. This process causes the heart to harden.

From the innocent, trusting heart of a child, life's experiences creates doubt, suspicion, fear, pain, guilt and regret. The ability to trust people is eroded and many people find the only way to survive is to isolate their emotions, keep their feelings to themselves and avoid the danger of being vulnerable. Through the lie of the serpent, the human soul wanders from the life giving river into the desolating desert of heat, sand and salt bush.

As our Father in heaven looks down upon His children wandering in the soul deserts of life, His heart is touched with pity. He observes the abominable desolating impacts of the serpent's lie and reaches out to us to bring us back to the life giving river.

The journey of coming back to the river is carefully described in the worship system that God gave to Israel. During their time in Egypt, the Israelites had their hearts desolated by the abominable Egyptian power that enslaved them. Even though their bodies were now free, their minds were still enslaved to the lie of the serpent; their hearts were still bruised and hardened by the sorrows and suffering of fear, worthlessness and pride.

At a later time in Israel's history, God expressed this process of changing the hearts of His people – a heart transplant if you will.

> **Ezek 36:26-27** A new heart also will I give you, and a new spirit will I put within you: and I will take away the stony heart out of your flesh, and I will give you an heart of flesh. **27** And I will put my spirit within you, and cause you to walk in my statutes, and ye shall keep my judgments, and do *them*.

God promised to send His life giving spirit to Israel. Like a stream of pure crystal water flowing from the throne, the Spirit of God immerses the human heart in blessing, love, forgiveness and acceptance and slowly the heart softens, warms, strengthens and in turn learns to love and live again.

King David describes this process as a tree by a river:

> **Psa 1:1-3** Blessed *is* the man that walketh not in the counsel of the ungodly, nor standeth in the way of sinners, nor sitteth in the seat of the scornful. **2** But his delight *is* in the law of the LORD; and in his law doth he meditate day and night. **3** And he shall be like a tree planted by the rivers of water, that bringeth forth his fruit in his season; his leaf also shall not wither; and whatsoever he doeth shall prosper.

Notice again, the role of the law of God in this process. The law is the protection of this river of life coming into the soul. As we noticed in the last chapter, it enables us to discern the source of the river and by revealing who we are and who God is, we become like the submissive ship to the lighthouse; willing to receive the wise counsel and instruction the lighthouse offers us.

With all this in mind, it becomes clear that restoring the channel of blessing involves a writing of the principles of God's law in our hearts and mind.

b. The Sanctuary System

Let us now look closely at the system of worship that God gave to Israel and observe the journey that is outlined in it.

The Journey from Tables of Stone to the Tables of the Heart

Exod 25:8, 9 And let them make me a sanctuary; that I may dwell among them. According to all that I shew thee, after the pattern of the tabernacle, and the pattern of all the instruments thereof, even so shall ye make it.

There are many details in the Israelite Sanctuary system and it is not the purpose of this book to explore them all. Our main aim it to look at the main sections and the progression from one side of the Sanctuary to the other.

The outline of the Sanctuary is essentially two squares joined together. At the centre of the first square is the altar of burnt offering. At the center of the second square is the Ark of the Covenant containing the law of Ten Commandments.

Notice the following outline:

Life Matters

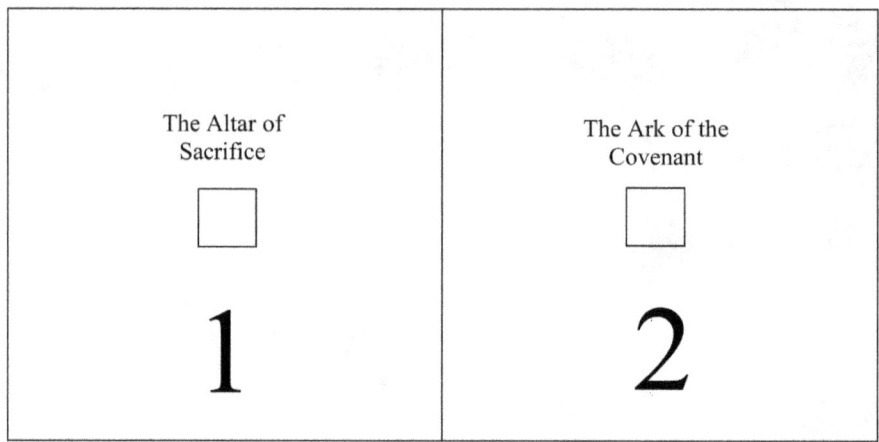

Both boxes are about the restoration of life. At the centre of box one is the symbol of the death of the lamb. The slain lamb is a symbol of the giving of God's Son so that we might continue to have life.

> **John 3:16** For God so loved the world, that he gave his only begotten Son, that whosoever believeth in him should not perish, but have everlasting life.

When Adam and Eve cut the life source to God by sin, the Son of God immediately placed Himself where the break occurred; joined the two broken pieces together and kept the life flowing to the human race. This break in the life source was now carried in the heart of the Son of God. The only way to rid the  universe of this break in the line was to take it to the grave to destroy it and then rise again without it. There was no other way to fix the problem other than letting the entire human race be obliterated.

At the centre of the second box was contained the Ten Commandment Law of God.

> **Exod 25:10-16** And they shall make an ark *of* shittim wood: two cubits and a half *shall be* the length thereof, and a cubit and a half the

The Journey from Tables of Stone to the Tables of the Heart

breadth thereof, and a cubit and a half the height thereof. **11** And thou shalt overlay it with pure gold, within and without shalt thou overlay it, and shalt make upon it a crown of gold round about. **12** And thou shalt cast four rings of gold for it, and put *them* in the four corners thereof; and two rings *shall be* in the one side of it, and two rings in the other side of it.... **16** And thou shalt put into the ark the testimony which I shall give thee.

Exod 31:18 And he gave unto Moses, when he had made an end of communing with him upon mount Sinai, two tables of testimony, tables of stone, written with the finger of God.

Arriving at the centre of this square is the ultimate destination of the journey from a heart of stone to a heart of flesh. The writing of this law in the heart and mind would permanently connect the human soul to the channel of blessing and protect them for being exposed to the curse. It also symbolized the most intimate point, for this is where the presence of God dwelt. This is the point where we as God's children experience the height of blessing as sons and daughters of God.

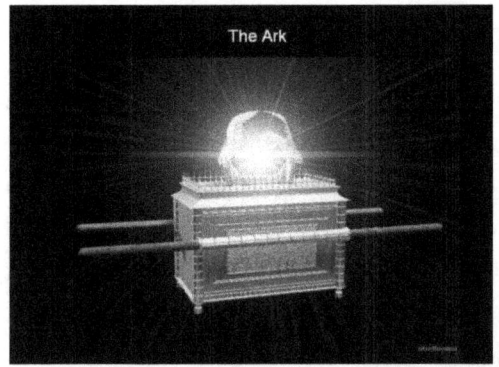

The Ark

It would be nice to think that this was a simple journey from point 1 to 2 but the lie of the serpent in our hearts makes this journey extremely difficult. The constant temptation to doubt God along the way or constant attempts to try and use the law as a means of proving our love and devotion constantly get in the way and take us off the path to life.

Let us add the next layer of detail to this Sanctuary system. We remember from the comparison of Abraham and Nimrod that the focus of Abraham's worship was relational and invisible, but Nimrod's worship focused on the visible and tangible. The Sanctuary journey moves from visible to invisible. It trains us to focus on the unseen rather than the seen.

VISIBLE	INVISIBLE
The Altar of Sacrifice	The Ark of the Covenant
☐	☐
1	2

The Israelite worshipper could enter the first square and offer his sacrifice. This area was called the court. He could see everything in this square. The death of Christ on the cross, which is the focus of the altar, was a recorded event on the earth that was seen. The vision of the cross and the gift of life given to us is the beginning of our journey. God meets us where we are, He comes near to us.

In our human existence with our focus on the visible and tangible, God meets us and confronts us with His gift of life. But the ultimate aim is to shift our thinking to the spiritual-relational world, the world of the mind. This is the real place where the work of transformation must take place and so the second square contained a Sanctuary that the worshipper could not enter. He could not see inside except by the eye of faith. Only the priest could enter this area and do a work for the worshipper. He could not do this for himself.

The invisibility of the second square is a symbol of the work that is done in heaven for us. We cannot now enter heaven and see what is happening on our behalf. God is working to transform our hearts and write His law within us, but we have no outward evidence of this work; neither in heaven, nor in our hearts – we can't see what is taking place with the human eye.

Let us add another layer of detail for the second square.

The Journey from Tables of Stone to the Tables of the Heart

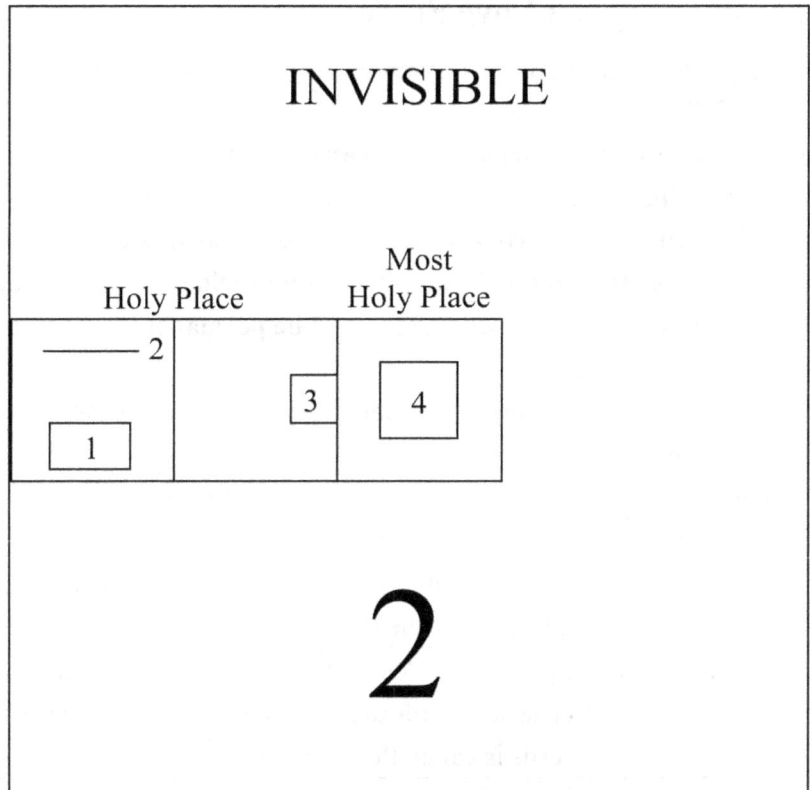

The tabernacle that the Israelites were instructed to build was made up of three squares. The Holy Place occupied two squares and the Most Holy occupied one square. The entrance of the Holy Place contained a curtain and the entrance of the Most Holy Place contained a curtain.

In the first half of the Holy Place was contained a table (1) with unleavened bread called shew bread and on the other side a candlestick (2) with seven lamps. This candlestick lighted the Holy Place. At the other end of the Holy Place was the Altar of Incense where prayer was offered.

c. The Journey is a Love Story

Each piece of furniture was symbolic in some way of the work and character of Christ.

The most important principle to learn about the Sanctuary is that the writing of the law in the heart means essentially that we become like Christ. The reason we become like Christ is because He is the divine example of submission to the Father. By becoming like the Son of God, we also will learn the lessons of submission and be permanently connected to the channel of blessing.

As we look at the furniture of the Sanctuary, we see that each piece tells us something about Jesus.

Furniture	Symbol of Christ
Altar of Sacrifice	John 1:29 "The next day John seeth Jesus coming unto him, and saith, Behold the Lamb of God, which taketh away the sin of the world."
The Laver of Water	Eph 5:26 (John 1:1) "That he might sanctify and cleanse it with the washing of water by the word." Jesus is called the Word of God.
The Shew Bread	John 6:35 "And Jesus said unto them, I am the bread of life: he that cometh to me shall never hunger; and he that believeth on me shall never thirst."
The Candlesticks	John 8:12 "Then spake Jesus again unto them, saying, I am the light of the world: he that followeth me shall not walk in darkness, but shall have the light of life."
The Altar of Incense	John 14:6 "Jesus saith unto him, I am the way, the truth, and the life: no man cometh unto the Father, but by me." – We pray to the Father through Christ.
The Ark	Matt 5:17 "Think not that I am come to destroy the law, or the prophets: I am not come to destroy, but to fulfil."

These articles of furniture can be laid out in a line to represent the journey. This journey is called the Way. As each piece of furniture refers to Jesus and

The Journey from Tables of Stone to the Tables of the Heart

Jesus is the one who is the divine example of how to stay connected to the Father – Jesus is referred to as the Way, which is the truth that brings us life. Notice what Jesus says:

> **John 14:6** Jesus saith unto him, I am the way, the truth, and the life: no man cometh unto the Father, but by me.

The way to come to the Father is symbolized by the Sanctuary system. As the Bible states:

> **Psa 77:13** Thy way, O God, *is* in the sanctuary: who *is so* great a God as *our* God?

So let's line up the pieces of furniture:

Walking with Jesus in the Sanctuary

	Court		Holy Place			Most Holy Place
	Altar of Sacrifice	Laver	Table of Shewbread	Candlesticks	Altar of Incense	Ark
Christ	Messiah		Priest			Judge
	Cross	Cleansing	The Truth	The Way	The Life	Judge
	John 1:29	Eph 5:26; I John 1:9	John 6:35	John 8:12; Ps 119:105	Heb 7:25; Rom 5:10	Mal 3:5
Us	Courtship		Engagement			Marriage
	Repent	Baptism	Bible Study	Witnessing	Prayer	Victory
	John 3:16; Acts 2:37,38	John 3:5	John 5:39	Matt 5:14	1 Thess 5:17	John 15:5

The row that refers to Christ reveals the work that Jesus does on our behalf in the journey from hearts of stone to hearts of flesh. The second row is our experience as we embrace an understanding of the work of Christ. For us this journey is a story of love, courtship and marriage. We move from the lies of isolation to a deeply intimate relationship with love overflowing in our hearts for our Saviour and in our love for Him we learn the true meaning of submission to the Father – the great source of all.

As we come in contact with Jesus through the story of the cross, we are struck by the incredible sense of love He has for us. His selfless act of giving His life acts like a cleansing agent of water and drives the first great crack into our hard hearts. His wooing love draws us into courtship with Him.

When we are convinced of the love of Christ and see good evidence for it in the Word of God, we wish to live with Him forever and we respond to His invitation to be married and so the engagement begins. Engagement is about learning more deeply the character of our prospective partner. Everywhere we go; we speak of our beloved and share our love and admiration of Him. For the Christian this process occurs through prayer, Bible study and sharing our faith. The more we study and share and pray, the more our love grows and the more eagerly we anticipate the marriage.

The marriage is where full revelation takes place. We see the character of Christ in all His glory in the Most Holy, we are captivated by the power of His love and we yield ourselves fully to Him. We remove everything from our lives that blocks our view of our wonderful husband/Saviour.

If you are not already on this journey, I invite you to begin. The writing of the law on your heart is painful at times as the hammer of the Word breaks open the encrusted heart. As the stones are removed and your heart is softened by the oil of God's Spirit – it feels so good to love and live again – to live without fear.

We have described the loving journey of the Sanctuary system, but we have not addressed the issue of how we get to the starting point of this journey. Once bitten by the serpent and under his influence, the human race was not free to just walk away. We were enslaved to the system of the serpent. We did not even know there was a way of escape, neither were we interested in one. As the Bible states:

> **Rom 3:11** There is none that understandeth, there is none that seeketh after God.
>
> **Rom 8:7** Because the carnal mind *is* enmity against God: for it is not subject to the law of God, neither indeed can be.

In the next chapter we will learn how God broke the power of the serpent and awoke within us the seeds of our true identity, which in turn drew our hearts to the door of the Sanctuary so that we could begin the journey.

Chapter 16

A Highway in the Desert

a. The Mountains and the Valleys

The Sanctuary system designed by God was designed to be a highway back to the paradise of the channel of blessing, but the lie of the serpent made it impossible for the human race to find this highway let alone start this journey.

In Chapter 8 we observed the cycle of worthlessness that comes with embracing the lie of inherent life. Let us notice again:

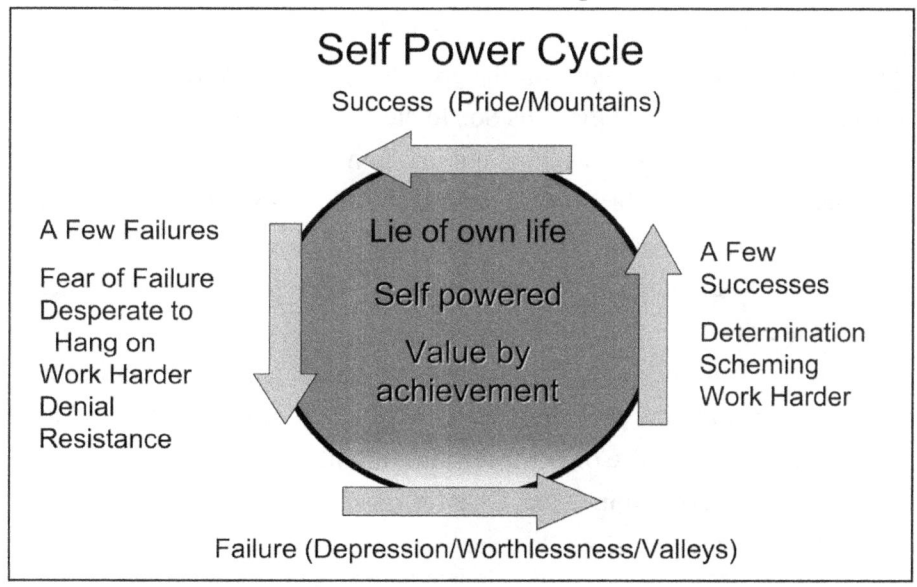

The inherent life system introduced by Satan causes people to feel proud when they achieve and worthless when they fail. This cycle of pride and worthlessness is like a series of mountains and valleys that are impassable.

These mountains and valleys actually become worse in a religious context. As we noted earlier, the law of God has been twisted by the lie of Satan to become a means of gaining acceptance with God or a constant reminder of their failure. As a result we often see religious bigots camping on the mountains of self importance, parading their religious zeal before all; but the majority of people usually camp in the valleys just feeling like it's all too hard, and that they will never be a good Christian.

This is the reason why the gate is strait and the path narrow that leads to life. The majority of people either invest great effort in good works to please God or just give up trying because they are sick of feeling bad all the time. There is also a significant group that move from one side to the other, trying and failing, trying and failing.

Unless the lie of the serpent is exposed and we can see our true relationship to God through the channel of blessing, everything we do will be blocked and hindered by mountains and valleys.

The most powerful demonstration of God's love – the gift of Jesus on the cross is also subject to these mountains and valleys. Many people are motivated by Christ's death on the cross to be a better person and to try and show Him that they love Him for the great thing He has done. Other's feel so unworthy that God would give His Son to die for them that they can't accept it; they feel that He died for others but not for them. For this reason, it was vitally important that before Christ died on the cross, He neutralized this false sense of identity which the human race had because of the serpent's lie. Before His death, Jesus would need to reveal our true position as sons and daughters of God that are greatly loved and accepted.

How could this be done in a way that such thoughts could reach the human mind? How could God reconnect us with the channel of blessing and at the same time give us a sense of our true value as children of God?

The plan is revealed in Isaiah Chapter 40:

> **Isa 40:3-11** The voice of him that crieth in the wilderness, Prepare ye the way of the LORD, make straight in the desert a highway for our God. **4** Every valley shall be exalted, and every mountain and hill shall be made low: and the crooked shall be made straight, and the rough places plain: **5** And the glory of the LORD shall be revealed, and all flesh shall see *it* together: for the mouth of the LORD hath spo-

ken *it*... **9** O Zion, that bringest good tidings, get thee up into the high mountain; O Jerusalem, that bringest good tidings, lift up thy voice with strength; lift *it* up, be not afraid; say unto the cities of Judah, Behold your God! **10** Behold, the Lord GOD will come with strong *hand*, and his arm shall rule for him: behold, his reward *is* with him, and his work before him. **11** He shall feed his flock like a shepherd: he shall gather the lambs with his arm, and carry *them* in his bosom, *and* shall gently lead those that are with young.

In this chapter, God reveals that He will deal with these mountains and valleys and make a clear path for the human race to walk on. (Verse 4) This would be done by the Son of God becoming one of us – this is the glory of the Lord being revealed. (Verse 5). How exactly would this happen:

1. By becoming one of us and taking our nature, Jesus would reconnect the human race with the channel of blessing and create a door into the human mind – the real battleground.
2. The Father's acceptance of the Son as a human would mean that humanity was also accepted by God as His children. This acceptance would break the cycle of worthlessness.
3. By living a perfectly submitted life to the Father, He would develop a human mind that would maintain the connection to the channel of blessing. The development of this mind would become the inheritance of all who accept Christ as their Saviour.
4. The Work of Jesus in heaven after His work here on earth would continue to provide us with a mindset that knows we are children of God and the ability to stay submitted to the Father.

b. Breaking the Cycle

The first step in this plan was accomplished when Jesus was born. He was made of the seed of David according to the flesh. As Paul states in Hebrews:

Heb 2:14 Forasmuch then as the children are partakers of flesh and blood, he also himself likewise took part of the same; that through death he might destroy him that had the power of death, that is, the devil;

The humanity of Jesus is our connecting link to the channel of blessing from the Father. In the book of John it is represented as a ladder.

> **John 1:51** And he saith unto him, Verily, verily, I say unto you, Hereafter ye shall see heaven open, and the angels of God ascending and descending upon the Son of man.

The feet of the ladder had to be firmly placed in human soil for the channel of blessing to reach us. Unless Jesus was truly human like us, then the connection would not be complete and the channel still not connected.

Once the channel was connected and God had access to the human mind through the humanity of Jesus, a message of acceptance needed to be delivered. A message that told us that God is not an aggravated King that is angry with us for stepping out of line, but that He is a tender Father that wants us back as part of His family and that the gifts He sends are from a loving Father not an angry judge.

This was accomplished at the baptism of Jesus, at the very beginning of His work. It would be pointless for Jesus to develop a perfect human mind if we did not have a sense of love and acceptance. Our performance based natures would not interpret the gift correctly. At the Baptism – the Father speaks directly to us through His Son. In speaking to Jesus, He is speaking to us.

> **Matt 3:16-17** And Jesus, when he was baptized, went up straightway out of the water: and, lo, the heavens were opened unto him, and he saw the Spirit of God descending like a dove, and lighting upon him: **17** And lo a voice from heaven, saying, This is my beloved Son, in whom I am well pleased.

What wonderful words to hear from the Father of the universe! You are my Son and I love and am pleased with you. To think that God is speaking these words to us – not because of our good deeds but simply because of our connection to Him through His Son.

> **Eph 1:6** To the praise of the glory of his grace, wherein he hath made us accepted in the beloved.

> **John 1:12** But as many as received him, to them gave he power [authority] to become the sons of God, *even* to them that believe on his name:

> **1 John 3:1** Behold, what manner of love the Father hath bestowed upon us, that we should be called the sons of God.

In accepting these words of the Father's love, our minds cease to be hostile to Him and His protective law. The acceptance of the words:

A Highway in the Desert
"YOU ARE MY BELOVED CHILD"

breaks the power of worthlessness and the lie of the serpent. It re-establishes our true identity as dependent children and opens the door for a relationship with God in his relational kingdom.

This statement is the blessing we all crave and it takes away the need for pride in achievement – God is proud of us just because we are His children. This statement takes away our sense of worthlessness – we don't have to feel useless because we are not achieving.

These words of blessing were originally designed to come through the channel of our earthly fathers as revealed in Proverbs 17:6 – The glory of children is their father. But sin has blurred this channel and in many cases cut it off, so that most of us live a very cursed life – trying to exist without a true sense of acceptance.

The great news is that in Jesus – we have the original and perfect Father – the source of all good fathers; and God is telling us through His Son that He loves us and accepts us.

Further to this, because Jesus accepted the words of His Father, we have access to this mindset of acceptance.

> **1 John 5:20** And we know that the Son of God is come, and hath given us an understanding [mind], that we may know him that is true, and we are in him that is true, *even* in his Son Jesus Christ. This is the true God, and eternal life.

> **1 Cor 2:16** For who hath known the mind of the Lord, that he may instruct him? But we have the mind of Christ.

In accepting Christ, a blessing of thoughts descend upon us that we are accepted and we receive a desire to respond. The very response that Jesus gave to His Father is gifted to us through the channel of blessing. This is extremely good news.

We don't have to struggle with doubt, if we believe that even the acceptance of such a gift was performed by Jesus Himself at the baptism.

The acceptance of sonship or daughtership is a vital step towards accepting the death of Jesus for our rebellion and disaffection from God because of the serpent's lie.

c. Clinging to Sonship by Faith

Satan was aware that if people should accept that they are children of God by faith, then his work to cause them to rebel would be much harder. If Jesus was free to believe that He was a Son of God as a human being, he knew that this could be passed to us through the channel. Satan had to do something to prevent Jesus from believing He was accepted as a human being and this is the background to the battle in the wilderness.

> **Matt 4:3-10** And when the tempter came to him, he said, If thou be the Son of God, command that these stones be made bread. **4** But he answered and said, It is written, Man shall not live by bread alone, but by every word that proceedeth out of the mouth of God. **5** Then the devil taketh him up into the holy city, and setteth him on a pinnacle of the temple, **6** And saith unto him, If thou be the Son of God, cast thyself down: for it is written, He shall give his angels charge concerning thee: and in *their* hands they shall bear thee up, lest at any time thou dash thy foot against a stone. **7** Jesus said unto him, It is written again, Thou shalt not tempt the Lord thy God. **8** Again, the devil taketh him up into an exceeding high mountain, and sheweth him all the kingdoms of the world, and the glory of them; **9** And saith unto him, All these things will I give thee, if thou wilt fall down and worship me. **10** Then saith Jesus unto him, Get thee hence, Satan: for it is written, Thou shalt worship the Lord thy God, and him only shalt thou serve.

God has spoken to His Son – saying "You are my Son." When Satan came to Jesus, he began with the word "IF"; if you are the Son of God. Contained in that word "if" was an attack on God's words. God had said "You are my Son"; Satan says, is this really true?

Satan suggested to Jesus that instead of simply trusting God's Word that he use His effort to prove that He is the Son of God. If Jesus responded to this temptation then He would have doubted His Father's word and agreed with Satan that being a son comes from a demonstration of power; inherent power. In resisting Satan's temptation, Jesus acquired for the human race a human mindset that trusted God's word as the only basis of sonship without any need to prove it by power. It is such a wonderful thing to have a Saviour who refuses to prove His sonship by His own power, but simply trusts His Father's acceptance of Him through their relationship. There is no doubt that Jesus had power to turn stones into bread; He had power to do whatever He wanted. But there is one thing that the Son of God would never do: use His power to prove His identity; this is completely contrary to His very being. It always has been and always will be.

d. His Victory is Ours

The choice of Jesus to believe God's Word alone as the basis of acceptance is a treasure that comes to us through the channel of blessing when we accept Christ. Do you struggle to believe God's Word alone that you are a child of God? Jesus has conquered this doubt already and if you believe this, then His victory over Satan automatically becomes yours. We can have faith in God's Word through the faith of Jesus. This is not simply faith in Jesus – it is the faith of Jesus that we receive as children of God.

As the Scripture tells us:

> **Gal 4:4-7** But when the fulness of the time was come, God sent forth his Son, made of a woman, made under the law, **5** To redeem them that were under the law, that we might receive the adoption of sons. **6** And because ye are sons, God hath sent forth the Spirit of his Son into your hearts, crying, Abba, Father. **7** Wherefore thou art no more a servant, but a son; and if a son, then an heir of God through Christ.

It is the Spirit of Christ flowing to us through the channel that causes us to cry out – "Father" in faith. The very words are the words of Christ revealed in us. It takes a little time for us to fully understand this concept, but a simple example is the story of the tree that was cut down into a body of bitter water to make it sweet.

> **Exod 15:23-25** And when they came to Marah, they could not drink of the waters of Marah, for they *were* bitter: therefore the name of it was called Marah. **24** And the people murmured against Moses, saying, What shall we drink? **25** And he cried unto the LORD; and the LORD shewed him a tree, *which* when he had cast into the waters, the waters were made sweet: there he made for them a statute and an ordinance, and there he proved them,

The faith of Jesus in His Father's word is like the tree that made the bitter waters of human doubt extremely sweet and possible to drink.

We have now given a brief overview of both the system of restoring the channel of blessing (through the Sanctuary) and the means by which the valleys and mountains that stand in the way of this system (acceptance through sonship) have been dealt with by God.

Before we move on from the time of Christ on earth, we need to come back to the history of Israel and how they fared with this Sanctuary system. Satan would not rest idle and allow Israel to keep this worship system intact. He determined to attack Israel until once again they were in slavery and the narrow path through the mountains and valleys would be lost along with the highway that led back to the commandments of God in the Sanctuary.

The descendents of Nimrod would be used to try and prevent the descendents of Abraham from keeping alive the family kingdom.

Chapter 17

Give Us a King, Like the Other Nations

a. Detailed Instructions to Protect the Family Structure

Israel was an extremely privileged nation to receive the law of God at Mt Sinai and many specific instructions on how to keep this law and therefore stay connected to the channel of blessing.

Many instructions were designed to teach Israelite families the critical nature of family relationships. Some of the instructions seem extremely harsh until we realize that the breakdown of the family unit is a direct path to tyranny, oppression and misery. Notice the following verses that God gave to Israel:

> **Lev 20:8-10** And ye shall keep my statutes, and do them: I *am* the LORD which sanctify you. **9** For every one that curseth his father or his mother shall be surely put to death: he hath cursed his father or his mother; his blood *shall be* upon him. **10** And the man that committeth adultery with *another* man's wife, *even he* that committeth adultery with his neighbour's wife, the adulterer and the adulteress shall surely be put to death.

A man who strikes his parents or curses them, shows clear evidence that he has rejected the channel of authority and blessing. Such a man is a danger to himself and society. Such actions reveal the seeds of tyranny and will certainly destroy a society if left unchecked. It was not God's desire to put people to death, but for the Israelites to see in these instructions the terrible consequences of rebellion.

Many of us are familiar with the immense pain that comes to families when couples commit adultery. It smashes the family structure, strips away respect and puts a stain on the community. So dangerous are these actions that

Israel had to understand that death would be the result.

These instructions seem excessive to many people, but we must remember that most people conceive the human race as possessing an independent life source free to do as they wish rather than dependent on God for every breath. Such people do not see the crucial nature of family structures and see God as harsh. Once again the lie of the serpent confuses reality.

From the example of Isaac, Jacob and Esau we learnt the vital nature of choosing a correct partner. Israelites were not to marry people from other nations who would not understand the vital nature of the family structure. The story of Nehemiah reveals the urgency of this matter for the survival of God's family relational system.

> **Neh 13:23-27** In those days also saw I Jews *that* had married wives of Ashdod, of Ammon, *and* of Moab: **24** And their children spake half in the speech of Ashdod, and could not speak in the Jews' language, but according to the language of each people. **25** And I contended with them, and cursed them, and smote certain of them, and plucked off their hair, and made them swear by God, *saying*, Ye shall not give your daughters unto their sons, nor take their daughters unto your sons, or for yourselves. **26** Did not Solomon king of Israel sin by these things? yet among many nations was there no king like him, who was beloved of his God, and God made him king over all Israel: nevertheless even him did outlandish women cause to sin. **27** Shall we then hearken unto you to do all this great evil, to transgress against our God in marrying strange wives?

The marrying of strange wives by the Israelites was a direct echo of the antediluvian sons of God marrying the daughters of men. The result would be the same – tyranny. Nehemiah was urgent to prevent this from occurring.

Moses was given much instruction for the protection of the family structure. If Israel had been faithful, they never would have suffered the way they did. God laid out before them the blessings of following His counsel and the curses of failing to obey these instructions. In Leviticus 26, God lays out the key ingredients that we have discussed for connecting to and preserving the channel of blessing. Notice carefully:

> **Lev 26:1-6** Ye shall make you no idols nor graven image, neither rear you up a standing image, neither shall ye set up *any* image of stone in your land, to bow down unto it: for I *am* the LORD your God. **2** Ye shall keep my sabbaths, and reverence my sanctuary: I *am* the LORD.

3 If ye walk in my statutes, and keep my commandments, and do them; **4** Then I will give you rain in due season, and the land shall yield her increase, and the trees of the field shall yield their fruit. **5** And your threshing shall reach unto the vintage, and the vintage shall reach unto the sowing time: and ye shall eat your bread to the full, and dwell in your land safely. **6** And I will give peace in the land, and ye shall lie down, and none shall make *you* afraid: and I will rid evil beasts out of the land, neither shall the sword go through your land.

1. The command to avoid idols was intended to preserve the relational/invisible perception of God. Idols made of material things would cause Israel to drift towards a power based value system and the hardening of relationships – as hard as the wood, stone and gold they would worship.
2. The command concerning the Sabbath was a reminder of the source of the life channel and who had created them.
3. The Sanctuary, as we discussed, provided the highway or journey for writing God's protective law in their hearts.
4. The Ten Commandments (and the detailed instructions concerning this law), as we have noted, is the protector of the channel of blessing. The Sabbath and command not to worship idols is part of the commandments, but has been singled out for special focus.

God warned the Israelites that if they failed to cling to these principles they would be cursed and suffer oppression, sorrow and be scattered abroad.

Lev 26:14-17,28-33 But if ye will not hearken unto me, and will not do all these commandments; **15** And if ye shall despise my statutes, or if your soul abhor my judgments, so that ye will not do all my commandments, *but* that ye break my covenant: **16** I also will do this unto you; I will even appoint over you terror, consumption, and the burning ague, that shall consume the eyes, and cause sorrow of heart: and ye shall sow your seed in vain, for your enemies shall eat it. **17** And I will set my face against you, and ye shall be slain before your enemies: they that hate you shall reign over you; and ye shall flee when none pursueth you. ... **28** Then I will walk contrary unto you also in fury; and I, even I, will chastise you seven times for your sins. **29** And ye shall eat the flesh of your sons, and the flesh of your daughters shall ye eat. **30** And I will destroy your high places, and cut down your images, and cast your carcases upon the carcases of your idols, and my soul shall abhor you. **31** And I will make your cities waste, and bring your sanctuaries unto desolation, and I will not smell the savour of your sweet odours. **32** And I will bring the land into desolation: and your enemies which dwell therein shall be astonished at it. **33** And I will scatter you among the heathen, and will draw out a sword after you: and your land shall be desolate, and your cities waste.

When God's people step out from the channel of blessing, He cannot protect them. He represents Himself as bringing these calamities upon His people, but the calamities are a natural reaping process of rejecting God's family kingdom. God would use the curses as a father wishing to correct His wayward children; He would allow them to suffer the consequences of their bad choices and since He allows them to suffer, He takes the responsibility for what takes place.

b. Israel Turns Away From God

If Israel had faithfully followed these things, they would have had peace and prosperity and a life free from fear and war. Israel did start well but after Moses, Aaron, Joshua and all their peers died, a new generation arose who failed to preserve these principles.

> **Judges 2:8-12** And Joshua the son of Nun, the servant of the LORD, died, *being* an hundred and ten years old. **9** And they buried him in the border of his inheritance in Timnathheres, in the mount of Ephraim, on the north side of the hill Gaash. **10** And also all that generation were gathered unto their fathers: and there arose another generation after them, which knew not the LORD, nor yet the works which he had done for Israel. **11** And the children of Israel did evil in the sight of the LORD, and served Baalim: **12** And they forsook the LORD God of their fathers, which brought them out of the land of Egypt, and followed other gods, of the gods of the people that *were* round about them, and bowed themselves unto them, and provoked the LORD to anger.

The peace and prosperity that Israel experienced under Joshua's leadership did not cause them to thank God, but rather caused them to slide into complacency. This trend has occurred many times in history and is a warning to us. Observe the western nations of today that were raised on Christian principles. Many of these nations became prosperous and wealthy and now all of them are slowly turning away from their original principles to serve materialism.

Israel turned from God to serve Baalim. Baalim was a god patterned after Nimrod's worship system; a worship of the inherent power of nature and especially the sun. In turning away from the true God, Israel turned from the source of life. The husband and wife relationship was no longer patterned on headship and submission principles as reflected in the Father and Son relationship in heaven, but the deities worshipped were all based around inherent power. The loss of an example of a submissive agent spelt doom for Israel. It cut off the relational value system of heaven and raised a generation that became insecure, worthless and fearful.

The book of Judges details a litany of evils and sorrows that befell the Israelites. They were subdued by neighboring tribes and their families were desolated. The society became feminized because the role of a father to bless his children was lost. Men lost their courage due to their insecurity and lack of blessing. To help Israel escape from the tyranny of their enemies, God had to use the services of a woman, because the male leadership had been decimated.

Deborah was raised as a prophetess to assist Israel escape the tyranny they were under. Under the seed and nurture principles, she never would have taken the mantle of the leader of God's people, but desperate times require desperate measures and God used the faithfulness of Deborah to deliver Israel. Deborah asked Barak to lead an army to route their enemies, but notice Barak's response:

> **Judges 4:8-9** And Barak said unto her, If thou wilt go with me, then I will go: but if thou wilt not go with me, *then* I will not go. **9** And she said, I will surely go with thee: notwithstanding the journey that thou takest shall not be for thine honour; for the LORD shall sell Sisera into the hand of a woman. And Deborah arose, and went with Barak to Kedesh.

Without the channel of blessing operating correctly, Barak was fearful and desired Deborah to hold his hand like a mother; as a result, the honour of victory would go to a woman who acted with courage.

This is the result of rejecting God's family blessing system. As Isaiah states later on:

> **Isa 3:12** *As for* my people, children *are* their oppressors, and women rule over them. O my people, they which lead thee cause *thee* to err, and destroy the way of thy paths.

When women are required to lead God's people, it is a sign that they

Life Matters

are in deep apostasy and the channel of blessing is smashed. The headship and submission principles can never work correctly under female leadership, because this confuses male and female roles. But it was better for the Israelites to be delivered by the hands of a woman than to continue to suffer in bondage to their enemies – this would have been much worse.

It is no accident that the book of Judges presents Samson as a weak-willed womanizer who loved to joke around, have fun and terrorise people. This too is the result of the channel of blessing being broken. Again God made events work together to deliver His people from the bondage of their enemies, but Samson is a poor example of male leadership.

We see Samson's unwise choice of a partner:

> **Judges 14:3** Then his father and his mother said unto him, *Is there never a woman among the daughters of thy brethren, or among all my people, that thou goest to take a wife of the uncircumcised Philistines?* And Samson said unto his father, Get her for me; for she pleaseth me well.

Samson had no sense of the vital nature of choosing a faithful wife; all that mattered was that it pleased him. Samson had grown to be a selfish, self-centred boy in a man's body.

Samson was indeed ruled by his desire for women. A man ruled by passion is a typical outcome when the relational blessing system is destroyed and God's people turn away from the Father and Son, headship and submission pattern; to the inherent power equality models of Baal.

Samson, grinding at the mill of the Philistines, is a fitting example of God's people turning away from the true God. He was wretched, poor, blind and naked; enslaved to a false value system and lacking the seeds of blessing that every man needs to be a wise and discerning leader.

c. Israel Enshrines the Inherent Power Belief System

After many years of trial and sorrow, God raised up a prophet – Samuel – to lead God's people. Looking at the context of Samuel's story, again we see the curse of the inherent power system in the life of Eli. He was not a man that could restrain his sons and be a strong leader. Samuel's father was not a discerning man and does not appear to be the spiritual leader he should have been.

Give Us a King, Like the Other Nations

God used Samuel to bring Israel back to the worship system of God and he did a great work of reform, but even Samuel struggled to raise a family after God's order and his sons failed to follow in the right path.

Samuel's faltering steps as a father provided the leading men of Israel with the opportunity for which they had been seeking for some time.

> **1 Sam 8:4-5** Then all the elders of Israel gathered themselves together, and came to Samuel unto Ramah, **5** And said unto him, Behold, thou art old, and thy sons walk not in thy ways: now make us a king to judge us like all the nations.

The Israelite leaders were not content to remain in family groups and be led by the benevolent leadership of the prophet. They wanted a Monarch that ruled absolutely. The desire for a King was a call for the principles of Nimrod. They wanted to be like the other nations. They did not want to be different and peculiar. Their insecurities could not deal with being different. This request was a complete rejection of God and His family kingdom principles.

> **1 Sam 8:7** And the LORD said unto Samuel, Hearken unto the voice of the people in all that they say unto thee: for they have not rejected thee, but they have rejected me, that I should not reign over them.

The desire for a king would ensure Israel's ultimate destruction. Once they entered this path there would be no escape until they were completely ruled, not only in mind, but also in body. This is exactly what happened with the later captivity in Assyria and Babylon. Satan was on the verge of a great victory. If he could draw Israel into a desire for a king, he could enthrone his principles of family and government, patterned after Nimrod, and ensure the smashing of the family channel of blessing system.

Samuel pleaded with them to not do this, but they were determined.

> **1 Sam 8:10-20** And Samuel told all the words of the LORD unto the people that asked of him a king. **11** And he said, This will be the manner of the king that shall reign over you: He will take your sons, and appoint *them* for himself, for his chariots, and *to be* his horsemen; and *some* shall run before his chariots. **12** And he will appoint him captains over thousands, and captains over fifties; and *will set them* to ear his ground, and to reap his harvest, and to make his instruments of war, and instruments of his chariots. **13** And he will take your daughters *to be* confectionaries, and *to be* cooks, and *to be* bakers. **14** And he will take your fields, and your vineyards, and your oliveyards, *even* the best *of them*, and give *them* to his servants. **15** And he will take

the tenth of your seed, and of your vineyards, and give to his officers, and to his servants. **16** And he will take your menservants, and your maidservants, and your goodliest young men, and your asses, and put *them* to his work. **17** He will take the tenth of your sheep: and ye shall be his servants. **18** And ye shall cry out in that day because of your king which ye shall have chosen you; and the LORD will not hear you in that day. **19** Nevertheless the people refused to obey the voice of Samuel; and they said, Nay; but we will have a king over us; **20** That we also may be like all the nations; and that our king may judge us, and go out before us, and fight our battles.

Everything that Samuel warned about – came to pass. They wanted a king to fight their battles for them. Their insecurities and lack of blessing caused them to lack courage and they revealed that they were boys in men's bodies looking for a strong deliverer to protect them. The key point they overlooked is that the desolating effects of their broken society leave them hard pressed to produce a man that was courageous, strong and upright. Saul, to all appearances, looked the perfect choice, but he was but a child of insecurity, fear and worthlessness in a man's body. His worthlessness caused him to rule as a moody tyrant.

This is a warning for the world today. Today we live in the soup of a feminized society that is revealing ever increasing tyranny and godlessness. Eventually the people will cry out for a deliverer to save them – but it will be a ruthless and heartless king like Nimrod without regard for true family values; not a king like Jesus who is the very embodiment of true blessing principles and Godly manhood.

d. The Kings of Israel

The results of Israel's choice for a king are very sad. The foundations were never laid correctly and therefore the channel of blessing rarely flowed. As we stated, Saul bore all the hallmarks of an insecure cursed child.

When Saul saw David kill Goliath, he saw David as an opportunity, but when the people started to sing David's praises for his courage in war, Saul then saw him as a threat.

> **1 Sam 18:6-9** And it came to pass as they came, when David was returned from the slaughter of the Philistine, that the women came out of all cities of Israel, singing and dancing, to meet king Saul, with tabrets, with joy, and with instruments of musick. **7** And the women

answered *one another* as they played, and said, Saul hath slain his thousands, and David his ten thousands. **8** And Saul was very wroth, and the saying displeased him; and he said, They have ascribed unto David ten thousands, and to me they have ascribed *but* thousands: and *what* can he have more but the kingdom? **9** And Saul eyed David from that day and forward.

The opportunity and threat mentality is clear evidence of the serpent's lie at work in Saul. His failure to recognize that all things come from God caused him to pursue David for the rest of his life. His insecurities and his lack of worth so overwhelmed him that he was constantly harassed by evil spirits.

> **1 Sam 18:10-12** And it came to pass on the morrow, that the evil spirit [allowed] from God came upon Saul, and he prophesied in the midst of the house: and David played with his hand, as at other times: and *there was* a javelin in Saul's hand. **11** And Saul cast the javelin; for he said, I will smite David even to the wall *with it*. And David avoided out of his presence twice. **12** And Saul was afraid of David, because the LORD was with him, and was departed from Saul.

The rest of Saul's life is a woeful tale of a man drowning in his own worthlessness; using his power to attack and destroy perceived and real threats, to secure his throne.

The Lord was with David, and his faith in God and trust in God's power rather than his own, enabled him to be used to do mighty things. For whatever reason though, the lessons of Abraham, Isaac and Jacob concerning family structure were not impressed upon him and he failed to establish his kingdom upon correct headship and submission principles.

> **2 Sam 3:2-5** And unto David were sons born in Hebron: and his firstborn was Amnon, of Ahinoam the Jezreelitess; **3** And his second, Chileab, of Abigail the wife of Nabal the Carmelite; and the third, Absalom the son of Maacah the daughter of Talmai king of Geshur; **4** And the fourth, Adonijah the son of Haggith; and the fifth, Shephatiah the son of Abital; **5** And the sixth, Ithream, by Eglah David's wife. These were born to David in Hebron.

If David had known, he would have prayerfully sought for one wife that would act as a submissive nurturing agent to carefully raise his children and secure his kingdom. But David appears ignorant of these vital issues and builds the foundations of his kingdom upon several wives, including one wife – Maacah – as a contract of peace with the king of Geshur.

The house of David was laid upon a flawed foundation and the fruits would soon manifest in his children. The multiple wives competing for David's affection combined with each woman's aspirations for her son to be the next king developed a royal court of jealousy, scheming and intrigue.

David's firstborn Amnon, tempted of the devil, seduced his half sister Tamar and raped her. This enraged Absalom and he quietly plotted his death. Absalom was the son of Maacah, David's foreign wife who was meant to be the means of a contract of peace. Little would David realize that the seeds of Maacah's training in Absalom would make him extremely ambitious, crafty and scheming. This woman that was meant as a bond of peace nearly destroyed David's entire kingdom.

There is a mystery that surrounds Abigail's son – Chileab or Daniel as is expressed in 1 Chron 3:1. Abigail appeared to be the wisest of David's wives and understood the principles of submission, but after Amnon's death, Chileab is never mentioned as being in line for kingship. There appears to be no mention of what happened to him.

Instead, the successor to David would come via an adulterous relationship with Bathsheba. We might pretend that this woman is innocently washing herself on her roof top and she had no idea that she was in view of the king, but that would reflect a high degree of ignorance as to what she was doing.

> **2 Sam 11:2** And it came to pass in an eveningtide, that David arose from off his bed, and walked upon the roof of the king's house: and from the roof he saw a woman washing herself; and the woman *was* very beautiful to look upon.

If Bathsheba was innocent, she would have declined the king's invitation to sleep with him, but she appeared quite willing for the story records no protest on her part. For David to act in this way, revealed that he was completely lacking in understanding of God's channel of blessing system.

The seeds of guilt that resided in David and Bathsheba from the adultery and David's killing of Bathsheba's husband were part of the recipe that went into their child Solomon. It is true that the Lord loved Solomon and blessed him with wisdom because there were many good traits passed to him from his parents, but the bad seeds of worthlessness and bad family structure would eventually surface.

Though Solomon possessed great wisdom in many areas, the one vital area where it was needed he failed and he failed greatly. He had 700 wives and 300 concubines. He built up his army and engaged in great building projects, and then taxed the people and put them to work. While many people point to the glory of Solomon, in reality the end result of his kingship was a disaster and ended up in his kingdom being divided. He ended up worshipping the false gods of some of his wives and built them temples. What an insult to the God of heaven.

> **1 Kings 11:1-4** But king Solomon loved many strange women, together with the daughter of Pharaoh, women of the Moabites, Ammonites, Edomites, Zidonians, *and* Hittites; **2** Of the nations *concerning* which the LORD said unto the children of Israel, Ye shall not go in to them, neither shall they come in unto you: *for* surely they will turn away your heart after their gods: Solomon clave unto these in love. **3** And he had seven hundred wives, princesses, and three hundred concubines: and his wives turned away his heart. **4** For it came to pass, when Solomon was old, *that* his wives turned away his heart after other gods: and his heart was not perfect with the LORD his God, as *was* the heart of David his father.

Solomon set the trend for a very bad ride for Israel. The kingdom of Israel that split from Judah after Solomon's death did not produce one good king. A number of the kings of Judah did right in the sight of the Lord, but even the good kings appeared to lack discernment. For instance Jehoshaphat allowed his son to marry the daughter of Jezebel. What on earth was he thinking! The fallout from the marriage led to the first female "king" of Judah – Athaliah and she nearly destroyed the entire nation.[40] Hezekiah was greatly blessed by the Lord and he did many good things to preserve the worship of the true God, but when the Babylonians came knocking at his door, he showed them all of his wealth and treasure and left a seed in the minds of the Babylonians that they should come back one day and take this treasure home.[41]

The failure of Israel to preserve a family channel system ensured that the principles of Nimrod would rule the world. The desire for territory and power would not be satisfied until there arose a leader that dominated the entire world. The principles of inherent power with all its worthlessness demand of

---

40 2 Kings 11:1-14
41 2 Chron 32:27-31

men the craving for limitless power. This power is the only drug to soothe their fragile egos and worthless souls. The first of these world empires emerged in the nation of Babylon.

Though Israel desired a king to rule over them and fight their battles, they did not discern that the families of kings do not often produce children that are fit to rule and tyranny is usually the result. And the willing slavery of Israel's leaders to the principles of Nimrod's kingdom would leave their children as physical captives of this system.

Chapter 18

The Rise and Tyranny of World Empire

a. The Battle Between the Two Seeds, Two Women, Two Cities

The battle between God's family kingdom and Satan's inherent power system is described in Genesis 3 as the battle between two seeds.

> **Gen 3:15** and I will put enmity between you and the woman, and between your seed and her Seed; He shall bruise your head, and you shall bruise His heel.

The seed of the woman represents the small group of people that faithfully seek to hold to God's family system in the midst of many attacks. The heart of this seed is of course the Son of God because He is the ultimate expression of submission to the life source of God and He establishes the flowing of this channel of blessing. The preservation of the seed is the preservation of the example of the Son of God. Whenever families are following the headship and submission principles in the context of the commandments of God and walking the journey of the Sanctuary system, they are being filled with the Spirit of Christ and revealing His character.

> **Gal 3:16** Now to Abraham and his Seed were the promises made. He does not say, "And to seeds," as of many, but as of one, "And to your Seed," who is Christ.

> **Gal 3:29** And if you are Christ's, then you are Abraham's seed, and heirs according to the promise.

As we discussed in Chapter 16, once the human race became enslaved to Satan's kingdom principles, it was impossible for us to be set free. Therefore

Jesus came as a human being and developed a human character that could then flow to us through the channel of blessing and we could then obtain victory over the serpent.

So wherever we see people responding to the commandments of God and the family kingdom system, it is actually the character and Spirit of Christ that is being reflected in their lives. This is a mystery to many and was a mystery until Jesus came to earth and fully revealed these family submission principles.

> **Col 1:26-29** *Even* the mystery which hath been hid from ages and from generations, but now is made manifest to his saints: **27** To whom God would make known what *is* the riches of the glory of this mystery among the Gentiles; which is Christ in you, the hope of glory: **28** Whom we preach, warning every man, and teaching every man in all wisdom; that we may present every man perfect in Christ Jesus: **29** Whereunto I also labour, striving according to his working, which worketh in me mightily.

Genesis 3:15 reminds us that Satan would seek to kill this seed. He would be successful in bruising the heel of this seed when he killed Jesus on the cross, but this darkest hour turned out to be the greatest triumph for God's people and opened the channel of blessing to the entire world.

But Satan not only tried to kill the seed directly in the person of Jesus, he also tried to kill this seed in the hearts and minds of His followers. The first example of this is the story of Cain and Abel.

> **Gen 4:8** And Cain talked with Abel his brother: and it came to pass, when they were in the field, that Cain rose up against Abel his brother, and slew him.

> **1 John 3:11-13** For this is the message that ye heard from the beginning, that we should love one another. **12** Not as Cain, *who* was of that wicked one, and slew his brother. And wherefore slew he him? Because his own works were evil, and his brother's righteous. **13** Marvel not, my brethren, if the world hate you.

These two brothers symbolize the war between the principles of Christ and Satan played out in human history. We will trace the history of these two principles over the next number of chapters.

The Rise and Tyranny of World Empire

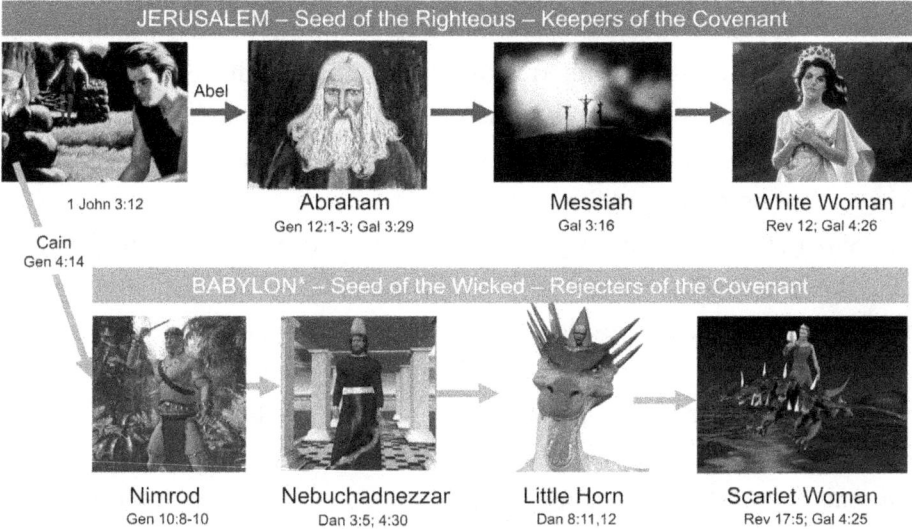

After the episode of Cain and Abel, Satan then tried to kill the seed of the woman by tempting the sons of God to marry the daughters of men which produced the tyrants of the antediluvian world. This plan nearly succeeded, but God called Noah and eight people were saved to continue the Seed.

> **1 Pet 3:18-20** For Christ also hath once suffered for sins, the just for the unjust, that he might bring us to God, being put to death in the flesh, but quickened by the Spirit: **19** By which also he went and preached unto the spirits in prison; **20** Which sometime were disobedient, when once the longsuffering of God waited in the days of Noah, while the ark was a preparing, wherein few, that is, eight souls were saved by water.
>
> **1 Pet 1:11** Searching what, or what manner of time the Spirit of Christ which was in them did signify, when it testified beforehand the sufferings of Christ, and the glory that should follow.

We notice how the Bible tells us that it was the Spirit of Christ in Noah that preached to the people of his time concerning the coming flood. These poor souls were in the prison of Satan's inherent life source kingdom (spirits in prison) and the Spirit of Christ flowing through Noah preached to the people to warn them. Sadly, none of the people responded and only Noah's family was saved.

Satan then attacked Noah's family by tempting Noah to get drunk and tempted his son to a vile immoral act. The result of this tragedy was the man Nimrod who developed the foundational principles for Satan's kingdom on earth. This entire system is referred to in Scripture through the city of Babylon, the first city that Nimrod built. Much of the world fell under this idolatrous system so God called Abraham out of Babylon and taught him His family kingdom principles.

Satan attacked again by tempting Abraham to be afraid while in Egypt (Egyptians were descendents of Ham, the grandfather of Nimrod). Abraham nearly lost his wife as a result but God counterattacked and sent great plagues to Egypt to avert the killing off of the precious seed. Satan did manage to wipe out Lot's family kingdom in the gross immorality of Sodom and the consequent fires that were needed to check this deeply immoral system.

Satan attacked again through the introduction of Hagar as a means of producing an heir to the kingdom promised to Abraham by God, but finally a true heir was born in the person of Isaac.

Satan attacked again by enslaving the Israelites in Egypt and preventing them from keeping the commandments which protected the channel of blessing. He also tried to feminize their society to weaken the channel.

God then called Moses to reestablish His family kingdom principles and He gave detailed instructions concerning how the law, which protects the channel of blessing, could be written in the hearts of His people. This came via the Sanctuary worship system.

Satan attacked through the murmuring of the people against Moses. He attacked by getting them to worship the golden calf. He attacked by tempting them to doubt God's word that they could go into the Promised Land. On the banks of the Jordan, Satan tempted Israel with foreign women and then after the death of Moses, Joshua and all that generation, he finally succeeded in breaking the family channel system when Israel forsook the Lord and worshipped other gods – gods that reflected Satan's inherent life source principles.

God sent several prophets to try and preserve the righteous seed containing the submissive Spirit of Christ and keep a faithful remnant. Since the channel had become so weakened, the Lord could find very few men to lead a work of reform. The Lord resorted to raising women in Israel like the prophetess

The Rise and Tyranny of World Empire

Deborah which, while not optimal, was the best thing to do in a desperate situation.

Satan then tempted Israel to ask for a king, like the other nations. This was a ploy to enslave Israel's hearts and minds to the principles of Nimrod and Babylon and prevent the Spirit of Christ from manifesting in His people. The kings of Israel were largely a disaster and prepared the way for Israel to be recaptured physically.

Satan had long been preparing his seed for the conquest of world dominion. If Satan could control the entire world through his seed, then he could cut off the family kingdom principles of God. He could wipe out His Sanctuary, His commandments and His people and anything that represented the channel of blessing principles and the Spirit of Christ.

Looking forward from the time of Babylon, we see a series of world powers that Satan uses to attack God's people, His commandments, His Sanctuary and His city, Jerusalem – city of peace. After Christ conquered Satan on earth and placed His seed safely within the church (His bride), Satan led an 'all out' world wide attack on those who kept the commandments of God and the faith of Jesus' family channel system. We read about this in Revelation Chapter 12.

> **Rev 12:1-5** And there appeared a great wonder in heaven; a woman clothed with the sun, and the moon under her feet, and upon her head a crown of twelve stars: **2** And she being with child cried, travailing in birth, and pained to be delivered. **3** And there appeared another wonder in heaven; and behold a great red dragon, having seven heads and ten horns, and seven crowns upon his heads. **4** And his tail drew the third part of the stars of heaven, and did cast them to the earth: and the dragon stood before the woman which was ready to be delivered, for to devour her child as soon as it was born. **5** And she brought forth a man child, who was to rule all nations with a rod of iron: and her child was caught up unto God, and *to* his throne.
>
> **Rev 12:13-17** And when the dragon saw that he was cast unto the earth, he persecuted the woman which brought forth the man *child*. **14** And to the woman were given two wings of a great eagle, that she might fly into the wilderness, into her place, where she is nourished for a time, and times, and half a time, from the face of the serpent. **15** And the serpent cast out of his mouth water as a flood after the woman, that he might cause her to be carried away of the flood. **16** And the earth helped the woman, and the earth opened her mouth, and swallowed up the flood which the dragon cast out of his mouth. **17**

> And the dragon was wroth with the woman, and went to make war with the remnant of her seed, which keep the commandments of God, and have the testimony of Jesus Christ.

The faithful woman representing the church of God, was under severe attack by the dragon and his agents. Satan had learnt early on that one of the best methods to derail God's people was to introduce another woman. He learnt this principle through introducing Hagar the Egyptian to Abraham as a wife. And so the Bible reveals:

> **Rev 17:3-7** So he carried me away in the spirit into the wilderness: and I saw a woman sit upon a scarlet coloured beast, full of names of blasphemy, having seven heads and ten horns. **4** And the woman was arrayed in purple and scarlet colour, and decked with gold and precious stones and pearls, having a golden cup in her hand full of abominations and filthiness of her fornication: **5** And upon her forehead *was* a name written, MYSTERY, BABYLON THE GREAT, THE MOTHER OF HARLOTS AND ABOMINATIONS OF THE EARTH. **6** And I saw the woman drunken with the blood of the saints, and with the blood of the martyrs of Jesus: and when I saw her, I wondered with great admiration. **7** And the angel said unto me, Wherefore didst thou marvel? I will tell thee the mystery of the woman, and of the beast that carrieth her, which hath the seven heads and ten horns.

Just as Sarah had to contend with Hagar, so the church of God will have to contend with another woman claiming to be the true bride of Christ. And sadly as it was Sarah who suggested that Hagar be used to produce a child, so it was the church itself that allowed this other woman to come into and dominate the family of God.

We will unpack these verses in detail in the coming chapters and reveal how Satan attacked God's people, His commandments and His Sanctuary after Jesus went back to heaven 2000 years ago. But first we must go back to the captivity of Israel and the rise of world dominion.

b. Satan's Seed Rules the World

During the time of the kings of Israel, God tried to warn them by sending prophets. Both Isaiah and Jeremiah warned the kings of Israel that they would be taken captive if they did not turn back to God.

> **Jer 25:9-11** Behold, I will send and take all the families of the north, saith the LORD, and Nebuchadrezzar the king of Babylon, my servant, and will bring them against this land, and against the inhabitants thereof, and against all these nations round about, and will utterly destroy them, and make them an astonishment, and an hissing, and perpetual desolations. **10** Moreover I will take from them the voice of mirth, and the voice of gladness, the voice of the bridegroom, and the voice of the bride, the sound of the millstones, and the light of the candle. **11** And this whole land shall be a desolation, *and* an astonishment; and these nations shall serve the king of Babylon seventy years.

Sadly they did not listen. The kings of Israel rejected the commandments of God and His Sanctuary system in favour of Satan's kingdom system. By continually rejecting God's channel of blessing and living outside of it, God could no longer protect Israel. Stepping outside of the channel of blessing allows Satan the right to freely attack, destroy and desolate. Finally the time came when Israel was taken to the very heart of Satan's kingdom principles – Babylon.

> **2 Chron 36:5-7** Jehoiakim *was* twenty and five years old when he began to reign, and he reigned eleven years in Jerusalem: and he did *that which was* evil in the sight of the LORD his God. **6** Against him came up Nebuchadnezzar king of Babylon, and bound him in fetters, to carry him to Babylon. **7** Nebuchadnezzar also carried of the vessels of the house of the LORD to Babylon, and put them in his temple at Babylon.

> **2 Chron 36:18-20** And all the vessels of the house of God, great and small, and the treasures of the house of the LORD, and the treasures of the king, and of his princes; all *these* he brought to Babylon. **19** And they burnt the house of God, and brake down the wall of Jerusalem, and burnt all the palaces thereof with fire, and destroyed all the goodly vessels thereof. **20** And them that had escaped from the sword carried he away to Babylon; where they were servants to him and his sons until the reign of the kingdom of Persia:

Notice how Nebuchadnezzar destroyed the Sanctuary of Israel and took the vessels of the Sanctuary and put them in his own sanctuary or temple. This was a fitting symbol of the domination of Satan's seed over Christ's seed during this time. But the Spirit of Christ fought back in an amazing way. Satan's desire was to rule the earth forever through Babylon and build a kingdom that would last forever. The Babylonian system would indeed rule for a long time but ultimately the Seed of the woman would bruise the serpent's head. This means that the lies of the serpent concerning inherent power would ultimately be wiped out.

God sent the king of Babylon a dream concerning these things but left him without an interpretation. Through providence, God allowed a young man of the captives of Israel to interpret the dream and grant him influence with the king of Babylon so that he might be able to present to him the true principles of God's kingdom. The story of the dream and its interpretation is found in Daniel Chapter 2. We will look briefly at the key points but I encourage you to read the entire chapter if you are not familiar with it.

The king had "wise men" that claimed to have connections with the spiritual realm and should have been able to tell the king his dream, but they could not. When Daniel was brought before the king, Daniel politely explained that the power to interpret dreams was not from himself but through the channel of blessing from God.

The Rise and Tyranny of World Empire

Dan 2:26-28 The king answered and said to Daniel, whose name *was* Belteshazzar, Art thou able to make known unto me the dream which I have seen, and the interpretation thereof? **27** Daniel answered in the presence of the king, and said, The secret which the king hath demanded cannot the wise *men*, the astrologers, the magicians, the soothsayers, shew unto the king; **28** But there is a God in heaven

that revealeth secrets, and maketh known to the king Nebuchadnezzar what shall be in the latter days. Thy dream, and the visions of thy head upon thy bed, are these;

Daniel then outlined the dream which revealed a statue of a man. This man consisted of various metals degrading in quality and getting harder and harder, representing four great kingdoms. After this came a division into ten kingdoms represented by the toes. The dream then comes to the key point: that a rock would come and smash the statue of the man and a new kingdom would be set up that would never end. This kingdom is God's family kingdom and God was telling Nebuchadnezzar that though he was ruling now, the seed of the woman would ultimately triumph over the serpent's lie.

Students of Bible history have identified these four world empires as Babylon, Medo-Persia, Greece and Rome. The Bible clearly indicates that the head is Babylon, because Daniel told the king this was the case.[42] We also know from reading further in Daniel that the 2nd and 3rd kingdoms were Medo-Persia and Greece because the angel Gabriel tells Daniel directly.[43]

These four kingdoms would dominate God's people right through to the return of Christ the second time. In the meantime, God would keep the seed alive and preserve a witness of his family kingdom in the earth, but they would always be in the minority. In the time of Media and Persia, God would cause the king to allow God's people to return to Israel and rebuild their temple. They would have a certain level of autonomy, but the seed of the serpent was always there seeking ways to control them. During the transition time between Greece and Rome, the temple services were interrupted by a king called Antiochus Epiphanes. He desecrated the temple by sacrificing a pig on the altar and did many other insulting and evil things.

But sadly this was not the worst problem. After Israel came back to their home land, they determined not to fall into idolatry again. Rather than strengthen the channel of blessing family system, they developed numerous laws regarding the keeping of the law, the Sabbath and how to worship in the Sanctuary. This was a new tactic of Satan to make the Israelites prove they were faithful to God by keeping all His requirements and more besides.

---

42   Daniel 2:38
43   Daniel 8:20,21

Since these laws were not a product of the channel of blessing, they were still infected by the serpent's lie of inherent power. But now the inherent power concept was directed towards trying to faithfully follow the true God. The effect of these laws made men's hearts hard and callous and just as much under the control of Satan as they were before, only now it was harder to detect.

c. Messiah the Prince Comes to His People

Knowing that all this would take place, God told Daniel in a prophecy that the true seed would come and deliver His people spiritually. There was no point in delivering God's people physically if their minds were still slaves to the serpent's lie. Peace and prosperity would never come. By sending His Son, God would restore the true principles of His kingdom and maintain a remnant of faithful followers until the second return of Christ.

The coming of Christ was taught every day in the Sanctuary service given to Moses, but we must remember that this entire system was a collection of symbols designed to show the pattern of how God would free the minds of His people to worship Him truly as a Father and cling to the pattern of submission revealed in His Son.

The piece of furniture in the Court of the Sanctuary was the Altar of Sacrifice and this was the symbol of the death of the coming Messiah. It was the first stage in the journey towards restoring the law of God in our hearts.

Let us turn to Daniel and see the prophecy that pin points when the Messiah would come.

> **Dan 9:24-26** Seventy weeks are determined upon thy people and upon thy holy city, to finish the transgression, and to make an end of sins, and to make reconciliation for iniquity, and to bring in everlasting righteousness, and to seal up the vision and prophecy, and to anoint the most Holy. **25** Know therefore and understand, *that* from the going forth of the commandment to restore and to build Jerusalem unto the Messiah the Prince *shall be* seven weeks, and threescore and two weeks: the street shall be built again, and the wall, even in troublous times. **26** And after threescore and two weeks shall Messiah be cut off, but not for himself: and the people of the prince that shall come shall destroy the city and the sanctuary; and the end thereof *shall be* with a flood, and unto the end of the war desolations are determined.

Some of the language here is a little tricky to understand and requires some study, but the main point is that there would be a period of seventy prophetic weeks in which the Israelite nation had to either fully accept or reject the coming Messiah.

When it comes to the use of prophetic time, the Bible applies the principle of a day for a year.

> **Ezek 4:6** And when thou hast accomplished them, lie again on thy right side, and thou shalt bear the iniquity of the house of Judah forty days: I have appointed thee each day for a year.

The starting point for these 70 weeks is set as the command to restore and rebuild Jerusalem. A careful study of the Bible reveals that the year when this was fulfilled was 457 B.C.

> **Ezra 6:14** And the elders of the Jews builded, and they prospered through the prophesying of Haggai the prophet and Zechariah the son of Iddo. And they builded, and finished *it*, according to the commandment of the God of Israel, and according to the commandment of Cyrus, and Darius, and Artaxerxes king of Persia.

There were three decrees that the Persian kings issued, but as Ezra 6:14 points out the full command was executed by the time of Artaxerxes. The first two decrees got the process going, but the restoring of all Jerusalem came with the third decree. This decree was given in the 7th year of Artaxerxes which was 457 B.C.[44]

So in summary we have the following:

---

44 Ezra 7:8

The Rise and Tyranny of World Empire

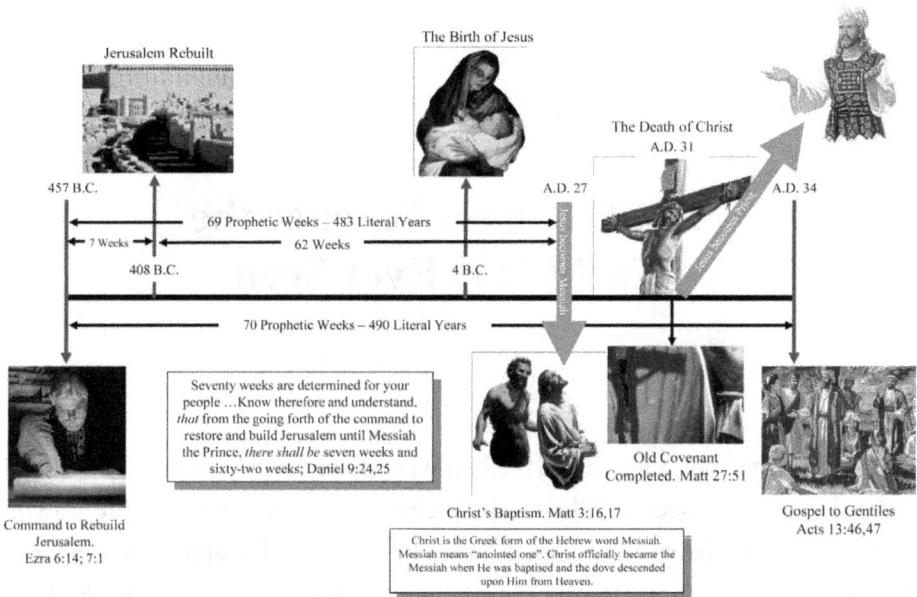

The story of the life, death and resurrection of Jesus is told symbolically in the story of Revelation 12 which we looked at recently. Satan tried to kill Christ soon after His birth through King Herod, but he failed. Jesus completed His work of establishing the family kingdom principles, He developed a perfect human character which He then returned to heaven with to flow the channel of blessing to His followers by the role of a priest in the heavenly Sanctuary.

In the next chapter we will look at the teachings of Jesus and how they restore the channel of blessing.

Chapter 19

The Greatest Teacher the World Has Ever Seen

In the last chapter we traced the battle between the two seeds mentioned in Genesis 3:15. The seed of Christ which clung to the principles of life flowing forth from God, being maintained through a close and loving relationship in family structures, protected by the commandments, and written in the heart through the journey revealed in the Sanctuary service. The seed of Satan grew through the lie that life is inherent within us and that value comes through self power and achievement.

We have traced the sad history of Israel's failure to preserve the channel of blessing, the scattering of their families and their captivity by Babylon. Israel was now firmly enslaved in both mind and body to the principles of the serpent's lie.

a. Delivering the Captives

It was now time for the Seed of Christ to come in person, restore God's family kingdom and set the captives free. The release from this captivity must begin in the mind and heart. There was no point making Israel free in body if their minds were still slaves to the inherent power system. The kingdom that Christ would establish would be a spiritual one that would free the heart from the lie of the serpent and reconnect humanity to the channel of blessing flowing from His Father.

The prophet Isaiah spoke of this work hundreds of years before Christ came:

Isa 40:3-5 The voice of one crying in the wilderness: "Prepare the way of the Lord; Make straight in the desert A highway for our God. **4** Every valley shall be exalted And every mountain and hill brought low; The crooked places shall be made straight And the rough places smooth; **5** The glory of the Lord shall be revealed, And all flesh shall see it together; For the mouth of the Lord has spoken."

Isa 41:15-18 "Behold, I will make you into a new threshing sledge with sharp teeth; You shall thresh the mountains and beat them small, And make the hills like chaff. **16** You shall winnow them, the wind shall carry them away, And the whirlwind shall scatter them; You shall rejoice in the Lord, And glory in the Holy One of Israel. **17** "The poor and needy seek water, but there is none, Their tongues fail for thirst. I, the Lord, will hear them; I, the God of Israel, will not forsake them. **18** I will open rivers in desolate heights, And fountains in the midst of the valleys; I will make the wilderness a pool of water, And the dry land springs of water.

Isa 45:13 I have raised him up in righteousness, and I will direct all his ways: he shall build my city, and he shall let go my captives, not for price nor reward, saith the LORD of hosts.

Isa 61:1 The Spirit of the Lord GOD *is* upon me; because the LORD hath anointed me to preach good tidings unto the meek; he hath sent me to bind up the brokenhearted, to proclaim liberty to the captives, and the opening of the prison to *them that are* bound;

The cutting of the channel of blessing turns the human heart into a wilderness of desolation. The water of God's Spirit cannot penetrate it and everything dies spiritually. Mountains of pride and valleys of depression also block the path of the Spirit of God from reaching those enslaved.

We see from the passages in Isaiah that God would cut down these mountains and lift the valleys. He would cause a river of life to flow into the desert places. God would send His Son to proclaim or teach the principles of deliverance and release those held captive by the lie. What a wonderful gift from heaven! Without the coming of Christ, the human race would have remained enslaved to the seed of the serpent and we all would have perished. How precious are the teachings that Jesus brought to the world, much more important than many perceive. We will now briefly examine the process and teachings Jesus delivered to set the captives free.

b. Re-establishing the Channel of Blessing

We covered this process in Chapter 16, so we will only mention it briefly here as part of the process. To allow a river to flow in the desert regions of the human heart, Jesus had to reconnect us to the life giving channel of blessing.

Since the law of God was written in the heart of His Son and Jesus was fully submissive to His Father, He possessed the life giving channel. By becoming a human like us, Jesus was able to connect us to the channel. By being connected to Him, we could have access to the river of life that flowed through Him.

But Jesus also had to cut down the mountains and raise the valleys for the river to reach the desert. It was on the banks of the river that the world heard through Jesus that God was well pleased with His Son and loved Him dearly. Immersed in these words and still dripping with the waters of the Jordan, Jesus pressed into the desert (the symbol of the human heart held captive by Satan) to open the river of life to the desolated ones.

By clinging to His Sonship and remaining submitted to the Father, Christ broke the power of the serpent's lie as a human being and therefore this victory was now flowing down the river of life to human hearts. At the baptism of Christ and in the wilderness of temptation, the channel of blessing was re-connected.

Now that the channel was established, the protective walls needed to be erected. These walls of course are the commandments of God. These commandments had been perverted and twisted by the lie of the serpent, but now Jesus would show us their true meaning from the family-relational kingdom.

c. Re-establishing the Law – The Channel Protector

Just as Moses went up on a mountain to receive the law of God, Jesus went up a mountain to proclaim the law of God in its true context. As Isaiah prophesied:

> **Isa 42:21** The LORD is well pleased for his righteousness' sake; he will magnify the law, and make *it* honourable.

This work has been most clearly recorded in Matthew Chapter 5 to 7, called the Sermon on the Mount.[45] It is no accident that Jesus first speaks of blessing and how it is received.

> **Matt 5:1-11** And seeing the multitudes, he went up into a mountain: and when he was set, his disciples came unto him: **2** And he opened his mouth, and taught them, saying, **3** Blessed *are* the poor in spirit: for theirs is the kingdom of heaven. **4** Blessed *are* they that mourn: for they shall be comforted. **5** Blessed *are* the meek: for they shall inherit the earth. **6** Blessed *are* they which do hunger and thirst after righteousness: for they shall be filled. **7** Blessed *are* the merciful: for they shall obtain mercy. **8** Blessed *are* the pure in heart: for they shall see God. **9** Blessed *are* the peacemakers: for they shall be called the children of God. **10** Blessed *are* they which are persecuted for righteousness' sake: for theirs is the kingdom of heaven. **11** Blessed are ye, when *men* shall revile you, and persecute *you*, and shall say all manner of evil against you falsely, for my sake.

These blessings only come through the life giving channel of blessing that Christ has established. If we read these verses with the serpent's lie clouding our thinking, we are tempted to read that Jesus tells us **we must** be meek **to** inherit, **we must** hunger **to be** filled, but all these attributes come to those who receive Christ and are connected to the channel. We cannot be pure in heart and be peacemakers unless we are connected to the blessing of God.

After this Jesus explains how those who are connected are to be channels also. As Jesus allows the blessing to flow through Him, we are to allow it to flow through us.

> **Matt 5:13-16** Ye are the salt of the earth: but if the salt have lost his savour, wherewith shall it be salted? it is thenceforth good for nothing, but to be cast out, and to be trodden under foot of men. **14** Ye are the light of the world. A city that is set on an hill cannot be hid. **15** Neither do men light a candle, and put it under a bushel, but on a candlestick; and it giveth light unto all that are in the house. **16** Let your light so shine before men, that they may see your good works, and glorify your Father which is in heaven.

The symbols of salt and light are healing and preserving agents that are a

---

45   It is interesting to note how clear the sequence of restoration is revealed in the book of Matthew. Chapter 1 and 2 speak of the humanity of Jesus and the consequent connecting link with us. Chapters 3 and 4 speak of the baptism and victory in the wilderness where the channel of blessing is reconnected. Chapters 5 to 7 speak of the law of God – the protector of that channel. The first 7 chapters of Matthew have been carefully constructed to lay the foundations for God's heavenly kingdom.

blessing. As we live in submission to the channel of blessing, others will be exposed to the waters flowing through us and be blessed. Jesus now speaks of the protection of this blessing channel.

> **Matt 5:17-19** Think not that I am come to destroy the law, or the prophets: I am not come to destroy, but to fulfil. **18** For verily I say unto you, Till heaven and earth pass, one jot or one tittle shall in no wise pass from the law, till all be fulfilled. **19** Whosoever therefore shall break one of these least commandments, and shall teach men so, he shall be called the least in the kingdom of heaven: but whosoever shall do and teach *them*, the same shall be called great in the kingdom of heaven.

Jesus speaks of the vital role of the law and His role to fulfill the law in its proper context. The Jewish people had tried to keep the law from the context of the serpent's lie. They tried to keep it to gain acceptance with God, but now Jesus is speaking about the law in a completely different kingdom context. This causes the Jewish leaders to think that He is trying to destroy the law. Jesus clearly tells them this is not the case and then goes on to explain the relational nature of the law and how it cuts far deeper than the Jews had imagined.

> **Matt 5:21-22** Ye have heard that it was said by them of old time, Thou shalt not kill; and whosoever shall kill shall be in danger of the judgment: **22** But I say unto you, That whosoever is angry with his brother without a cause shall be in danger of the judgment: and whosoever shall say to his brother, Raca, shall be in danger of the council: but whosoever shall say, Thou fool, shall be in danger of hell fire.

> **Matt 5:27-28** Ye have heard that it was said by them of old time, Thou shalt not commit adultery: **28** But I say unto you, That whosoever looketh on a woman to lust after her hath committed adultery with her already in his heart.

> **Matt 5:43-45** Ye have heard that it hath been said, Thou shalt love thy neighbour, and hate thine enemy. **44** But I say unto you, Love your enemies, bless them that curse you, do good to them that hate you, and pray for them which despitefully use you, and persecute you; **45** That ye may be the children of your Father which is in heaven: for he maketh his sun to rise on the evil and on the good, and sendeth rain on the just and on the unjust.

The Jews taught people to avoid the **act** of killing, but Jesus spoke against the **relational violation** of hating. The Jews spoke against the **act** of adultery, but Jesus spoke against the **relational violation** of thinking of a woman simply as a sexual object. The Jews spoke of displaying love to your neighbour, but Jesus spoke of displaying love to your enemy. Loving your neighbour who loves you does not reveal whether the principle of love is active. Only when we love our enemies can we tell that love abides in the heart.

Jesus explained the law in a relational way, not as a means of gaining merit with God, but as a means of keeping relationships together and most notably our relationship with God.

d. Re-establishing the True God as Father

Jesus then turns our attention to the primary way we should perceive God. In Matthew's progression of thought, Jesus first mentions God as a Father in Matt 5:16 where Jesus is discussing being a channel of blessing. He then mentions it again in Matt 5:45 where the true attributes of love are revealed when we love our enemies and then Jesus finishes Chapter 5 with the often misunderstand statement:

> **Matt 5:48** Be ye therefore perfect, even as your Father which is in heaven is perfect.

Reading this statement in the context of the serpent's lie, leaves us with the impression that we must perform in order to be like God and win His favour. But in the kingdom of God, this statement is a further expression of let your light shine before men which was mentioned previously. If we are in the channel of blessing, then God's perfect love will flow through us and we will be perfectly reflecting the channel as is God's desire.

In Chapter 6, Jesus teaches us how to pray. He tell us to call God "Our Father":

> **Matt 6:9** After this manner therefore pray ye: Our Father which art in heaven, Hallowed be thy name.

It is so vitally important to see God as a Father that loves us and cherishes us and cares for our needs. To see Him simply as the King of the universe, does not allow us to see His heart and desire for us. The reference to 'Father' is a wonderful invitation to come and talk to Him.

Once we see God as our Father who loves us, we can be released from the fear and worry of trying to provide for ourselves. We no longer need to focus on possessions and worry about them. By seeing God as our Father we are freed from these enslaving concerns.

> **Matt 6:31-33** Therefore take no thought, saying, What shall we eat? or, What shall we drink? or, Wherewithal shall we be clothed? **32** (For after all these things do the Gentiles seek:) for your heavenly Father knoweth that ye have need of all these things. **33** But seek ye first the kingdom of God, and his righteousness; and all these things shall be added unto you.

The lie of the serpent causes people to rely on their inherent power to provide their needs and protect themselves. This preoccupation can consume a person's entire throught process and leave no room for spiritual consideration. But when we see God as a Father, we trust that He will provide for us, so that we can focus on staying connected to Him.

e. Re-establishing the Correct View of the Sabbath

As we have discussed previously, the Sabbath is a vital reminder of where life comes from and along with the command to obey our parents, sits at the very centre of the commandments. The Jewish leaders had turned the Sabbath into a burden through the lens of the serpent's lie. The list of rules to be kept on this day was sickening. But that Sabbath was meant to represent the source of life; it is a memorial of freedom and rest in our heavenly Father. It was designed to be the best day of the week.

As a means of restoring the true meaning of the Sabbath, Jesus would heal people physically; a symbol of the spiritual healing that comes when we acknowledge God as the source of life.

> **John 5:5-11** And a certain man was there, which had an infirmity thirty and eight years. **6** When Jesus saw him lie, and knew that he had been now a long time *in that case*, he saith unto him, Wilt thou be made whole? **7** The impotent man answered him, Sir, I have no man, when the water is troubled, to put me into the pool: but while I am coming, another steppeth down before me. **8** Jesus saith unto him, Rise, take up thy bed, and walk. **9** And immediately the man was made whole, and took up his bed, and walked: and on the same day was the sabbath. **10** The Jews therefore said unto him that was cured, It is the sabbath day: it is not lawful for thee to carry *thy* bed. **11** He answered them, He that made me whole, the same said unto me, Take up thy bed, and walk.

Jesus also challenged the leaders of Israel on their perception of working on the Sabbath. The Jewish leaders' perception was to display their efforts to refrain from working, but this concept is influenced by the lie of the serpent and the display of inherent power. Jesus showed clearly that the Sabbath was made for man's benefit and enjoyment with his Creator.

> **Mark 2:23-28** And it came to pass, that he went through the corn fields on the sabbath day; and his disciples began, as they went, to pluck the ears of corn. **24** And the Pharisees said unto him, Behold, why do they on the sabbath day that which is not lawful? **25** And he said unto them, Have ye never read what David did, when he had need, and was an hungred, he, and they that were with him? **26** How he went into the house of God in the days of Abiathar the high priest, and did eat the shewbread, which is not lawful to eat but for the priests, and gave also to them which were with him? **27** And he said unto them, The sabbath was made for man, and not man for the sabbath: **28** Therefore the Son of man is Lord also of the sabbath.

The Sabbath is a wonderful memorial when understood correctly. Sadly, many Christians see the Sabbath as an attempt to please God by your efforts. They recognize that the Jewish leaders were wrong and seek for the freedom that comes from the good news that Jesus brought, but because many do not understand the life source correctly and belief in the immortal soul, they struggle to be able to see the Sabbath as it was intended. Such Christians are not helped by many Sabbath keepers today who still focus on a list of rules to be obeyed to show that you are doing the right thing.

When you love your Father in heaven, the list is not the focus. The focus is on being connected to the life giver and communing with Him and resting in His love. I am so glad that Jesus taught the correct understanding of the Sabbath. It is a vital part of the restoration of God's family kingdom.

f. Re-establishing Submission Principles

The most critical thing that Jesus came to demonstrate was submission to the Father. As expressed in an earlier chapter, the Son of God is the divine example of submission to the Father and therefore is the best qualified to demonstrate it.

In the wilderness of temptation, we observe the submission of Jesus in all its power:

> **Matt 4:3-4** And when the tempter came to him, he said, If thou be the Son of God, command that these stones be made bread. **4** But he answered and said, It is written, Man shall not live by bread alone, but by every word that proceedeth out of the mouth of God.

Jesus refused to be drawn away from the will of the Father. Notice the following expressions of this submission:

> **John 5:19** Then answered Jesus and said unto them, Verily, verily, I say unto you, The Son can do nothing of himself, but what he seeth the Father do: for what things soever he doeth, these also doeth the Son likewise.

> **John 5:30** I can of mine own self do nothing: as I hear, I judge: and my judgment is just; because I seek not mine own will, but the will of the Father which hath sent me.

> **John 8:29** And he that sent me is with me: the Father hath not left me alone; for I do always those things that please him.

But it is on the eve of His death that we see submission at a level never seen nor comprehended before:

> **Matt 26:39** And he went a little further, and fell on his face, and prayed, saying, O my Father, if it be possible, let this cup pass from me: nevertheless not as I will, but as thou *wilt*.

What incredible faith! Jesus was willing to trust His very life to the Father and trust that He knows best; its awe inspiring to contemplate. The submission of Jesus to the Father, cemented in His human nature a willingness to submit to the Father and trust Him at any cost. This victory now flows to us through the channel of blessing. We can now trust God completely because Jesus did it for us and now can do it through us by His Spirit.

g. Re-establishing the True Purpose of the Sanctuary

The Sanctuary system was designed by God to write the protective law of God in the hearts of people. The Jewish people, influenced by the serpent's lie had turned the Sanctuary temple into a national icon, a symbol of pride, a possession that made them feel good about themselves. On top of this was added the greed, selfishness and desire for gain from the money changers at the temple who sold sacrificial animals for profit. The Sanctuary system like everything else had been twisted and perverted by the serpent's lie.

Jesus signaled His intentions to restore a correct view of the Sanctuary by cleansing it.

> **John 2:13-17** And the Jews' passover was at hand, and Jesus went up to Jerusalem, **14** And found in the temple those that sold oxen and sheep and doves, and the changers of money sitting: **15** And when he had made a scourge of small cords, he drove them all out of the temple, and the sheep, and the oxen; and poured out the changers' money, and overthrew the tables; **16** And said unto them that sold doves, Take these things hence; make not my Father's house an house of merchandise. **17** And his disciples remembered that it was written, The zeal of thine house hath eaten me up.

By cleansing the temple, Jesus pointed to its real purpose, a place for people to approach God and worship. Jesus cleansed the temple again at the close of his ministry. It was vital for Jesus to restore a correct view of the Sanctuary for as we noted it is God's appointed method of returning us to the family kingdom.

h. Re-establishing the Truth about Death and Life Only in Christ

After spending many years in captivity, some of the Israelites became influenced by the teachings on immortality that come from the serpent. To break this lie and reaffirm our total dependence on God for life, Jesus taught that life comes through Him and Him alone. It does not reside in anyone else of itself.

The Old Testament is very clear on what man is and what happens to man when he dies.

> **Gen 3:19** In the sweat of thy face shalt thou eat bread, till thou return unto the ground; for out of it wast thou taken: for dust thou *art*, and unto dust shalt thou return.

Man was made from the dust and to the dust he will return. There is no life retained or a soul that remains alive in any form.

> **Eccl 3:19-20** For that which befalleth the sons of men befalleth beasts; even one thing befalleth them: as the one dieth, so dieth the other; yea, they have all one breath; so that a man hath no preeminence above a beast: for all *is* vanity. **20** All go unto one place; all are of the dust, and all turn to dust again.

When man dies, he does not rise again until the resurrection at the end of the world.

> **Job 14:12-14** So man lieth down, and riseth not: till the heavens *be* no more, they shall not awake, nor be raised out of their sleep. **13** O that thou wouldest hide me in the grave, that thou wouldest keep me secret, until thy wrath be past, that thou wouldest appoint me a set time, and remember me! **14** If a man die, shall he live *again*? all the days of my appointed time will I wait, till my change come.

Jesus made it very clear in His teaching that life only comes from His Father and through Himself and that we can only have life as we are connected to Him.

> **John 6:31-33** Our fathers did eat manna in the desert; as it is written, He gave them bread from heaven to eat. **32** Then Jesus said unto them, Verily, verily, I say unto you, Moses gave you not that bread from heaven; but my Father giveth you the true bread from heaven. **33** For the bread of God is he which cometh down from heaven, and giveth life unto the world.

> **John 6:46-48** Not that any man hath seen the Father, save he which is of God, he hath seen the Father. **47** Verily, verily, I say unto you, He that believeth on me hath everlasting life. **48** I am that bread of life.

When a friend of Jesus, Lazarus, had died, He spoke of the state that Lazarus was in.

> **John 11:11-14** These things said he: and after that he saith unto them, Our friend Lazarus sleepeth; but I go, that I may awake him out of sleep. **12** Then said his disciples, Lord, if he sleep, he shall do well. **13** Howbeit Jesus spake of his death: but they thought that he had spoken of taking of rest in sleep. **14** Then said Jesus unto them plainly, Lazarus is dead.

Jesus called death a sleep. During, sleep a person is completely unaware of their surroundings, they are not active in any way, nor participate in any activities. They rest in sleep, waiting for the morning when they arise. This is exactly what death is like. Notice what Jesus says:

> **John 11:25-26** Jesus said unto her, I am the resurrection, and the life: he that believeth in me, though he were dead, yet shall he live: **26** And whosoever liveth and believeth in me shall never die. Believest thou this?

Only those who believe in Jesus will be resurrected to eternal life. And the life that we have now is a gift to every person, allowing them time to decide for God's kingdom or Satan's kingdom. Those who choose Satan's kingdom will be disconnected from the life source and cease to exist.

> **Obad 1:16** For as ye have drunk upon my holy mountain, *so* shall all the heathen drink continually, yea, they shall drink, and they shall swallow down, and they shall be as though they had not been.

Those that have drunk of the wine of the serpent's lie and continually drink from it will in the end cease to be.

This understanding of death will raise questions for some. It is not the purpose of this book to give an exhaustive study on the subject, but to reaffirm the point that we can only have life when we are connected to the life source. Outside that life source there is no life at all. As the apostle John puts it:

> **1 John 5:11-12** And this is the record, that God hath given to us eternal life, and this life is in his Son. **12** He that hath the Son hath life; *and* he that hath not the Son of God hath not life.

Understanding this truth is vital to aid the breaking of the serpent's lie of inherent life and power.

i. Re-establishing the True Nature and Purpose of Prayer

One of the clearest evidences of a belief that life and blessing exist outside of you is personal prayer: Prayer that expresses the need for strength; prayer that expresses the need for communion and connection. This is how Jesus lived.

> **Matt 14:23** And when he had sent the multitudes away, he went up into a mountain apart to pray: and when the evening was come, he was there alone.

> **Mark 1:35** And in the morning, rising up a great while before day, he went out, and departed into a solitary place, and there prayed.

The disciples of Jesus were devout followers and had forsaken everything to follow Him, but when they heard Jesus pray, they asked:

> **Luke 11:1** And it came to pass, that, as he was praying in a certain place, when he ceased, one of his disciples said unto him, Lord, teach us to pray, as John also taught his disciples.

There was something in the prayers of Jesus that made the disciples feel they were lacking something. Prayer for the Israelites had degenerated through the serpent's lie to a form or a ritual that needed to be performed in order to be worthy. Jesus exposed this when He said:

> **Matt 6:5-8** And when thou prayest, thou shalt not be as the hypocrites *are*: for they love to pray standing in the synagogues and in the corners of the streets, that they may be seen of men. Verily I say unto you, They have their reward. **6** But thou, when thou prayest, enter into thy closet, and when thou hast shut thy door, pray to thy Father which is in secret; and thy Father which seeth in secret shall reward thee openly. **7** But when ye pray, use not vain repetitions, as the heathen *do*: for they think that they shall be heard for their much speaking. **8** Be not ye therefore like unto them: for your Father knoweth what things ye have need of, before ye ask him.

When we know we are God's children by faith through Christ, we have confidence in prayer and we speak to Him in love and joy. We bring our cares and sorrows to Him and we open our heart to Him. In God's kingdom, prayer is the outworking of a real relationship, it is relational. Prayer is not a deed to be performed to be seen to be holy or accepted by God.

The example of Jesus in prayer was another vital piece in bringing the human family back to the family kingdom. If Jesus felt His need of prayer as a human, how much more should we feel that need?

j. Re-establishing the Dignity of Women

In God's family kingdom, the role of a woman is vital in the family. A wife and mother establishes the authority of her husband and through the principles of submission teaches her children vital lessons regarding submission to headship.

Satan has ever tried to make the lives of women difficult and cause them to resist the submissive role or be crushed beneath an indifferent or hostile husband. The Jewish leaders had placed women in a very difficult position. For instance a man could divorce his wife for the most trifling of reasons and leave a woman feeling extremely insecure and consequently compliant if she wanted to maintain respect in the community.

In cases of adultery, women were usually blamed as the cause of the adultery. Jesus addressed these issues directly and we see a breath taking defense of a woman who had been taken advantage of by the Jewish leaders in the following passage:

> **John 8:3-11** And the scribes and Pharisees brought unto him a woman taken in adultery; and when they had set her in the midst, **4** They say unto him, Master, this woman was taken in adultery, in the very act. **5** Now Moses in the law commanded us, that such should be stoned: but what sayest thou? **6** This they said, tempting him, that they might have to accuse him. But Jesus stooped down, and with *his* finger wrote on the ground, *as though he heard them not.* **7** So when they continued asking him, he lifted up himself, and said unto them, He that is without sin among you, let him first cast a stone at her. **8** And again he stooped down, and wrote on the ground. **9** And they which heard *it*, being convicted by *their own* conscience, went out one by one, beginning at the eldest, *even* unto the last: and Jesus was left alone, and the woman standing in the midst. **10** When Jesus had lifted up himself, and saw none but the woman, he said unto her, Woman, where are those thine accusers? hath no man condemned thee? **11** She said, No man, Lord. And Jesus said unto her, Neither do I condemn thee: go, and sin no more.

Jesus defended this woman against the callous and uncaring Pharisees. He did not condone her part in the sin, but He made her feel worth something by defending her and saving her life. He did not condemn her sin but offered her the hope of a new life.

On another occasion, some mothers brought their children to Jesus to be blessed by Him. These women drawn by the Spirit of God, sensed something in Jesus that their children needed and that Jesus could provide that by blessing them.

> **Mark 10:13-16** And they brought young children to him, that he should touch them: and *his* disciples rebuked those that brought *them*. **14** But when Jesus saw *it*, he was much displeased, and said unto them, Suffer the little children to come unto me, and forbid them not: for of such is the kingdom of God. **15** Verily I say unto you, Whosoever shall not receive the kingdom of God as a little child, he shall not enter therein. **16** And he took them up in his arms, put *his* hands upon them, and blessed them.

The disciples of Jesus saw this event as an intrusion to more important matters. To show the seriousness of this situation, the Bible indicates that Jesus was "much displeased" or more directly, quite angry about the mother's request being denied. There are few times that Jesus is recorded as being angry, this was one of them. Through this act, Jesus showed that he understood the cares and toils of a mother and He did what He could to lighten that load.

It is interesting to note that it was the defense of a woman that ultimately led to the death of Christ. Notice this passage:

> **Matt 26:6-16** Now when Jesus was in Bethany, in the house of Simon the leper, **7** There came unto him a woman having an alabaster box of very precious ointment, and poured it on his head, as he sat *at meat*. **8** But when his disciples saw *it*, they had indignation, saying, To what purpose *is* this waste? **9** For this ointment might have been sold for much, and given to the poor. **10** When Jesus understood *it*, he said unto them, Why trouble ye the woman? for she hath wrought a good work upon me. **11** For ye have the poor always with you; but me ye have not always. **12** For in that she hath poured this ointment on my body, she did *it* for my burial. **13** Verily I say unto you, Wheresoever this gospel shall be preached in the whole world, *there* shall also this, that this woman hath done, be told for a memorial of her. **14** Then one of the twelve, called Judas Iscariot, went unto the chief priests, **15** And said *unto them*, What will ye give me, and I will deliver him unto you? And they covenanted with him for thirty pieces of silver. **16** And from that time he sought opportunity to betray him.

When Mary came to wipe the feet of Jesus, the disciples, led by Judas, scorned her as wasteful. Jesus immediately defended her actions and rebuked the disciples for their hard heartedness towards her and then gave the pronouncement that wherever the gospel is preached, the story of Mary should be told. How encouraging this must have been for Mary. Mary demonstrated perfectly the true position of a repentant sinner and displayed the joy of forgiveness. Jesus wanted the world to know, that what she had done was the most appropriate response to His work.

After Judas was rebuked by Jesus, he went straight to the priests to cut a deal to betray Jesus. This story shows how much Jesus was willing to sacrifice to raise the dignity of women.

This work was vital for helping restore true family relationships and the vital role of a wife and mother in the family.

All of these teachings that Jesus re-established are referred to in the book of Revelation as the 'faith of Jesus'. The 'faith of Jesus' is the set of principles both taught and lived by Jesus. This faith, as we will discover later on, would survive till the end of time under fierce attack from Satan. But the seed of the woman will triumph and God's family kingdom will finally rule the universe. So it can be said "here are they that keep the commandments of God and the faith of Jesus." Rev 14:12

Chapter 20

Transition to the Invisible

a. Relationships are Invisible

By the very fact that God's kingdom is based on relationships, its emphasis is on the things that are not seen. Though we can see evidences of a relationship, the actual relationship itself cannot be observed with the eye. If we look closely at a husband and wife relationship, we cannot tell exactly how strong or stable that relationship is, we can guess by the things they say and how they relate to each other, but we can't see the actual relationship itself.

This is why God's kingdom focuses on the invisible; that which occurs in the mind. Notice some Bible passages that describe this aspect of God.

> **Rom 1:20** For the invisible things of him from the creation of the world are clearly seen, being understood by the things that are made, *even* his eternal power and Godhead; so that they are without excuse:

> **1 Tim 6:16** Who only hath immortality, dwelling in the light which no man can approach unto; whom no man hath seen, nor can see: to whom *be* honour and power everlasting. Amen.

For this reason, those who are seeking a relationship with God will focus on the invisible things of life; a relationship with God, family and friends.

Referring back to our comparison between Abraham and Nimrod, we see this issue raised in the area of worship. Abraham focused on the invisible. His value was in his relationship with God and he did not need constant external reminders of that relationship. On the other hand Nimrod's insecurity required constant external evidences of his value and since he had no real relationship with God, his worship focused on ritual and ceremony and that which can be seen.

Abraham	Nimrod
1. Family Structure (Gen 18:19)	1. Individual Dictator/Tyrant (Gen 10:10)
2. Nomadic Rural Dwellers (Heb 11:8-10)	2. City Builders and Defenders (Gen 11:4)
3. Identity by Parental Blessing (Gen 12:2)	3. Identity by Renown (Gen 11:4)
4. Observe Sabbath and Commandments (Gen 26:5)	4. Follow Personal Desires (Rom 1:21-32)
5. Belief in Death and Resurrection (Heb 11:17-19)	5. Belief in Immortality of the Soul (Gen 3:4)
6. Saviour as Humble Life Restorer – Revealed in Slain Lamb (John 11:25)	6. Saviour as Prideful Liberator and Subduer Empowered by Sun and Nature Worship
7. Focus of Worship on the Invisible	7. Focus of Worship on the Visible

Therefore, the issue of the visible versus the invisible will be an important indicator as to which kingdom is most influencing our thinking. And we see this reflected in Scripture:

> **2 Cor 4:18** While we look not at the things which are seen, but at the things which are not seen: for the things which are seen *are* temporal; but the things which are not seen *are* eternal.
>
> **Heb 11:1** Now faith is the substance of things hoped for, the evidence of things not seen.

This issue is so important that God actually made it one of His commandments:

> **Exod 20:4** Thou shalt not make unto thee any graven image, or any likeness *of any thing* that *is* in heaven above, or that *is* in the earth beneath, or that *is* in the water under the earth.

The representation of God through earthly and material things is the fastest way to shift the focus from the invisible to the visible. The Bible calls it idolatry and God hates it because it disconnects His children from a real relationship with Him.

b. The Serpent's Lie Shifts Focus to the Visible

Idolatry is a constant problem for the human race because of the serpent's lie. This is because the belief that we have inherent life and power combined with a need for value demands that this power is demonstrated and seen. If we can't see our own power demonstrated, we start to feel worthless. And in the realm of worship, the focus of worship is on power, the display and worship of power. A quick glance at idolatry through the ages reveals the objects worshipped were worshipped for some aspects of their power which the worshipper wanted to obtain or possess themselves. In worshipping the 'god' it was hoped that a worshipper would be favoured and receive some of their power. This is in complete harmony with the opportunity and threat mindset of inherent power. Seeing an object that possesses power, presents the opportunity to a person that through the right approach they might obtain some of this power.

When it comes to the worship of the true God, sadly many people become confused and seek to combine a love for God with a seeking to obtain His power. It is true that we need His power, but not to make us feel powerful and valuable, but that we might honour Him, reflect His character and enjoy His relationship. Many people perform good deeds, pray long and sacrifice much in order to win God's favour and obtain His power. Such religion is empty and devoid of true love.

> **1 Cor 13:1-3** Though I speak with the tongues of men and of angels, and have not charity, I am become *as* sounding brass, or a tinkling cymbal. **2** And though I have *the gift of* prophecy, and understand all mysteries, and all knowledge; and though I have all faith, so that I could remove mountains, and have not charity, I am nothing. **3** And though I bestow all my goods to feed *the poor*, and though I give my body to be burned, and have not charity, it profiteth me nothing.

c. The Journey Towards the Invisible

It is for these reasons that the Sanctuary service system was designed to lead its worshippers back towards the invisible, to the relational. You will remember from our introduction to the Sanctuary that this shift from visible to invisible is clearly portrayed.

Transition to the Invisible

VISIBLE	INVISIBLE
The Altar of Sacrifice	The Ark of the Covenant
☐	☐
Tables of Stone	Tables of the Heart

The question that must be raised is: if God's kingdom is in the invisible, then why did He give the Israelites a system that was so heavily visible? The answer to that question lies in that fact that God meets us where we are at and in order to teach Israel the true principles of His kingdom, He had to give them a model in the visible of how this worked. It must be remembered though, that the most sacred aspect of the worship service was never seen by the worshippers. The beautiful gold furniture, the ark, the commandments were never seen except by faith. Also there was a wall all around the Sanctuary that prevented the people from seeing anything from the outside. The only real visible things that the worshippers saw were the altar of sacrifice, the slain lamb and the laver of water for cleansing. The rest was hidden except for the priests who acted on their behalf.

It is vitally important to remember that the purpose of the Sanctuary journey is to write the law of God in our hearts, a place that cannot be seen. To do this effectively, the process of the journey must be through the mind of the worshipper.

With this in mind we can understand why Jesus would seek to shift the focus of the Israelites from the objects of the temple on earth, and place them on the heavenly invisible realities. The interesting thing about the Sanctuary on earth is that it was only ever a copy of an invisible heavenly original.

Heb 8:1-5 Now of the things which we have spoken *this is* the sum: We have such an high priest, who is set on the right hand of the throne of the Majesty in the heavens; **2** A minister of the sanctuary, and of the true tabernacle, which the Lord pitched, and not man. **3** For every high priest is ordained to offer gifts and sacrifices: wherefore *it is* of necessity that this man have somewhat also to offer. **4** For if he were on earth, he should not be a priest, seeing that there are priests that offer gifts according to the law: **5** Who serve unto the example and shadow of heavenly things, as Moses was admonished of God when he was about to make the tabernacle: for, See, saith he, *that* thou make all things according to the pattern shewed to thee in the mount.

It was always God's intention to shift people's focus from the visible to the invisible, so the work of writing His law in the hearts of His people would be effective. This was one of the key elements of the ministry of Jesus: shift the people's thinking to the heavenly.

Luke 17:20-21 And when he was demanded of the Pharisees, when the kingdom of God should come, he answered them and said, The kingdom of God cometh not with observation: **21** Neither shall they say, Lo here! or, lo there! for, behold, the kingdom of God is within you.

Jesus clearly told the Pharisees that God's kingdom was not visible to the eye, but within a person. There would be no giant display to convince the Jewish leaders of this kingdom; it had to be entered into by faith. This shift in thinking is well documented in the conversation between Jesus and the woman at the well.

John 4:19-24 The woman saith unto him, Sir, I perceive that thou art a prophet. **20** Our fathers worshipped in this mountain; and ye say, that in Jerusalem is the place where men ought to worship. **21** Jesus saith unto her, Woman, believe me, the hour cometh, when ye shall neither in this mountain, nor yet at Jerusalem, worship the Father. Ye worship ye know not what: we know what we worship: for salvation is of the Jews. **23** But the hour cometh, and now is, when the true worshippers shall worship the Father in spirit and in truth: for the Father seeketh such to worship him. **24** God *is* a Spirit: and they that worship him must worship *him* in spirit and in truth.

When the woman sensed that Jesus understood spiritual matters, she immediately questioned Him about the correct place or location of worship. Her mind was focused on the physical and geographical. But Jesus told her that true worship does not consist on a focus on earthly building and locations. It is not buildings that make a place holy, but the Spirit of God that makes a place holy and sacred. He pointed this woman to true worship: worship in

Transition to the Invisible

spirit (the invisible) and truth.

d. Satan Seeks to Shut the Door to the Invisible

The very fact that God had given a visible Sanctuary as a lesson book meant that it was used by Satan to get Israel to focus on this visible worship system. If he could keep their attention focused on the earthly temple system, then he could block their minds from shifting to the heavenly realities and the true invisible Sanctuary in heaven.

If we study carefully the dialog between Jesus and the Jewish leaders, this issue surfaces again and again.

> **John 3:3-12** Jesus answered and said unto him, Verily, verily, I say unto thee, Except a man be born again, he cannot see the kingdom of God. **4** Nicodemus saith unto him, How can a man be born when he is old? can he enter the second time into his mother's womb, and be born? **5** Jesus answered, Verily, verily, I say unto thee, Except a man be born of water and *of* the Spirit, he cannot enter into the kingdom of God. **6** That which is born of the flesh is flesh; and that which is born of the Spirit is spirit. **7** Marvel not that I said unto thee, Ye must be born again. **8** The wind bloweth where it listeth, and thou hearest the sound thereof, but canst not tell whence it cometh, and whither it goeth: so is every one that is born of the Spirit. **9** Nicodemus answered and said unto him, How can these things be? **10** Jesus answered and said unto him, Art thou a master of Israel, and knowest not these things? **11** Verily, verily, I say unto thee, We speak that we do know, and testify that we have seen; and ye receive not our witness. **12** If I have told you earthly things, and ye believe not, how shall ye believe, if I tell you *of* heavenly things?

Jesus told Nicodemus that he must be born again which, in its most literal reading, means to be born from above or the invisible. Jesus then went on to explain the invisible workings of the Spirit of God which the eye cannot see. Nicodemus struggled to understand this invisible focus.

Satan had to prevent the Israelites from following Jesus from earth back to heaven in their minds. If their focus shifted to the invisible realities they would lose interest in the earthly visible worship system which was the means of control that the Jewish leaders had over the people. With this in mind, every time Jesus spoke of this shift, it was seen as an attack on the Jewish leaders and their power base.

> **John 2:18-21** Then answered the Jews and said unto him, What sign shewest thou unto us, seeing that thou doest these things? **19** Jesus answered and said unto them, Destroy this temple, and in three days I will raise it up. **20** Then said the Jews, Forty and six years was this temple in building, and wilt thou rear it up in three days? **21** But he spake of the temple of his body.

The Jews wanted an outward or visible sign of the authority of Jesus, but in His answer to them Jesus spoke of the invisible rather than the visible. The whole Sanctuary system was a reflection of Jesus – the divine submissive agent. The whole object of this system was to make people like Jesus; Jesus is the centre and focus of everything and the aspect of Christ that was so vital was His character which was not visible to the naked eye.

Sadly, the Jews refused to move with Christ in their thinking to the invisible realm and clung to their earthly temple. It is interesting to note that on the basis of this statement above that the Jews finally condemned Jesus to death.

> **Matt 26:61-65** And said, This *fellow* said, I am able to destroy the temple of God, and to build it in three days. **62** And the high priest arose, and said unto him, Answerest thou nothing? what *is it which* these witness against thee? **63** But Jesus held his peace. And the high priest answered and said unto him, I adjure thee by the living God, that thou tell us whether thou be the Christ, the Son of God. **64** Jesus saith unto him, Thou hast said: nevertheless I say unto you, Hereafter shall ye see the Son of man sitting on the right hand of power, and coming in the clouds of heaven. **65** Then the high priest rent his clothes, saying, He hath spoken blasphemy; what further need have we of witnesses? behold, now ye have heard his blasphemy.

This obsessive focus on the earthly temple, cunningly devised by Satan through his lie of inherent power that causes a focus on the visible, caused a great tragedy for Israel. They missed the meaning of the services they were given and they rejected the very Person that was at the heart of their worship system. In a passionate and desperate effort, Jesus sought to awaken their minds to their foolish obsession with the visible.

> **Matt 23:16-25** Woe unto you, *ye* blind guides, which say, Whosoever shall swear by the temple, it is nothing; but whosoever shall swear by the gold of the temple, he is a debtor! **17** *Ye* fools and blind: for whether is greater, the gold, or the temple that sanctifieth the gold? **18** And, Whosoever shall swear by the altar, it is nothing; but whosoever sweareth by the gift that is upon it, he is guilty. **19** *Ye* fools and blind:

> for whether *is* greater, the gift, or the altar that sanctifieth the gift? **20** Whoso therefore shall swear by the altar, sweareth by it, and by all things thereon. **21** And whoso shall swear by the temple, sweareth by it, and by him that dwelleth therein. **22** And he that shall swear by heaven, sweareth by the throne of God, and by him that sitteth thereon. **23** Woe unto you, scribes and Pharisees, hypocrites! for ye pay tithe of mint and anise and cummin, and have omitted the weightier *matters* of the law, judgment, mercy, and faith: these ought ye to have done, and not to leave the other undone. **24** *Ye* blind guides, which strain at a gnat, and swallow a camel. **25** Woe unto you, scribes and Pharisees, hypocrites! for ye make clean the outside of the cup and of the platter, but within they are full of extortion and excess.

Sadly, they did not listen and the very system that was designed to bring the heart to a flourishing life was left in the state that Satan's kingdom makes it – desolate.

> **Matt 23:37-38** O Jerusalem, Jerusalem, *thou* that killest the prophets, and stonest them which are sent unto thee, how often would I have gathered thy children together, even as a hen gathereth her chickens under *her* wings, and ye would not! **38** Behold, your house is left unto you desolate.

e. The Followers of Christ Make the Shift from Earthly Symbols to Heavenly Realities

This shift in thinking was hard to accept even for the disciples of Christ. They could not understand why He needed to go back to heaven and become invisible to them.

> **John 13:36-37** Simon Peter said unto him, Lord, whither goest thou? Jesus answered him, Whither I go, thou canst not follow me now; but thou shalt follow me afterwards. **37** Peter said unto him, Lord, why cannot I follow thee now? I will lay down my life for thy sake.

> **John 14:1-5** Let not your heart be troubled: ye believe in God, believe also in me. **2** In my Father's house are many mansions: if *it were* not *so*, I would have told you. I go to prepare a place for you. **3** And if I go and prepare a place for you, I will come again, and receive you unto myself; that where I am, *there* ye may be also. **4** And whither I go ye know, and the way ye know. **5** Thomas saith unto him, Lord, we know not whither thou goest; and how can we know the way?

If Jesus did not return to heaven, our human natures would focus on His physical person rather than His character. Jesus had to return to heaven, so that our minds would learn to think in the invisible. The wonderful news was that Jesus would still be present via His Spirit. He could still comfort His people while not being visible to them. Through the Holy Spirit, Jesus could complete the work of writing His law; His character into their hearts.

> **John 14:16-18** And I will pray the Father, and he shall give you another Comforter, that he may abide with you for ever; **17** *Even* the Spirit of truth; whom the world cannot receive, because it seeth him not, neither knoweth him: but ye know him; for he dwelleth with you, and shall be in you. **18** I will not leave you comfortless: I will come to you.

> **John 16:4-7** But these things have I told you, that when the time shall come, ye may remember that I told you of them. And these things I said not unto you at the beginning, because I was with you. **5** But now I go my way to him that sent me; and none of you asketh me, Whither goest thou? **6** But because I have said these things unto you, sorrow hath filled your heart. **7** Nevertheless I tell you the truth; It is expedient for you that I go away: for if I go not away, the Comforter will not come unto you; but if I depart, I will send him unto you.

Just as the temple needed to become invisible, so did Jesus. This was all part of the process of shifting from a visible power based system to an invisible relational system. How wonderful to know that Jesus is still with us through His Spirit. The one who knows our trials and sorrows and understands the challenges of human life is still present with us and comforts us. As Jesus stated it was vital that He go away as a visible identity and return via the Spirit as an invisible identity, in order that the real work of changing our hearts could be accomplished where it was needed – in the invisible, relational realm.

Much of the rest of the New Testament is about this shift in thinking to the invisible and Satan's attempts to block this shift.

> **Acts 6:7-15** And the word of God increased; and the number of the disciples multiplied in Jerusalem greatly; and a great company of the priests were obedient to the faith. **8** And Stephen, full of faith and power, did great wonders and miracles among the people. **9** Then there arose certain of the synagogue, which is called *the synagogue* of the Libertines, and Cyrenians, and Alexandrians, and of them of Cilicia and of Asia, disputing with Stephen. **10** And they were not able to resist the wisdom and the spirit by which he spake. **11** Then they suborned men, which said, We have heard him speak blasphemous words against Moses, and *against* God. **12** And they stirred up the people,

and the elders, and the scribes, and came upon *him*, and caught him, and brought *him* to the council, **13** And set up false witnesses, which said, This man ceaseth not to speak blasphemous words against this holy place, and the law: **14** For we have heard him say, that this Jesus of Nazareth shall destroy this place, and shall change the customs which Moses delivered us. **15** And all that sat in the council, looking stedfastly on him, saw his face as it had been the face of an angel.

Acts 7:48-60 Howbeit the most High dwelleth not in temples made with hands; as saith the prophet, **49** Heaven *is* my throne, and earth *is* my footstool: what house will ye build me? saith the Lord: or what *is* the place of my rest? **50** Hath not my hand made all these things? **51** Ye stiffnecked and uncircumcised in heart and ears, ye do always resist the Holy Ghost: as your fathers *did*, so *do* ye. **52** Which of the prophets have not your fathers persecuted? and they have slain them which shewed before of the coming of the Just One; of whom ye have been now the betrayers and murderers: **53** Who have received the law by the disposition of angels, and have not kept *it*. **54** When they heard these things, they were cut to the heart, and they gnashed on him with *their* teeth. **55** But he, being full of the Holy Ghost, looked up stedfastly into heaven, and saw the glory of God, and Jesus standing on the right hand of God, **56** And said, Behold, I see the heavens opened, and the Son of man standing on the right hand of God. **57** Then they cried out with a loud voice, and stopped their ears, and ran upon him with one accord, **58** And cast *him* out of the city, and stoned *him*: and the witnesses laid down their clothes at a young man's feet, whose name was Saul. **59** And they stoned Stephen, calling upon *God*, and saying, Lord Jesus, receive my spirit. **60** And he kneeled down, and cried with a loud voice, Lord, lay not this sin to their charge. And when he had said this, he fell asleep.

The Jews claimed that Stephen was turning the minds of the people away from the earthly temple and therefore changing the customs of Moses – their most revered leader. Stephen tried to tell them in his trial that God does not dwell in temples made with hands; His kingdom is in the invisible. Again, in a desperate attempt to reach the Jews and awaken them to their enslaved focus on the visible, Stephen spoke to them directly that they and their forebears had consistently resisted the invisible – spiritual view. As a sign of the shift that had taken place and that Jesus was indeed in heaven, Stephen had a vision of heaven, where He saw Jesus at the right hand of the Father. This was the Jews final chance to accept that there needed to be a shift to the invisible. But rather than accept this, they silenced the voice of the man who pleaded with them.

This act sealed their fate as a nation. As Jesus predicted their house was left unto them desolate. Devoid of the protection of God, the Jewish temple was destroyed 40 years later.

Sadly this desire to focus on the visible temple remains with us today. Millions of people believe that the earthly temple will be rebuilt, but such a belief denies everything that Jesus taught in regard to being born from above. The true worshippers of God will worship in Spirit – in the invisible and be comforted by the invisible Spirit of Christ until He comes in the clouds of glory and we see Him again when our hearts are cleansed of the serpent's lie and the obsession with the visible is no longer a problem.

Nimrod	Christian Church Under Rome
1. Individual Dictator/Tyrant (Gen 10:10)	1. Individual Dictator/Tyrant (Rev 13:16,17)
2. City Builders and Defenders (Gen 11:4)	2. City Builders and Traders (Rev 18)
3. Identity by Renown (Gen 11:4)	3. Identity through Position (2 Thess 2:4)
4. Follow Personal Desires (Rom 1:21-32)	4. Commandments and Sabbath Changed to Suit Personal Desire (Dan 7:25)
5. Belief in Immortality of the Soul (Gen 3:4)	5. Belief in Immortality of Soul (Catechism)
6. Saviour as Prideful Liberator and Subduer Empowered by Sun and Nature Worship	6. Saviour as Prideful Liberator and Subduer – the Pope, Empowered by Sun-day Worship and Natural Law.
7. Focus of Worship on the Visible	7. Focus of Worship on the Visible

Chapter 21

The Heavenly Sanctuary and Work of Jesus Trodden Under Foot

In this chapter we will see Satan's desperate efforts to block people from looking into the invisible realm and the work of Jesus in heaven. This warfare would naturally be conducted through the spiritual descendents of Nimrod who clung to the inherent power system and consequently a focus on the visible.

a. The Priestly Ministry of Jesus in Heaven

> **Heb 4:14-16** Seeing then that we have a great high priest, that is passed into the heavens, Jesus the Son of God, let us hold fast *our* profession. **15** For we have not an high priest which cannot be touched with the feeling of our infirmities; but was in all points tempted like as *we are, yet* without sin. **16** Let us therefore come boldly unto the throne of grace, that we may obtain mercy, and find grace to help in time of need.

The work of Jesus on earth was to connect the human race with the channel of blessing, cut down the mountains of pride and worthless, form a perfectly submitted human character that could be added to the channel of blessing and take the separation from the channel, caused by Adam, to the cross and the grave. This work was symbolized by the court in the Sanctuary service; the altar of sacrifice and the laver of cleansing. Armed with these victories, Christ entered into the invisible heavenly realm to then impart to His believing followers, the victories He had obtained. The victories are imparted to us through His Spirit.

> **Rom 8:9-11** But ye are not in the flesh, but in the Spirit, if so be that the Spirit of God dwell in you. Now if any man have not the Spirit of Christ, he is none of his. **10** And if Christ *be* in you, the body *is* dead

because of sin; but the Spirit *is* life because of righteousness. **11** But if the Spirit of him that raised up Jesus from the dead dwell in you, he that raised up Christ from the dead shall also quicken your mortal bodies by his Spirit that dwelleth in you.

Phil 1:19 For I know that this shall turn to my salvation through your prayer, and the supply of the Spirit of Jesus Christ,

Eph 1:17-21 That the God of our Lord Jesus Christ, the Father of glory, may give unto you the spirit of wisdom and revelation in the knowledge of him: **18** The eyes of your understanding being enlightened; that ye may know what is the hope of his calling, and what the riches of the glory of his inheritance in the saints, **19** And what *is* the exceeding greatness of his power to us-ward who believe, according to the working of his mighty power, **20** Which he wrought in Christ, when he raised him from the dead, and set *him* at his own right hand in the heavenly *places*, **21** Far above all principality, and power, and might, and dominion, and every name that is named, not only in this world, but also in that which is to come:

Gal 4:6 And because ye are sons, God hath sent forth the Spirit of his Son into your hearts, crying, Abba, Father.

As the followers of Christ focus their minds on the person of Jesus and pray for help to be like Him, He sends His Spirit to them full of the victories He has obtained and the Spirit residing in His followers is manifested in love, joy, peace, patience and all the other fruit of the Spirit of Christ.

If Satan allowed God's people to focus on this wonderful work of Jesus in heaven, they would become too powerful for him to overcome. He had to block the minds of the worshippers from looking towards heaven and the work of Jesus.

b. The Spiritualization of Rome

Of course, in the wisdom and foreknowledge of God, He knew that Satan would seek to do this and predicted 600 years before Christ came to earth that Satan would work to obstruct the heavenly Sanctuary and wipe out God's true followers.

Satan would do this through the Babylonian system. Satan had managed to enslave Israel to Babylon physically, and after the shift of Jesus into the invisible, he would have to do it spiritually. Daniel Chapter 7 and 8 explains the process of how this would take place. The four world empires that culminated in Pagan Rome would have to take on a spiritual emphasis to compete with the true followers of Christ. It is true that pagan kingdoms all had a spiritual element, but this new spiritual emphasis via Rome would have to look similar to the spiritual focus of God's heavenly kingdom. Therefore Satan transformed Rome into a counterfeit spiritual power as well as an earthly power. By adding this spiritual dimension, he could then enter the new battlefield for the minds of God's true worshippers, block their view from the heavenly work of Christ and cut off the channel of blessing through His mediatorial work as a priest.

> **Dan 7:19-21** Then I would know the truth of the fourth beast, which was diverse from all the others, exceeding dreadful, whose teeth *were of* iron, and his nails *of* brass; *which* devoured, brake in pieces, and stamped the residue with his feet; **20** And of the ten horns that *were* in his head, and *of* the other which came up, and before whom three fell; even *of* that horn that had eyes, and a mouth that spake very great things, whose look *was* more stout than his fellows. **21** I beheld, and the same horn made war with the saints, and prevailed against them;

The fourth beast which, we know to be Rome, would become diverse or different from the previous kingdoms in that it would add this spiritual or invisible dimension that was a counterfeit of the true invisible system. This transition is revealed in prophecy as a horn coming out of the fourth beast – Rome.

> **Dan 8:12-13** And an host was given *him* against the daily *sacrifice* by reason of transgression, and it cast down the truth to the ground; and it practised, and prospered. **13** Then I heard one saint speaking, and another saint said unto that certain *saint* which spake, How long *shall be* the vision *concerning* the daily *sacrifice*, and the transgression of desolation, to give both the sanctuary and the host to be trodden under foot?

This horn power is described again in Daniel 8 as casting the truth to the ground. This casting to the ground process was bringing all the elements of the Sanctuary system back into the visible and in this way the work of writing the law in the hearts of God's people would be interfered with and confused.

c. Attack on the Heavenly Sanctuary

During the period of the 4th to 6th century A.D., the church of Rome focused on the doctrines of Christ on earth. It did this in four main ways:

1. It altered the law of God, by taking out the second and fourth commandment. The second commandment was vital to protecting the invisible focus and the fourth commandment points people to the source of the channel of blessing and the place where true power comes from.
2. It set up an earthly temple in Rome to focus the worshippers' minds on an earthly visible structure.
3. It set up a system of earthly priests to hear confession and promise forgiveness of sins. This was counterfeiting the work of Christ and again would focus the minds of worshippers on the earthly and a visible priesthood system rather than on our invisible Priest in an invisible Sanctuary.
4. The Mass was introduced as a visible token of the death of Christ and also the power of absolution. Instead of the Spirit of Christ being the focus, the body of Christ eaten by the people would become the source of spiritual power. The shift is subtle, but powerful and again confused the minds of God's followers.

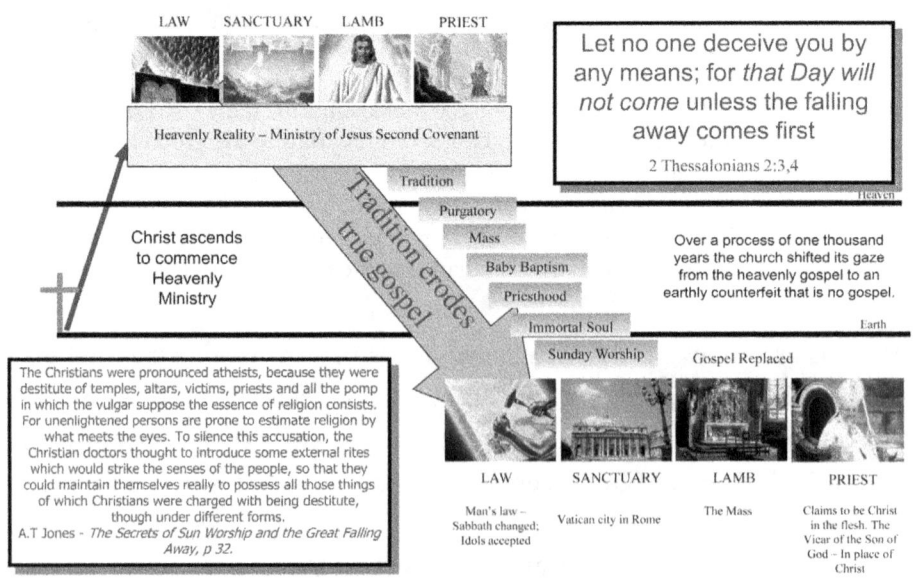

The Heavenly Sanctuary and Work of Jesus Trodden Under Foot

As Daniel considered the terrible situation of this horn power tearing down God's Sanctuary and persecuting His followers, he wondered how long this would go on for. In answer to this an angel poses this very question: How long will this horn power be allowed to trample God's Sanctuary, His law and His people?

The answer comes immediately:

> **Dan 8:14** And he said unto me, Unto two thousand and three hundred days; then shall the sanctuary be cleansed.

The word cleansed also means restored. The Sanctuary would be restored to its rightful heavenly place in the minds of the people. It would be restored to the invisible so that the work of writing the law in the hearts of the people could be finished. We will look at when this 2300 day period culminates in the next chapter, but before that we want to look at a few more points regarding the horn power.

Just as the Jews tried to oppose Jesus and His work for 3½ literal years and prevent Him from shifting the minds of the people to the fact they must be born from above, so the horn power of Daniel 8 would oppose Jesus for 3½ spiritual or prophetic years and keep people focused on an earthly visible worship program.

> **Dan 7:25** And he shall speak *great* words against the most High, and shall wear out the saints of the most High, and think to change times and laws: and they shall be given into his hand until a time and times and the dividing of time.

The time, times and a dividing of time is equal to 1260 prophetic days which equals 1260 literal years. The Roman church was most dominant from the time of 538 A.D. when the Ostrogoths were destroyed (the last of the Arian powers that stood in their way), right though until 1798 when the Pope was taken prisoner by France. The book of Revelation speaks of this situation as follows:

> **Rev 13:5-8** And there was given unto him a mouth speaking great things and blasphemies; and power was given unto him to continue forty *and* two months. 6 And he opened his mouth in blasphemy against God, to blaspheme his name, and his tabernacle, and them that dwell in heaven. 7 And it was given unto him to make war with the saints, and to overcome them: and power was given him over all kindreds, and tongues, and nations. 8 And all that dwell upon the earth shall worship him, whose names are not written in the book of life of

the Lamb slain from the foundation of the world.

42 months is equal to 1260 prophetic days or 1260 literal years.[46] This work of the horn power cut off the channel of blessing and once again broke down the family kingdom of God. The hearts of God's people were once again hardened by this false system of worship and left desolate. This is why this power is referred to as the transgression of desolation.

> **Dan 8:13** Then I heard one saint speaking, and another saint said unto that certain *saint* which spake, How long *shall be* the vision *concerning* the daily *sacrifice*, and the transgression of desolation, to give both the sanctuary and the host to be trodden under foot?

This period of history is rightly named 'The Dark Ages.' The light of truth was hidden under a worship system that attacked God's law, Sanctuary and the family.

d. The Horn Power Attacks the Family Kingdom

As we learnt previously, the creation of Adam and Eve in a headship and submission relationship was in the image of the Father and the Son. It is a Father and Son relationship which is the focus of heaven.

The Roman system introduced Mary as the mother of God and through this doctrine introduced the primary relationship of heaven as the mother and son, exactly the same way that Nimrod and Semiramis were seen in the original Babylon. The mother and son relationship does not reflect the Father and Son relationship of heaven and confuses the channel of blessing.

The Roman church also introduced a confused view of God as three beings in one literal substance.[47] This created greater confusion regarding the roles of God as a Father and a Son. Added to this was the conception of God burning sinners in hell forever and ever. This was not the picture of a loving Father, but a raging tyrant like Nimrod who cut down his enemies in vengeance. Even the death of Christ on the cross was portrayed as the satisfaction of vengeance and a clamouring for blood. All of these teachings have terribly damaged the view of God as a heavenly Father that loves us and a submissive Son that shows us how to stay connected to the source of blessing.

---

46   Rev 11:2,3
47   See the Athansian Creed

To further attack the family, the Roman church forbade its leaders to marry. Marriage, rightly conducted, is the most powerful demonstration of the kingdom of God and this could not be tolerated. The Bible clearly tells us that the elders or bishops of God's church should be the husband of one wife, so they would understand the principles of blessing. The church leaders scorned this principle and act as Bishop without being a husband. Such a man can never really be qualified to act as a shepherd of God's flock from a family kingdom context.

How could this terrible situation come about? As in the days of Samuel where the leaders of Israel wanted to be like the other nations and did not want to be different, so the Christian church found it hard to be so different having a worship system that was almost completely invisible.

> The Christians were pronounced atheists, because they were destitute of temples, altars, victims, priests and all the pomp in which the vulgar suppose the essence of religion consists. For unenlightened persons are prone to estimate religion by what meets the eyes. To silence this accusation, the Christian doctors thought to introduce some external rites which would strike the senses of the people, so that they could maintain themselves really to possess all those things of which Christians were charged with being destitute, though under different forms. A.T Jones - *The Secrets of Sun Worship and the Great Falling Away, p 32.*

The introduction of these external or visible rites opened the door for this horn power to emerge and once again take God's people captive. In captivity, God's people could no longer keep His protective law or stay connected to the priestly ministry of Jesus that would provide the power they needed to overcome the lie of the serpent.

e. Plagues of Judgment Sent to Release the Woman

Just as God sent mighty plagues or judgments on Egypt to release the woman, Sarah, from her captivity; so in Egypt when the woman (the church of Israel) was again captive, God sent judgments on spiritual Babylon to allow the woman to be released once again. These judgments are detailed in the trumpets of Revelation 8, 9 and 11.

The judgments came against Rome in both its pagan and papal phases. The first four trumpets brought pagan Rome to its knees; and the 5th and 6th trumpet describe the work of the Islamic powers and the French Revolution, which weakened the papal system and then gave it a deadly wound.

It was after this deadly wound that knowledge increased and the way was opened for a recovery of the true principles of God's kingdom to again be restored. In the same way that Moses was used to lead God's people to the commandments and the Sanctuary, the same thing would occur when Israel would be gathered again the second time.

The other key point of course that needed restoring was the blessing or seeding role of the father and the recovery of the family system. It would be the work of Elijah to bring this about just before the return of Jesus.

> **Mal 4:5-6** Behold, I will send you Elijah the prophet before the coming of the great and dreadful day of the LORD: **6** And he shall turn the heart of the fathers to the children, and the heart of the children to their fathers, lest I come and smite the earth with a curse.

It is to this story we turn next and see a movement that would arise at the end of the Sanctuary being trampled under foot at the end of the 2300 days that would recover the law, the heavenly Sanctuary and a true view of the Father and Son relationship.

Chapter 22

The Gathering of Israel the Second Time – Rise of the Advent Movement and The Elijah Message

In the last chapter we observed how Daniel spoke of this horn power that would arise and trample the Sanctuary worship system of Christ under foot by altering the key elements of the worship system from the invisible back to the visible, but in an altered form to the original. We observed that this power was the Roman church. Amongst many things it altered, it tried to change the law of God in two critical areas, removing the second commandment which protected against idolatry and visible worship and then the fourth commandment which pointed to the author of life and the source of blessing.

In Daniel 8, the question was raised, how long would this power continue? The answer came "Unto 2300 days; then shall the Sanctuary be cleansed (restored)." We will pinpoint the end of this time period shortly, but first we want to look at the events that led to the culmination of the 2300 days.

The restoring of the Sanctuary would require a process of recognizing that all the elements of the Sanctuary system were in heaven in the invisible realm. This process began with the Reformation of the 16th century.

a. The Reformation Starts Recovery of the Invisible View

Around the time of the 16th century some men were beginning to really question the Biblical integrity of the Roman Church. Up until this time very few people had Bibles or could read for themselves and they simply trusted the leaders of the church to guide them on spiritual matters. But around this time, the printing press was invented and books began to multiply quickly. The Bible was being mass produced in a number of languages much to the anger and frustration of the Roman Church. Among those who were studying the Bible carefully was Martin Luther.

A central feature of the Roman Church was the Mass. The Mass was a ceremony where the priest would summon the person of Christ down from heaven into the bread of communion. By eating this bread, the believer would have forgiveness and absolution from their sins. This ceremony took the focus completely away from the true work of Jesus in heaven. It also caused people to visibly see Jesus in the communion wafer. This wafer was actually worshipped by the church as God, a clear violation of the commandment against idolatry.

Martin Luther responded after careful study of the Bible:

> "The Mass in the Papacy must be the greatest and most horrible abomination, as it directly and powerfully conflicts with this chief article, [Jesus died and rose again for our Justification] and yet above and before all other popish idolatries it has been the chief and most specious. For it has been held that this sacrifice or work of the Mass, even though it be rendered by a wicked (and abandoned) scoundrel, frees men from sins, both in this life and also in purgatory, while ***only the Lamb of God shall and must do this***." Martin Luther, *The Smalcald Articles*, page 10.

As Luther continued to write and present, several men began to see the state of captivity the church was in. Martin Luther even penned a book called *The Babylonian Captivity*, in which he pointed out many of the false teachings that were enslaving the minds of the people.

The historian J.A Wylie made a very interesting assessment of what was occurring during this time:

> "Instead of the hierarchy whose reservoir of power was on the Seven Hills, whence it was conveyed downward through a mystic chain that linked all other priests to the Pope, much as the cable conveys the electric spark from continent to continent, they restored the universal priesthood of believers. **Their fountain of power is in heaven**; faith like a chain links them to it; the Holy Spirit is the oil with which they are anointed; and the sacrifices they present are not those of expiation, which has been accomplished once for all by the Eternal Priest, but of hearts purified by faith, and lives which the same divine grace makes fruitful in holiness. This was a great revolution. An ancient and stablished order was abolished; an entirely different one was introduced." *The History of Protestantism*, by Rev J.A. Wylie, Vol 1, page 843.

This statement clearly identifies the issue. The Roman system had turned the people from the fountain of life and had developed its own fountain which does not produce life.

> **Jer 2:13** For my people have committed two evils; they have forsaken me the fountain of living waters, *and* hewed them out cisterns, broken cisterns, that can hold no water.

The reformers turned their minds toward heaven and where the true source of power was coming from. They connected themselves to Jesus the true Priest and prayed directly to Him for power and strength. The Church could have been a channel of blessing to point people to Christ in the heavenly Sanctuary, but instead they stood in the way of the people and blocked their minds from seeing the truth.

The Reformation under Luther, Tyndale and others did begin a work of restoration of the invisible worship of the Sanctuary system. But there were many things that still needed addressing. The church had taken people so deeply into darkness that it would take quite a while to come out. The reformers restored the work of Jesus as a priest to the heavenly realm but they did not discover the need for the Sanctuary system to also be in heaven. Thankfully God would call a people out to point to the Sanctuary being in heaven as a fulfillment of the prophecy concerning the 2300 days.

b. The Scattering, Indignation and Gathering of God's People

The close of the 2300 days mentioned in Daniel 8:14 contains another clue in verse 19 of the same chapter.

> **Dan 8:19** And he said, Behold, I will make thee know what shall be in the last end of the indignation: for at the time appointed the end *shall be*.

It mentions that the 2300 days would also be the end of the indignation. This indignation takes us back to the time of Israel and the promises of the blessings for faithfulness and curses for a failure to cling to the worship elements that would keep Israel connected to the channel of blessing.

The book of Deuteronomy gives us the context for this indignation or anger that takes place in Daniel 8. It is connected to the covenant that God made with Israel to keep His commandments and faithfully worship according to the Sanctuary system given.

> **Deut 29:9-15** Keep therefore the words of this covenant, and do them, that ye may prosper in all that ye do.... **13** That he may establish thee to day for a people unto himself, and *that* he may be unto thee a God, as he hath said unto thee, and as he hath sworn unto thy fathers, to Abraham, to Isaac, and to Jacob. **14** Neither with you only do I make this covenant and this oath; **15** But with *him* that standeth here with us this day before the LORD our God, and also with *him* that *is* not here with us this day:

If Israel would do this, the channel of blessing and protection would stay open, but if they did not, then their children would be raised without a sense of blessing and would be in danger of becoming tyrants or feel a strong temptation to become like other nations rather than be different. This process would cause incredible pain to the families of Israel and this process God referred to as His anger or indignation. It is the people who cause this to take place, but God takes responsibility for the events, because He does not step in to prevent what happens.

> **Deut 29:16-28** (For ye know how we have dwelt in the land of Egypt; and how we came through the nations which ye passed by; **17** And ye have seen their abominations, and their idols, wood and stone, silver and gold, which *were* among them:) **18** Lest there should be among you man, or woman, or family, or tribe, whose heart turneth away this day from the LORD our God, to go *and* serve the gods of these nations; lest there should be among you a root that beareth gall and wormwood; **19** And it come to pass, when he heareth the words of this curse, that he bless himself in his heart, saying, I shall have peace, though I walk in the imagination of mine heart, to add drunkenness to thirst: **20** The LORD will not spare him, but then the anger of the LORD and his jealousy shall smoke against that man, and all the curses that are written in this book shall lie upon him, and the LORD shall blot out his name from under heaven. **21** And the LORD shall separate him unto evil out of all the tribes of Israel, according to all the curses of the covenant that are written in this book of the law: **22** So that the generation to come of your children that shall rise up after you, and the stranger that shall come from a far land, shall say, when they see the plagues of that land, and the sicknesses which the LORD hath laid upon it; **23** *And that* the whole land thereof *is* brimstone, and salt, *and* burning, *that* it is not sown, nor beareth, nor any grass groweth therein, like the overthrow of Sodom, and Gomorrah, Admah, and Zeboim, which the LORD overthrew in his anger, and in his wrath: **24** Even all nations shall say, Wherefore hath the LORD

The Gathering of Israel the Second Time

> done thus unto this land? what *meaneth* the heat of this great anger? **25** Then men shall say, Because they have forsaken the covenant of the LORD God of their fathers, which he made with them when he brought them forth out of the land of Egypt: **26** For they went and served other gods, and worshipped them, gods whom they knew not, and *whom* he had not given unto them: **27** And the anger of the LORD was kindled against this land, to bring upon it all the curses that are written in this book: **28 And the LORD rooted them out of their land in anger, and in wrath, and in great indignation, and cast them into another land, as** *it is* **this day.**

As we have studied, Israel did forsake the covenant and they worshipped other gods and exposed their children to the worthlessness that comes from the curse of being outside the channel of blessing. As part of this indignation, Israel would be allowed to be scattered. The scattering of Israel would take away the leadership of Israel that was meant to act as a channel of blessing. The scattering of Israel would take this blessing channel away and the sheep would then be without an appointed shepherd. The fatherless and the widows would not have a fatherly figure to bless them and so the curse would be extended. This scattering is mentioned in a number of places:

> **Lev 26:27-33** And if ye will not for all this hearken unto me, but walk contrary unto me; **28** Then I will walk contrary unto you also in fury; and I, even I, will chastise you seven times for your sins. **29** And ye shall eat the flesh of your sons, and the flesh of your daughters shall ye eat. **30** And I will destroy your high places, and cut down your images, and cast your carcases upon the carcases of your idols, and my soul shall abhor you. **31** And I will make your cities waste, and bring your sanctuaries unto desolation, and I will not smell the savour of your sweet odours. **32** And I will bring the land into desolation: and your enemies which dwell therein shall be astonished at it. **33** And I will scatter you among the heathen, and will draw out a sword after you: and your land shall be desolate, and your cities waste.

This scattering certainly took place under the Assyrians and Babylonians.

> **Isa 10:5-6** O Assyrian, the rod of mine anger, and the staff in their hand is mine indignation. **6** I will send him against an hypocritical nation, and against the people of my wrath will I give him a charge, to take the spoil, and to take the prey, and to tread them down like the mire of the streets.

> **Jer 9:13-16** And the LORD saith, Because they have forsaken my law which I set before them, and have not obeyed my voice, neither

walked therein; **14** But have walked after the imagination of their own heart, and after Baalim, which their fathers taught them: **15** Therefore thus saith the LORD of hosts, the God of Israel; Behold, I will feed them, *even* this people, with wormwood, and give them water of gall to drink. **16 I will scatter them also among the heathen**, whom neither they nor their fathers have known: and I will send a sword after them, till I have consumed them.

Even though Israel forsook God and turned to other gods, the Lord promised through His prophets that He would gather Israel again the second time.

Isa 11:11 And it shall come to pass in that day, *that* the Lord shall set his hand again the second time to recover the remnant of his people, which shall be left, from Assyria, and from Egypt, and from Pathros, and from Cush, and from Elam, and from Shinar, and from Hamath, and from the islands of the sea.

When would this gathering take place? You might have noticed that God said that He would punish Israel seven times for their sins. In reference to prophetic time, this seven times amounts to 2520 years.

Israel was divided into two kingdoms after Solomon. The northern kingdom was taken into captivity by Assyria in the year 723 B.C. and the king of the southern kingdom – Manasseh, was taken into Babylon in 677 B.C.

2 Chron 33:11 Wherefore the LORD brought upon them the captains of the host of the king of Assyria, which took Manasseh among the thorns, and bound him with fetters, and carried him to Babylon.

If we add 2520 years to the dates 723 and 677 we have the dates 1798 and 1844. The year 1798 we have discovered is significant because the Pope was taken captive in this year and a great revival in the study of Daniel took place as a result, seeking to understand this highly significant event.

This indignation would stretch beyond the time of literal Israel right through to the time period of spiritual Israel. The sequence of this indignation is outlined in Daniel 10 to 12.

Daniel 11 speaks of the various powers through the ages that would dominate God's people and prevent them in various ways from worshipping God faithfully. Daniel 11:36 speaks directly of the Roman Church and its connection to the indignation.

Dan 11:36 And the king shall do according to his will; and he shall exalt himself, and magnify himself above every god, and shall speak marvellous things against the God of gods, and shall prosper till the indignation be accomplished: for that that is determined shall be done.

Students of Daniel 11 understand that the time sequence flows from about 539 B.C. under Medo-Persia right through to the end of the world. This shift from literal Israel to spiritual Israel is important. The New Testament writers clearly presented the spiritual concept of Israel:

Rom 2:28-29 For he is not a Jew, which is one outwardly; neither *is that* circumcision, which is outward in the flesh: **29** But he *is* a Jew, which is one inwardly; and circumcision *is that* of the heart, in the spirit, *and* not in the letter; whose praise *is* not of men, but of God.

Gal 3:26-29 For ye are all the children of God by faith in Christ Jesus. **27** For as many of you as have been baptized into Christ have put on Christ. **28** There is neither Jew nor Greek, there is neither bond nor free, there is neither male nor female: for ye are all one in Christ Jesus. **29** And if ye *be* Christ's, then are ye Abraham's seed, and heirs according to the promise.

After Christ came and taught the people, citizenship in God's kingdom was not based on birth, but on the spiritual teachings of Christ, those who keep the commandments of God and the faith of Jesus.

Just as literal Israel was scattered by literal Babylon; so spiritual Israel was scattered by spiritual Babylon. This whole time process would take 2520 years and would end in 1844.

At this time God would gather Israel the second time, just like He did the first time. The first time He gathered Israel out of Egypt, He gave them His commandments, and He gave them a Sanctuary and guided them by the prophet Moses into many other important truths concerning health, education and civil life. To gather Israel the second time, means He would do all this again. And this is what happened around the time of 1844.

c. The Rise of the Advent Movement

One of the men that was studying his Bible very carefully after 1798 was William Miller. Miller had been a Deist, one who believed that God was an absentee landlord. One who created the world and then left man to his own devices. But after fighting in the American Militia at the battle of Plattsburgh and seeing a greatly outnumbered force of Americans defeat the well-ordered British, he began to wonder about whether God did involve Himself in human affairs, for it seemed impossible to him that the Americans should have won that battle.

As William Miller studied, he laid down some very important rules for interpretation. As he was not affiliated with any of the existing churches of his day, he was not directly influenced by their teachings. William Miller saw the importance of a consistent method of interpreting Scripture. He along with his Deist friends originally believed the Bible to be full of errors and inconsistencies. After his experience at Plattsburgh, he felt he needed to see if he could harmonise all these inconsistencies. To do this, he needed a consistent method of Bible study. If he could use a method that was consistent and then unravel all the apparent inconsistencies of the Bible, he would have found the answers he was looking for. A full list of William Millers rules of interpretation is included in the Appendices, but we will mention a few here.

> RULE I.
> Every word must have its proper bearing on the subject presented in the Bible.
>
> RULE II.
> All Scripture is necessary, and may be understood by a diligent application and study.
>
> RULE IV.
> To understand doctrine, bring all the Scriptures together on the subject you wish to know; then let every word have its proper influence, and if you can form your theory without a contradiction, you cannot be in an error.
>
> RULE V.
> Scripture must be its own expositor, since it is a rule of itself. If I depend on a teacher to expound it to me, and he should guess at its meaning, or desire to have it so on account of his sectarian creed, or to be thought wise, then his guessing, desire, creed or wisdom is my rule, not the Bible.
>
> RULE VI.
> God has revealed things to come, by visions, in figures and parables, and in this way the same things are oftentime revealed again and again, by different visions, or in different figures, and parables. If you wish to understand them, you must combine them all in one.

The Gathering of Israel the Second Time

By a careful and a consistent method, William Miller began studying Daniel 8 and began pondering the meaning of the 2300 days.

He noticed that a starting date for the 2300 days had not been given and that at the end of Daniel 8, Daniel still had not understood the vision concerning this time period. Through a series of connections between Daniel 8 and 9, he saw that the starting time for the seventy weeks of Daniel 9 was also the starting period for the 2300 days.

Like the seventy week prophecy, consistent application demanded that the 2300 prophetic days also be seen as 2300 years. The starting date for the seventy weeks was 457 B.C. When William Miller first made the calculation, he included a 0 year in the transition from B.C. to A.D. This led him to the year 1843.

William Miller had also faithfully studied out the prophecies concerning the indignation and had determined that the "seven times" of Leviticus 26 also concluded in this year of 1843. The added prophecies of the 1290 and 1335 years found in Daniel 12 also connected this date. A detailed analysis of these prophecies is beyond the scope of this book, but William Miller determined that the 1290 years finished in 1798 and that the 1335 years starting from the same time, finished in 1843.

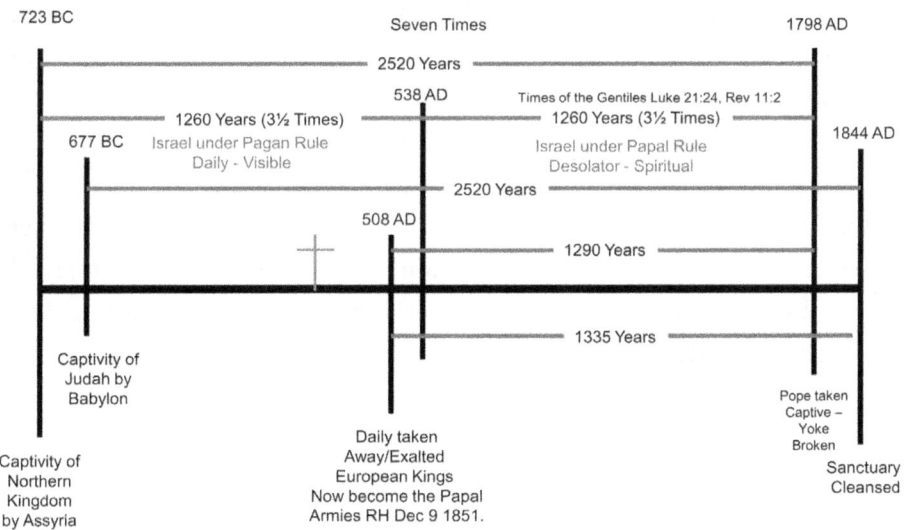

William Miller was amazed that he had several lines of prophecy all finishing in 1843, using a consistent method of Bible study.

Immediately after making this discovery, he felt compelled to share his findings with the world, but like Moses he was fearful and did not want to do it. He thought he might be wrong and wanted to make sure. This discovery was made in 1818 after 2 years of solid Bible study, but William Miller spent another 12 years trying to see if his reasoning was flawed in some way. He looked for every possible reason to disprove what he had found, but he could not find anything significant.

Finally in 1831 after wresting with the Lord, he started to preach. He began small at first, but after a few years, he began preaching in major cities and towns.

William Miller preached that the cleansing of the Sanctuary in 1843 must be the coming of Christ to gather His people. It is true that God would gather His people, but there had to be a restoration of truth concerning the law and the Sanctuary before this would occur.

After the passing of 1843, Miller and the many thousands that now believed realized that the "0" year had been incorrectly added and the actual date was 1844 not 1843.

This message was carried to every mission station in the world and other scholars besides William Miller had also discovered the end of this time period; everywhere people were called to account. The message went forward that the hour of God's judgment had come and that they needed to get ready.

Sadly the Millerites were disappointed because Jesus did not return in 1844. They were right about the date but wrong about the event. Just as literal Israel needed to come out of Egypt, learn the truth about the Sanctuary, the Law and the Sabbath and then go into the Promised Land, so spiritual Israel had to do the same.

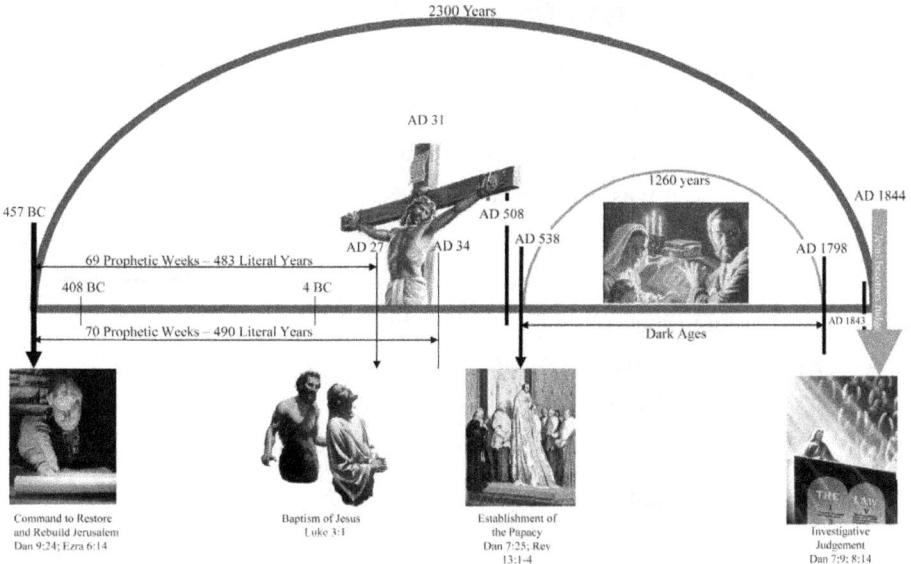

i. Restoration of the Heavenly Sanctuary

After the great disappointment of the Millerites, many of those who professed to believe in the movement fell away. But a small group of Bible students after much prayer and searching of heart began to realize that the event at the end of the 2300 days was a work that Jesus had to do in heaven in a heavenly Sanctuary. A man by the name of Hiram Edson, connected the work described in Daniel 7 concerning the judgment of the horn power with events described in Hebrews 8 concerning the heavenly Sanctuary. He also saw the connection to Revelation 14 and the hour of judgment that was described there.

> **Heb 8:1-2** Now of the things which we have spoken *this is* the sum: We have such an high priest, who is set on the right hand of the throne of the Majesty in the heavens; 2 A minister of the sanctuary, and of the true tabernacle, which the Lord pitched, and not man.

In the year 1844, the heavenly Sanctuary was restored in the minds of a group of Christian believers. The recovery of this Sanctuary truth ended the scattering of Israel and the gathering could now begin. There could be no gathering of Israel without the Sanctuary in its proper place. Now that this small group of Christians was now looking to the heavenly Sanctuary, they could now begin to once again receive the channel of blessing.

ii. Restoration of the Law of God

The object of the Sanctuary was to write God's law on our hearts, so the channel of blessing from God could be protected. This group of people, now called Adventists, began to see the importance of the law of God more than ever before, not because it was written on stone thousands of years ago, but because the law was now residing in heaven in the Sanctuary. It was no longer an event that occurred in the past, but something that was very current. The experience of God's people seeing the law of God is described by John when he says:

> **Rev 11:19** And the temple of God was opened in heaven, and there was seen in his temple the ark of his testament.

A recognition of the law of God led them to another important discovery – the Sabbath.

iii. Restoration of the Sabbath

Now that the Adventists were looking towards the heavenly Sanctuary and the work that Jesus was doing in heaven; their minds were directed to the passage in Daniel 7:

> **Dan 7:9-10** I beheld till the thrones were cast down, and the Ancient of days did sit, whose garment *was* white as snow, and the hair of his head like the pure wool: his throne *was like* the fiery flame, *and* his wheels *as* burning fire. 10 A fiery stream issued and came forth from before him: thousand thousands ministered unto him, and ten thousand times ten thousand stood before him: the judgment was set, and the books were opened.

For Israel, this work of judgment occurred once a year in the Most Holy Place. The parallel passage in Daniel 8 gave more clues to what this event was about.

> **Dan 8:14** And he said unto me, Unto two thousand and three hundred days; then shall the sanctuary be cleansed.

The judgment in Israel was the cleansing of the Sanctuary. It was one and the same event. This judgment was based around the law residing in the ark in the Most Holy Place. This concept of judgment was further developed by a recognition of the warning angels of Revelation 14 who come just before the second coming to warn of the judgment.

> **Rev 14:6-7** And I saw another angel fly in the midst of heaven, having the everlasting gospel to preach unto them that dwell on the earth, and to every nation, and kindred, and tongue, and people, 7 Saying with a loud voice, Fear God, and give glory to him; for the hour of his judgment is come: and worship him that made heaven, and earth, and the sea, and the fountains of waters.

The description of judgment in Revelation 14 is directly connected to a worship of the one who made the heavens and the earth. The only place where this concept is revealed in the context of the law and the judgment is the 4th commandment concerning the Sabbath.

The restoration of the Sabbath opened once again the minds of the people to the source of the channel of blessing. The channel of blessing could not flow properly without a clear understanding of where life comes from and how it is maintained. It is the Sabbath commandment that teaches us these things.

iv. Restoration of the State of the Dead and Second Coming

The belief in the Sabbath caused the Adventists to see God as the only source of life. This caused them to question the belief in the immortality of the soul. The other reason they had to look at this teaching is that they now believed in a time when a judgment would take place in heaven. The commencement time as we noticed took place in 1844. It was during the judgment that it was determined who would receive eternal life and who would not.

Most Christians believed that when believers died they went straight to heaven, but this would be impossible if the judgment began in 1844. They then noticed what Jesus said at the end of Revelation:

> **Rev 22:12** And, behold, I come quickly; and my reward *is* with me, to give every man according as his work shall be.

The reward of eternal life would not be granted until the Second Coming of Christ at the end of the world. Therefore people could not receive their reward until Christ came in the clouds of glory. Notice what the Bible says:

> **1 Thess 4:15-17** For this we say unto you by the word of the Lord, that we which are alive *and* remain unto the coming of the Lord shall not prevent them which are asleep. 16 For the Lord himself shall descend from heaven with a shout, with the voice of the archangel,

and with the trump of God: and the dead in Christ shall rise first: **17** Then we which are alive *and* remain shall be caught up together with them in the clouds, to meet the Lord in the air: and so shall we ever be with the Lord.

The Bible clearly says that when Christ returns, the dead are raised first and then those who are alive are caught up together with them. The Lord must descend first to receive His faithful people before they rise to heaven.

> **Job 14:10-13** But man dieth, and wasteth away: yea, man giveth up the ghost, and where *is* he? **11** *As* the waters fail from the sea, and the flood decayeth and drieth up: **12** So man lieth down, and riseth not: till the heavens *be* no more, they shall not awake, nor be raised out of their sleep. **13** O that thou wouldest hide me in the grave, that thou wouldest keep me secret, until thy wrath be past, that thou wouldest appoint me a set time, and remember me!

As Job states, that man will not rise again until the heavens be no more and that event occurs at the second coming.

> **2 Pet 3:10-12** But the day of the Lord will come as a thief in the night; in the which the heavens shall pass away with a great noise, and the elements shall melt with fervent heat, the earth also and the works that are therein shall be burned up. **11** *Seeing* then *that* all these things shall be dissolved, what manner *of persons* ought ye to be in *all* holy conversation and godliness, **12** Looking for and hasting unto the coming of the day of God, wherein the heavens being on fire shall be dissolved, and the elements shall melt with fervent heat?

The state of the dead was a vital truth to break the lie of the serpent which stated that you would not surely die. It also reinforced the truth that life only comes from God and that we can only receive it in a close relationship with Him.

v. Restoration of the Father and Son Relationship

The other vital truth that became apparent to the Adventists was that the passages in Daniel 7 spoke of two Beings in the heavenly Sanctuary that operated in the judgment.

> **Dan 7:9, 13,14** I beheld till the thrones were cast down, and the **Ancient of days** did sit, whose garment *was* white as snow, and the hair of his head like the pure wool: his throne *was like* the fiery flame, *and* his wheels *as* burning fire....**13** I saw in the night visions, and,

behold, *one* like **the Son of man** came with the clouds of heaven, and came to the Ancient of days, and they brought him near before him. **14** And there was given him dominion, and glory, and a kingdom, that all people, nations, and languages, should serve him: his dominion *is* an everlasting dominion, which shall not pass away, and his kingdom *that* which shall not be destroyed.

This dominion that was given to Christ is a parallel of the rock that smashed the image in Daniel 2. The judgment of Daniel 7 describes the recovery of the church of Christ and the ushering in of a family relational kingdom that would never pass away. The era of the worthless ruling tyrant would end! Praise God.

But as we mentioned, the Bible describes the **Ancient of Days** and the **Son of Man** as working in a literal Sanctuary in heaven. This fact caused the Adventists to really think about the relationship between the Father and the Son. Notice what James White, one of the founders of the Adventist movement, said about this:

> Says the prophet Daniel, "I beheld till the thrones were cast down, and the Ancient of days did sit, whose garment was white as snow, and the hairs of his head like the pure wool; his throne was like the fiery flame, and his wheels as burning fire." Chap.vii,9. "I saw in the night visions, and, behold, one like the Son of man came with the clouds of heaven, and came to the Ancient of days, and they brought him near before him, and there was given him dominion and glory and a kingdom." Verses 13, 14.
>
> *Here is a sublime description of the action of two personages; viz, God the Father, and his Son Jesus Christ. Deny their personality, and there is not a distinct idea in these quotations from Daniel.* In connection with this quotation read the apostle's declaration that the Son was in the express image of his Father's person. "God, who at sundry times, and in divers manners, spake in time past unto the fathers by the prophets, hath in these last days spoken unto us by his Son, whom he hath appointed heir of all things, by whom also he made the worlds; who being the brightness of his glory, and the express image of his person." Heb.i,1-3.[48]
>
> The Most Holy, containing the Ark of the Ten Commandments, was then opened for our Great High Priest to enter to make atonement for the cleansing of the Sanctuary. If we take the liberty to say there is not a literal Ark, containing the Ten Commandments in heaven, we may go only a step further and deny the literal City, and the literal Son

---

48 J. S. White, *The Personality of God*, Page 3 and 4

of God. Certainly, Adventists should not choose the spiritual view, rather than the one we have presented. We see no middle ground to be taken."[49]

To correctly understand the statements in Daniel 7, the Father and Son had to be understood as two separate persons otherwise it would not make sense. Their view of God was interpreted through their understanding of the heavenly Sanctuary system.

The Church of Rome who had blocked the channel of blessing by confusing the minds of people regarding the law, the Sanctuary and the state of the dead developed a very strange view of God which they called the Trinity. Three persons in one substance, a strange mystical union that defies reason and must just be accepted as beyond understanding – and that is exactly what it is.

This view of God that Rome called the Trinity made it impossible to believe in the work of the Sanctuary in heaven. To reclaim the heavenly view of the Sanctuary system, God's people would need a correct understanding of the personages in Daniel 7 otherwise they would never see it and the gathering could not begin. There are many who conclude that the view of these early Adventists was wrong and needed developing. There is always room for development, but the key point is that to understand the Sanctuary teaching correctly, the Father and Son relationship had to be understood correctly and any development that occurred had to be in line with a correct view of the Father and Son relationship.

The other reason that their relationship needed to be understood was that it retrieved a correct view of headship and submission principles. Adam and Eve were made in the image of the Father and the Son. The image involved the headship and submission principles. The channel of blessing could not flow correctly with an incorrect view of the divine submissive agent. The divine submissive agent as we noted is Christ and thankfully, the awareness of the work in the heavenly Sanctuary restored all of these vital points.

d. A Solid Platform

The pieces of the puzzle were starting to come together. The Sanctuary, the law, the judgment, the state of the dead and the second coming all connected

---
49   J. S. White, *The Parable*, Page 16

together to build a platform upon which spiritual Israel could be gathered. The final warning message to bring people onto this platform is found in Rev 14:6-12. It is commonly called the Three Angel's Messages and each message is like a step that leads you onto the solid platform.

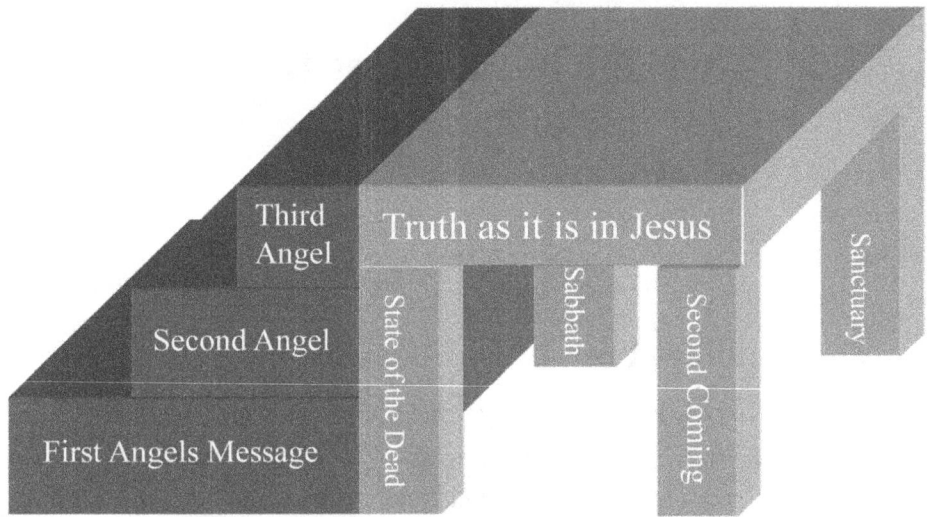

Through the Advent Movement, God had laid a platform to gather His people and re-establish His family kingdom principles. The way was now prepared for the protective principles of the law to be fully written in the heart so that we might be enabled to give glory to Him that made the heavens and the earth.

Chapter 23

The Marriage in the Most Holy Place – The Judgment

a. The Marriage Fully Opens the Channel

As we have noted, the Sanctuary system was developed by God to write His protective Ten Commandment Law in our hearts so that we will always stay connected to Him and stay in the channel of blessing.

This journey begins in the court and culminates in the Most Holy Place. This is the place where the law of God is sealed into the minds of His people and then the channel of blessing is permanently connected. To seal the law in our minds, there had to be a shift from visible to invisible as we have noted.

VISIBLE	INVISIBLE
The Altar of Sacrifice	The Ark of the Covenant
☐	☐
1	2

The time prophecies of Daniel 8 and 9 set up the key points of this journey. The centre of the visible square is reached through the seventy weeks of Daniel 9. The centre of the invisible square is reached through the prophecy of the 2300 days.

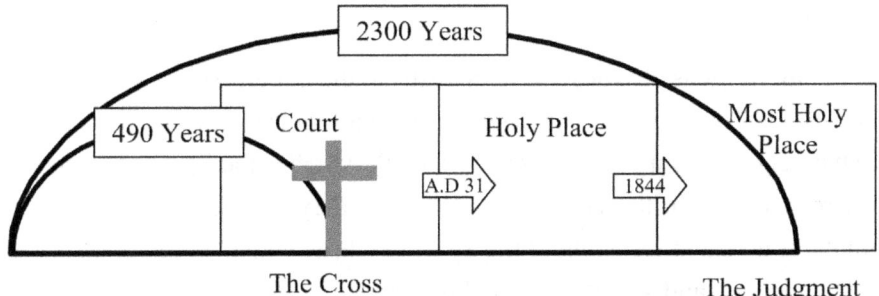

The arrival to the Most Holy Place, as we noted, is the sealing of the law into the minds of God's people. Since this law is a reflection of Christ, this sealing process is likened to a marriage, where two become one. The minds of Christ and the minds of His people become one.

As we have stated several times, this does not happen because God's people are good enough, but this state of oneness means that the channel of blessing is now fully open and the mind of Christ flows fully to His people. As Jesus stated:

> **John 17:21-22** That they all may be one; as thou, Father, *art* in me, and I in thee, that they also may be one in us: that the world may believe that thou hast sent me. **22** And the glory which thou gavest me I have given them; that they may be one, even as we are one:

This oneness comes directly from perfect submission to the life that flows from the Father. As the church submits fully to Christ, the channel flows perfectly and Christ is revealed in His bride:

> **Eph 5:23-24** For the husband is the head of the wife, even as Christ is the head of the church: and he is the saviour of the body. **24** Therefore as the church is subject unto Christ, so *let* the wives *be* to their own husbands in every thing.

The marriage of Christ to the church is also expressed as a marriage between Christ and the city of Jerusalem. This city represents the people of God who fully submitted to the family kingdom principles and channel of blessing.

> **Rev 21:2-3** And I John saw the holy city, new Jerusalem, coming down from God out of heaven, prepared as a bride adorned for her

husband. **3** And I heard a great voice out of heaven saying, Behold, the tabernacle of God *is* with men, and he will dwell with them, and they shall be his people, and God himself shall be with them, *and be* their God.

The marriage is also described by Jesus in the parable of the ten virgins, in Matthew 25. Those who go into the marriage are those who stay connected to the channel of blessing symbolized by the oil, which is the Spirit of Christ. For some reason, half of the virgins ran out of oil, they had become disconnected from the source and lost sight of the Spirit of Christ which would prepare them for the marriage and seal the law in their hearts.

The wonderful marriage of Christ and His bride fully reconnects the channel of blessing and the Spirit of Christ flows fully into His submissive bride and produces the fruit of that Spirit.

> **Col 1:27** To whom God would make known what *is* the riches of the glory of this mystery among the Gentiles; which is Christ in you, the hope of glory:

> **Isa 8:16** Bind up the testimony, seal the law among my disciples.

b. Many Reject the Wedding Invitation

Everyone is called to this wedding but sadly many will not come, either because they love the principles of Satan's inherent power kingdom or they feel unworthy because of a focus on their own inability to perform; which is really the same thing – a focus on inherent power. Jesus speaks of those who reject the wedding in the following manner:

> **Matt 22:2-10** The kingdom of heaven is like unto a certain king, which made a marriage for his son, **3** And sent forth his servants to call them that were bidden to the wedding: and they would not come. **4** Again, he sent forth other servants, saying, Tell them which are bidden, Behold, I have prepared my dinner: my oxen and *my* fatlings *are* killed, and all things *are* ready: come unto the marriage. **5** But they made light of *it*, and went their ways, one to his farm, another to his merchandise: **6** And the remnant took his servants, and entreated *them* spitefully, and slew *them*. **7** But when the king heard *thereof*, he was wroth: and he sent forth his armies, and destroyed those murderers, and burned up their city. **8** Then saith he to his servants, The wedding is ready, but they which were bidden were not worthy. **9** Go ye therefore into the highways, and as many as ye shall find, bid to

The Marriage in the Most Holy Place – The Judgment

the marriage. **10** So those servants went out into the highways, and gathered together all as many as they found, both bad and good: and the wedding was furnished with guests.

How sad it is that many will choose darkness rather than light, they would rather cling to the love of inherent power than submit to the divine submissive agent and be filled with the peaceful and loving Spirit of God.

c. An Investigation of Worthiness

The work of Jesus in the Most Holy Place is to examine those who truly believe in Him and have lost all confidence in the serpent's lie of inherent power. They have been sobered by the truths of the law, the Sanctuary, the Sabbath and the state of the dead, and they have chosen to believe that Christ has made them worthy; because by faith they believe that the victories of Jesus on earth are freely given to them and they believe they are greatly loved as children of God.

The great test of the judgment is the same test that Jesus went through in the wilderness of temptation. Do we believe that we are children of God simply because God has said in His Word and believe that He has made all the provision necessary; or will we doubt him and focus on our failures, mistakes, weakness and lack of performing good works? The simple belief that we are children of God and that God can restore us to His image is what makes us worthy, it has nothing to do with anything we can achieve or perform ourselves, because we have no inherent power to do one single good deed.

The belief that we are children of God by faith is symbolized by the wearing of a special garment given by God at the wedding.

> **Matt 22:11-14** And when the king came in to see the guests, he saw there a man which had not on a wedding garment: **12** And he saith unto him, Friend, how camest thou in hither not having a wedding garment? And he was speechless. **13** Then said the king to the servants, Bind him hand and foot, and take him away, and cast *him* into outer darkness; there shall be weeping and gnashing of teeth. **14** For many are called, but few *are* chosen.

The Bible clearly states that the king examines the guests to see that they had on the wedding garment. This examination is the judgment described in Daniel 7, where the books are opened and everyone is examined to see that they have the wedding garment on.

Without a clear sense of being a child of God and the value and worth that comes from this, an examination would be a most fearful thing. Those who cling to a concept of some form of inherent power would never wish to enter such a judgment. They refuse to give up the lie of the serpent and so instead choose to believe that no such judgment occurs. They choose rather to believe that Jesus has done everything for them and they are free to hide under that name with all their filthy sins.

> **Isa 4:1-5** And in that day seven women shall take hold of one man, saying, We will eat our own bread, and wear our own apparel: only let us be called by thy name, to take away our reproach. **2** In that day shall the branch of the LORD be beautiful and glorious, and the fruit of the earth *shall be* excellent and comely for them that are escaped of Israel. **3** And it shall come to pass, *that he that is* left in Zion, and *he that* remaineth in Jerusalem, shall be called holy, *even* every one that is written among the living in Jerusalem: **4** When the Lord shall have washed away the filth of the daughters of Zion, and shall have purged the blood of Jerusalem from the midst thereof by the spirit of judgment, and by the spirit of burning. **5** And the LORD will create upon every dwelling place of mount Zion, and upon her assemblies, a cloud and smoke by day, and the shining of a flaming fire by night: for upon all the glory *shall be* a defence.

Isaiah tells us that the whole church (seven women) try to take hold of the man (Jesus) and tell Him, we will live by our own means, we just want your name to help us to stop feeling guilty about our sins. These poor people are those who call themselves Jews but are not.

> **Rev 3:9** Behold, I will make them of the synagogue of Satan, which say they are Jews, and are not, but do lie; behold, I will make them to come and worship before thy feet, and to know that I have loved thee.

This passage above is speaking of the church of Philadelphia who prophetically live at the time the judgment is about to begin.

The passage in Isaiah 4 goes onto say that God will wash away the filth and burn away our sins, so that we can truly be connected to Him.

We need to be investigated to see if any remnants of the lie of the serpent still exist in us. These principles are so deep inside the human heart that without the call for a judgment, we would never know that they are there. Like the foolish virgins, we could come to the door fully expecting entrance and be

The Marriage in the Most Holy Place – The Judgment

shockingly told that Jesus never knew us.

Thank God for the judgment that prepares us for the marriage. Let us sing with David:

> **Psa 26:1-6** Judge me, O LORD; for I have walked in mine integrity: I have trusted also in the LORD; *therefore* I shall not slide. **2** Examine me, O LORD, and prove me; try my reins and my heart. **3** For thy lovingkindness *is* before mine eyes: and I have walked in thy truth. **4** I have not sat with vain persons, neither will I go in with dissemblers. **5** I have hated the congregation of evil doers; and will not sit with the wicked. **6** I will wash mine hands in innocency: so will I compass thine altar, O LORD:

Like David, we need not fear the judgment, as children of God, we can be truly confident. But the only way to be secure as children of God is to believe the message of God which says, you are my beloved child in whom I am well pleased. We have to turn our hearts to the Father and trust Him or we will be too fearful to enter the Most Holy Place and face the judgment.

Chapter 24

The Last Day War on the Family – the Remnant of God's Family Kingdom

a. Family Unit versus the New World Order

The judgment culminates in a celebration of marriage when the channel of blessing is open. Under the influence of the blessing, God's children do not fear the judgment, but welcome it.

We would expect that Satan would not sit idly by while this marriage is taking place, he wants to do everything he can to disrupt the marriage process and prevent as many people as possible from becoming part of the bride.

> **Rev 12:17** And the dragon was wroth with the woman, and went to make war with the remnant of her seed, which keep the commandments of God, and have the testimony of Jesus Christ.

Satan is a keen student of Bible prophecy and he knew when the judgment would commence. He knew that if he could cut the channel of blessing by disrupting the family unit and confusing the roles of husband and wife, he could draw people into a performance based value system more easily and consequently cause people to be unprepared for the judgment marriage, by either a fear of judgment or a dismissal of the whole concept as unchristian.

As in the days of Nimrod, those who today are entrenched in the inherent life source model recognize that to control society, any authority structure or allegiance that stands in the way of, or competes with the government, has to be seen as a threat and must be eliminated. It is well known for those who research that there are small groups of wealthy people who wish to create a

New World Order. They want to shift from the divided nation states into a global system with one government, one economy and one worship system.

The Bible speaks of this coming system in the last days as follows:

> **Rev 13:15-17** And he had power to give life unto the image of the beast, that the image of the beast should both speak, and cause that as many as would not worship the image of the beast should be killed. **16** And he causeth all, both small and great, rich and poor, free and bond, to receive a mark in their right hand, or in their foreheads: **17** And that no man might buy or sell, save he that had the mark, or the name of the beast, or the number of his name.

We are not going to focus on the issue of the mark of this beast power, but rather on the fact that it obtains power to kill or keep alive; it forces a worship system for all and it can prevent people from buying or selling, so in essence it controls the power of life and death, money and religion across the entire globe.

The setting up of such a system would be impossible if people maintain strong family ties and allegiances. It would also be impossible to force such a system on people "for their own protection against terrorism" if they have a strong concept of self-worth through the family channel system.

So what is the point we are making? While God is preparing the wedding for His Son to the church, Satan is hard at work building a world order that does not allow the family channel system to operate.

Notice the following outline from Henry Makow on this subject about the plan of the New World Order:

> The "Plan" calls for the destruction of all "collective" forces capable of resistance. These forces, which support our human identity, are family, race, religion and nation-state. They are to be eliminated through a campaign of "tolerance" which erases the differences between them. If you accept everything, eventually you become nothing.
>
> Thus we have ecumenicalism in religion, miscegenation in race, and regionalism in nation states. You destroy family by erasing gender differences. Their goal is one world government, one race, one religion, and ultimately one sex, the hetro-homo.
>
> Families give people their purpose, identity and sense of belonging. They provide values and a measure of social, spiritual and financial independence. The goal of Communism and the New World Order always has been the destruction of family. This forces people to get their sense

of belonging from the elite-run media, political causes or products.[50]

Makow has correctly discerned that it is the family unit that stands in the way of the Nimrod style one world system. If individuals are getting their values through a family social network, through a channel connected directly to heaven, then you can't easily control such people. Again I quote Makow:

> Marriage is the basic building block of society. If men and women are not faithful, then there is no basis for social stability. There is no foundation for the family. **Break up marriage and you break up society, rendering it vulnerable to political control.**[51]

Looking at society, do we see an increase in the rate of family breakdown? I think that is fairly obvious to most people, but here is a quote anyway from Jim Conway:

> In the 1950's, divorce was relatively uncommon and still not socially acceptable. That changed drastically in the next two decades. By the mid-sixties one out of every three marriages ended in divorce. By 1980 the rate was one out of two.[52]

Conway details several studies of the impact of broken families on children and their ability to live a reasonably happy and successful life. Again quoting from Conway:

> As I read these studies I realized what had happened to me. I understood why I always thought I had to "try harder" so people would like me. The pieces of the puzzle were starting to come together. Finally there were reasons for my feelings. And I was not the only one – millions felt what I felt.[53]

b. The Orchestrated Demolition of the Family

This explosion of family breakdown has not been by chance. It has been well orchestrated. It is not the purpose of this book to document the inception and roots of this orchestration in history; but merely to acknowledge its presence and pick up on vital aspects here and there to demonstrate the coordinated attack

---

50   Henry Makow PHD. *Cruel Hoax – Feminism and the New World Order* (Published by Silas Green, 2007) Page 11.
51   Ibid, 15
52   Jim Conway. *Adult Children of Legal or Emotional Divorce* (Published by Monarch Publications LTD, 1990) Page 23.
53   Ibid, 37

on the family that would hinder the judgment-marriage process that God wants to complete before the return of Jesus, to claim His faithful bride.

i. The Education Revolution

During the expansion of America during the 19th century, a small group of men became extremely wealthy, particularly through steel, railways and oil. One of these men was John D. Rockerfeller. Having limitless resources at his disposal, he set about with a select group to ensure that the power he had acquired would never be challenged. Rockerfeller was quoted as saying – "Competition is sin". Rockerfeller only believed in monopoly. In 1904 Rockerfeller wrote:

> In our dreams, we have limitless resources and the people yield themselves with perfect docility to our molding hands. The present education conventions fade from their minds, and unhampered by tradition, we work our good will upon a grateful and responsive rural folk.[54]

Rockerfeller and his friends[55] wanted to take control of the educational process and they did this through a system of foundations and trusts[56] that would form the backbone of developing a new education process.[57] Notice the following:

> "A New Public mind is to be created. How? Only by creating tens of millions of individual minds and welding them into a new social mind. Old Stereo types must be broken up and 'new climates of opinion' formed in the neighborhoods of America."[58]

> "Through the schools of the world we shall disseminate a new conception of government – one that will embrace all activities of men, one that will postulate the need for scientific control and operation of

---
54 Des Griffin. *Fourth Reich of the Rich* (Published by Emissary Publications, 1976) Page 77
55 Ibid 79. "John Dewey was a leading figure in the overall plans. As head of the teachers' College at Columbia University he grew in influence on the national educational scene. In 1919, with Rockerfeller money, Dewey founded the Progressive Education Association to spread the philosophy of his masters. As time went by Dewey was joined by Ruggs, Counts, Kilpatrick and other Socialists. They wormed their way into positions of authority and set about using the educational system as a tool to accomplish their political goals."
56 Ibid, 78.
57 Makow, 16. "The unprecedented decline of the family was caused by the mass psychological conditioning ordered by the central banking cartel using the CIA, the Rockerfeller Foundation, the mass media, government and education system."
58 Ibid 79.

economic activities in the interest of all people."⁵⁹

> "Many new textbooks made their appearance in classrooms – all specifically designed to undermine traditional values and brainwash the students into an acceptance of Socialism in which "Big Brother" Government would control every phase of peoples' lives."⁶⁰

The seeds of the sixties revolution was laid in the undermining of traditional family authority structures from the 1920's through to the 1950's. This revolution was not an accident, it was planned. The socialist communal philosophy that grew into the "flower power movement" was a direct attack on family values and authority. But education into this new system did not only come through the universities, it also came through new musical forms.

ii. The Music Revolution

Plato stated a long time ago: "Let me write the songs and I care not who makes the laws." There is nothing that can move the heart like music. If the music of a nation can be influenced, then you have a direct ability to move the hearts of a nation. In Satan's war against God's family kingdom, he knew that if he could control music, he could control the hearts of men and women and further prevent them from wishing to attend the wedding in the Most Holy Place of the Sanctuary.

The music needed would seek to undermine existing authority and parental authority particularly. This description is the history of Rock and Roll. Through the development of records, radio and post Second World War freedoms, young people across western societies were exposed to the phenomenon of rock music. A cultural war erupted between generations and the lively appeal of rock music took the new generation of the fifties down a path away from traditional families values that culminated in the "Woodstock" phenomenon.⁶¹

With the aid of the transistor radio, teens could listen to the new music form in their bedrooms and imbibe the principles of counterculture. The essence of the music was anti-authority, anti-family and freedom of the individual to do

---

59   Ibid.
60   Ibid 80.
61   Woodstock was the watershed Rock and Roll Festival that took place in Bethel, New York from August 15 to 18 in 1969 and has become the icon of 1960's counterculture music.

as they pleased.

The music was also extremely feminized[62] through the expressions of long hair, high voice and heightened emotional expression in a male form. This confusion of gender and the unrestrained sexual expressions associated with it, has been a key factor is breaking down and destroying headship and submission principles in a traditional family structure.

This feminization process in music combined with the Rockerfeller educational process formed the basis of another planned revolution: The Feminist Movement.

iii. The Feminist Revolution

This revolution is probably best symbolized by the Helen Ready song "I am Woman" which galvanized millions of women around the world to fight for their rights and be released from the bondage of house work. It must be admitted that the lot of women was made hard by many men in the era preceding the 1970's and some of the social reforms have been beneficial, but the real objectives of the feminist revolution were also planned by the banking elite to break down the family and enslave the population to a global controlling elite.

> The Rockerfeller foundation funded the birth control and pro choice campaigns, the development of the "pill" and other contraceptives, and the promotion of the (homo) sexual revolution. All of these were intended to divorce sex from marriage and procreation and make sex the national pastime.
>
> Recently Aaron Russo, the respected producer of Bette Middler's "The Rose" and the documentary "America: From Freedom to Facism" confirmed this.
>
> He reported that when Nicolas Rockerfeller tried to recruit him for the CFR, he said his family foundation created women's liberation. "He asked me what I thought of the women's movement, and I told him that I supported equal opportunity," Russo said.
>
> "He looked at me and said 'you know, you're such an idiot in some ways. We – meaning the people he works with – created the women's

---

62 Derek B. Scott. *Music, Culture and Society* (Published by Oxford University Press, 2000) Page 69 "The decline of Rock 'n' Roll rested on a process of feminization."

movement, and we promoted it. And it's not about equal opportunity. It's designed to get both parents out of the home and into the workforce, where they will pay taxes. And then we can decide how the children will be raised and educated.' That's how they control society – by removing parents from the home and then raise the children as the elitists see fit."[63]

The statement speaks for itself, the agenda is clear, break down the family, get both parents into the workforce to pay taxes to the banking elite, send the kids to minding centres, and raise them on movies, TV and computer games to program them into an anti-family mindset.

It does not take much looking around to see that this agenda is pretty well complete. It appears that Satan has triumphed over God's family kingdom system in these last days. Thankfully the final chapter has not been written, the seed of the woman will triumph over the seed of the serpent and all the plans of the world's tyrants will ultimately fail.

Just before the Lord returns to bring about the ultimate family reunion, God sends a message that will awaken people to family values and the importance of the channel of blessing system through the role of a father. It is to this message we turn next.

---

63 Makow, 22.

Chapter 25

The Return of Elijah

After our brief look at the plans of the world's elite and how successful they have been, it is easy to see that the world is now largely "enslaved" to these kings of the earth. God's family kingdom principles have been overwhelmed and this has left the people of the world completely vulnerable to the domination and leadership of those who wish power for themselves based on the serpent's lie of inherent power.

Just as Israel was taken captive by the nation of Babylon, the same principles have led the entire world into a relational and spiritual captivity. Spiritual Babylon once again rules the world. The prophet Jeremiah explains how the whole world had become infected with this desire for power, control through a belief in one's own power. He calls it the wine of Babylon.

> **Jer 51:7** Babylon *hath been* a golden cup in the LORD'S hand, that made all the earth drunken: the nations have drunken of her wine; therefore the nations are mad.

Spiritual Babylon is addressed in the book of Revelation using the same symbol:

> **Rev 17:1-2** And there came one of the seven angels which had the seven vials, and talked with me, saying unto me, Come hither; I will shew unto thee the judgment of the great whore that sitteth upon many waters: **2** With whom the kings of the earth have committed fornication, and the inhabitants of the earth have been made drunk with the wine of her fornication.

God does not leave His children alone to their own destruction; as in the past with literal Israel, when God promised deliverance, God today promises deliverance to His people. Notice carefully:

Jer 50:28,33-34 The voice of them that flee and escape out of the land of Babylon, to declare in Zion the vengeance of the LORD our God, the vengeance of his temple…Thus saith the LORD of hosts; The children of Israel and the children of Judah *were* oppressed together: and all that took them captives held them fast; they refused to let them go. **34** Their Redeemer *is* strong; the LORD of hosts *is* his name: he shall throughly plead their cause, that he may give rest to the land, and disquiet the inhabitants of Babylon.

Rev 18:1-6 And after these things I saw another angel come down from heaven, having great power; and the earth was lightened with his glory. **2** And he cried mightily with a strong voice, saying, Babylon the great is fallen, is fallen, and is become the habitation of devils, and the hold of every foul spirit, and a cage of every unclean and hateful bird. **3** For all nations have drunk of the wine of the wrath of her fornication, and the kings of the earth have committed fornication with her, and the merchants of the earth are waxed rich through the abundance of her delicacies. **4** And I heard another voice from heaven, saying, Come out of her, my people, that ye be not partakers of her sins, and that ye receive not of her plagues. **5** For her sins have reached unto heaven, and God hath remembered her iniquities. **6** Reward her even as she rewarded you, and double unto her double according to her works: in the cup which she hath filled fill to her double.

Just as God punished literal Babylon and caused His people to be set free, so in the last days, a message of liberation will come through the mighty angel (messenger) that will lighten the earth with his glory. Under this message the power of Babylon will be broken and she shall fall.

As God sent Moses to prepare Israel to leave the slavery of Egypt, followed by a series of plagues, so in the last days God promises to send Elijah to prepare God's people to escape the clutches of Babylon and then a series of plagues will rain down on Babylon and God's people will be delivered.

a. Turning the Hearts of the Children to the Fathers

This message of Revelation will greatly affect the earth's population. It will be a stirring message that will bring people to a decision. The one man in the Old Testament who performed this work was the prophet Elijah. God tells us that the work of the prophet Elijah would be needed again in the last days to bring the world to a decision. Notice carefully:

The Return of Elijah

Mal 4:5-6 Behold, I will send you Elijah the prophet before the coming of the great and dreadful day of the LORD: 6 And he shall turn the heart of the fathers to the children, and the heart of the children to their fathers, lest I come and smite the earth with a curse.

In the last days God would send a message in the spirit of Elijah that would cause people to reclaim family values. This message would rediscover the true principles of headship and submission and especially the role of the divine submissive agent – the Son of God. This message will bring the world to a decision as to whether they would worship the God of the Bible and His express image – the Divine Son – and be part of His family kingdom; or worship the beast and his image and remain a part of the inherent power system.

If we study closely the work of Elijah the prophet, he did a number of things:

i) Warned that no more rain (channel of blessing) would come for a specific time period. By this, the false gods of fertility – the Baals, were exposed as a fraud. (1 Kings 17:1)

ii) He provided for a woman and her son who had no seed or channel of blessing – provides for fatherless and widows. (1 Kings 17:8-24)

iii) He exposed the fact that God's people had forsaken the commandments – the life source protection system. (1 Kings 18:18)

iv) He brought them to a decision as to which God and worship system they would follow. (1 Kings 18:21)

v) He repaired the altar of the Lord with the correct sacrifice. (1 Kings 18:30)

vi) He released the people from a false worship system by removing the prophets of Baal. (1 Kings 18:40)

vii) He interceded for the rain (channel of blessing) to be restored. (1 Kings 18:42-46)

If we summarize the work of Elijah we see that:

i) He exposed the false worship system.

ii) He protected and provided for families made vulnerable – he restored the channel of blessing to these families by providing

bread and oil which is a symbol of the seed (Christ) and oil (the Spirit).
iii) He called for a return to the commandments of God.
iv) He restored the heart of the Sanctuary system by repairing the altar.
v) He brought the people to a decision as to who they would follow.

A careful look at what Elijah did, we see key components for restoring God's family kingdom: the commandments including the Sabbath, the Sanctuary, as well as the direct practical role of providing for the fatherless and the widow with seed.

This message is described for God's last day people as the Three Angel's Messages. It is a series of messages to prepare them to be set free from enslavement and enter the heavenly Canaan.

b. The Three Angel's Messages

The Three Angel's Messages are God's final call for the world to connect themselves to the channel of blessing system. Let's read through them to see exactly what they say.

> **Rev 14:6-12** And I saw another angel fly in the midst of heaven, having the everlasting gospel to preach unto them that dwell on the earth, and to every nation, and kindred, and tongue, and people, **7** Saying with a loud voice, Fear God, and give glory to him; for the hour of his judgment is come: and worship him that made heaven, and earth, and the sea, and the fountains of waters. **8** And there followed another angel, saying, Babylon is fallen, is fallen, that great city, because she made all nations drink of the wine of the wrath of her fornication. **9** And the third angel followed them, saying with a loud voice, If any man worship the beast and his image, and receive *his* mark in his forehead, or in his hand, **10** The same shall drink of the wine of the wrath of God, which is poured out without mixture into the cup of his indignation; and he shall be tormented with fire and brimstone in the presence of the holy angels, and in the presence of the Lamb: **11** And the smoke of their torment ascendeth up for ever and ever: and they have no rest day nor night, who worship the beast and his image, and whosoever receiveth the mark of his name. **12** Here is the patience of the saints: here *are* they that keep the commandments of God, and the faith of Jesus.

The first message calls for people to worship the Creator (the source of blessing), be willing to enter the marriage chamber with Jesus by faith during the judgment in the Most Holy Place (of the Sanctuary), and call others to the same wonderful opportunity. This is the message of the everlasting gospel that removes the serpent's lie from our hearts and keeps us fully connected to the channel of blessing. The appeal to worship Him who made heaven and earth and the sea and the fountains of waters is a direct reference to the fourth commandment concerning the Sabbath. This call to worship this God is a call to remember that all life comes from God; it is the very heart of the relational kingdom system. This describes exactly the work that Elijah did when he reminded the people concerning God's commandments and when he repaired the altar of the Lord.

The Second Angel's Message is a warning against the system of Babylon first erected by Nimrod and continued through most nations of the earth. It also warns against spiritual Babylon which is the horn power of Daniel 7 and 8. This power as we noted was responsible for blocking the blessing channel system and kept people focused on an inherent power system in line with the serpent's lie. It also warns against trying to please God with our works to show that we are worthy of His approval because of what we do for Him. Notice how it speaks of the wine of Babylon, this is the lie of the serpent concerning inherent power that has made the nations[64] angry. Elijah exposed the false worship system of Israel by causing the rain to stop and reveal that this system had no power at all.

The Third Angel's Message warns against following the New World Order system set up by the kings of the earth, that in the last days will seek to enshrine the inherent life power system and cause everyone to obey, just like Nebuchadnezzar did in the time of Babylon. The beginning of this message begins with the word "if" meaning that a decision is required. If you follow this system, this is what will happen – choose now to follow God.

When we study the story of Elijah, we see that the people clearly saw who the true God was because of the fire that fell from heaven onto the sacrifice. In this final battle of the two systems Satan will try to deceive people by producing miracles that will cause them to think that the false

---

64 Race or Tribe of people.

system is the right one. Notice:

> **Rev 13:13-14** And he doeth great wonders, so that he maketh fire come down from heaven on the earth in the sight of men, **14** And deceiveth them that dwell on the earth by *the means of* those miracles which he had power to do in the sight of the beast; saying to them that dwell on the earth, that they should make an image to the beast, which had the wound by a sword, and did live.

It will be difficult for many to discern the true from the false system of worship; to discern between the worship of the Creator and His Image (His Son) and the beast and his image. But there is no need to be deceived if we follow carefully the Bible principles concerning the family.

So we see that the Three Angel's Messages reflect the very work that Elijah did when seeking to combat the inherent power worship system of his day. These messages:

i) Call to a worship of the Creator through a restoration of the commandments, the Sanctuary worship system and especially the Sabbath.

ii) Call to give God glory, which means to reflect His character. This reflection of character comes through the restoration of the family channel system. "The glory of children is their father."

iii) Are an exposure of the false worship system of Babylon and its inherent power life source system.

iv) Call for a choice – How long halt ye between two opinions?

What about the praying for the restoration of the rain? This comes in the message of the fourth angel which speaks powerfully of Babylon's spiritual fall. This message goes with great power under the direction of the Spirit of God. This outpouring of the Spirit is symbolized by rain.

> **James 5:7** Be patient therefore, brethren, unto the coming of the Lord. Behold, the husbandman waiteth for the precious fruit of the earth, and hath long patience for it, until he receive the early and latter rain.

This message that goes with power speaks of the fall of Babylon. As Babylon was holding people spiritually as slaves to the inherent power system, this message will cause people to joyfully be released from this worthless, desolating belief system, so they will cry "Babylon is fallen and now I am free." This is exactly what happened to Mary Magdelene when she poured the precious perfume on the feet of Jesus. Her joy could not be contained and her joy made the disciples ashamed, especially Judas. Very soon a cry of freedom will ring through the world as people come back to the family system of God and get their value alone from Him.

c. The Revelation of the Father in the Flames of Hell

Before we move on, we need to address a few texts in the final part of the Third Angel's Message. Some people believe these texts teach that God will burn people in hell forever. Is this truly a reflection of a loving Father? What do these verses really mean? Let's look closely at Rev 14:10 and 11 again.

> **Rev 14:10,11** The same shall drink of the wine of the wrath of God, which is poured out without mixture into the cup of his indignation; and he shall be tormented with fire and brimstone in the presence of the holy angels, and in the presence of the Lamb: **11** And the smoke of their torment ascendeth up for ever and ever: and they have no rest day nor night, who worship the beast and his image, and whosoever receiveth the mark of his name.

What is the wine of the wrath of God which is poured out without mixture into the cup of His indignation? This is the consequences and punishment for those who have rejected God and His family kingdom. We can find a clue to this cup by looking at the penalty that Jesus paid for those who choose to follow God. Notice what Jesus says about his experience just before He died:

> **Matt 20:22** But Jesus answered and said, Ye know not what ye ask. Are ye able to drink of the cup that I shall drink of, and to be baptized with the baptism that I am baptized with? They say unto him, We are able.

> **John 18:11** Then said Jesus unto Peter, Put up thy sword into the sheath: the cup which my Father hath given me, shall I not drink it?

> **Luke 22:41-42** And he was withdrawn from them about a stone's cast, and kneeled down, and prayed, **42** Saying, Father, if thou be willing, remove this cup from me: nevertheless not my will, but thine, be done.

The cup that Jesus was speaking about was the experience of separation from the Father on the cross. When Jesus died with the sins of the world upon Him, instead of sensing the joy and love of His Father, He felt His Father's anger towards the sins He was carrying. He felt His Father leaving Him alone. As His Father's presence left Him, He cried out:

> **Matt 27:46** And about the ninth hour Jesus cried with a loud voice, saying, Eli, Eli, lama sabachthani? that is to say, My God, my God, why hast thou forsaken me?

The word "forsake" means to leave behind or desert. In the context of all we have discussed concerning the channel of blessing and God as the source of life and blessing, this must be the most terrifying event possible. Note carefully, the most painful and tormenting event in a relational kingdom is the breaking of a relationship. Jesus did not cry out the "nails and the beating are hurting me" – He cried out "Why are you deserting me?" This is the cup of wrath, the indignation of God, that Jesus had to drink.

The torment of those who reject God is the full realization of Who they are rejecting and how much they have hurt their heavenly Father. God will fully reveal to them how much He has loved them and how precious they were to Him and now He has to say goodbye. Notice how the Bible describes love in the Song of Solomon:

> **Song 8:6** Set me as a seal upon thine heart, as a seal upon thine arm: for love *is* strong as death; jealousy *is* cruel as the grave: the coals thereof *are* coals of fire, *which hath a* most vehement flame.

As the love of God is fully revealed to those who reject Him, it is like coals of fire that burn them. The torment and the agony cause them to weep and gnash their teeth:

> **Matt 8:12** But the children of the kingdom shall be cast out into outer darkness: there shall be weeping and gnashing of teeth.

Another point that is important is that if Jesus paid the full debt for sin and that debt was to suffer a total separation from God, then the debt was paid in full. If the debt is to burn in hell forever then Jesus should still be in hell paying the price.

Another point that people overlook is that life only comes from God and that once you are separated from Him you cease to exist. It is the lie of the serpent that causes people to believe that people can live on forever and ever in the flames of hell. No fair-minded person could punish a person forever for a brief life of sin. This would be unjust; such a belief makes God out to be a cruel tyrant somewhat like Nimrod.

Remember that God's kingdom is a relational kingdom and the punishment will be relational. The punishment is the pain of separation from the most loving Being in the universe and the guilt of rejecting such a person.

It is true that a physical fire will cleanse the earth and cause those who reject God to be turned to ashes, but this is not the focus of punishment, this is the aftermath when the earth is cleansed.

> **Mal 4:1** For, behold, the day cometh, that shall burn as an oven; and all the proud, yea, and all that do wickedly, shall be stubble: and the day that cometh shall burn them up, saith the LORD of hosts, that it shall leave them neither root nor branch.

What about the smoke of their torment ascending forever and ever. This means that the effect of the separation is permanent. As we have noted, it is impossible to live apart from God, so people can't keep living on and suffering. The word forever in the Bible means "as long as it lasts" or "until it is completed." Notice how the word forever is used in Jonah:

> **Jonah 2:5-6** The waters compassed me about, *even* to the soul: the depth closed me round about, the weeds were wrapped about my head. **6** I went down to the bottoms of the mountains; the earth with her bars *was* about me for ever: yet hast thou brought up my life from corruption, O LORD my God.

Speaking of the judgments against various nations during the time of Israel, Isaiah pens some familiar words:

> **Isa 34:8-11** For *it is* the day of the LORD'S vengeance, *and* the year of recompences for the controversy of Zion. **9** And the streams thereof shall be turned into pitch, and the dust thereof into brimstone, and the land thereof shall become burning pitch. **10** It shall not be quenched night nor day; the smoke thereof shall go up for ever: from generation to generation it shall lie waste; none shall pass through it for ever and ever. **11** But the cormorant and the bittern shall possess it; the owl also and the raven shall dwell in it: and he shall stretch out upon it the line of confusion, and the stones of emptiness.

If you travel through these lands today, you will not see a fire burning in the towns and locations that were mentioned. The fire was not stopped and it completed its work of destruction and the effect was permanent. When we read the Bible carefully, we can be thankful that God is not a vengeful tyrant like Nimrod, but a loving Father. Jesus has paid the price of separation for us so that we can live eternally with our heavenly Father and His Son. Choose today which kingdom you will live in. Will you follow the true God, the source of all life; or believe the lie of Satan, believe that life is in yourself and face the torments of final separation and then cease to exist?

Chapter 26

Family Reunion – The Second Coming (The Stone)

From the time Christ ascended to heaven after His crucifixion and resurrection, His followers have anxiously looked forward to His promised Second Coming. The Second Coming of Christ is mentioned more than 300 times in the New Testament. It is the time all of God's followers look forward to because for the first time in human history, the whole human family will be together and we will never be parted again. Paul tells us that Christ will appear a second time to reclaim His children.

> **Heb 9:28** So Christ was once offered to bear the sins of many; and unto them that look for him shall he appear the second time without sin unto salvation.

Jesus spoke about His coming again and the home that He is preparing for us:

> **John 14:1-4** Let not your heart be troubled: ye believe in God, believe also in me. **2** In my Father's house are many mansions: if *it were* not *so*, I would have told you. I go to prepare a place for you. **3** And if I go and prepare a place for you, I will come again, and receive you unto myself; that where I am, *there* ye may be also. **4** And whither I go ye know, and the way ye know.

Christ said, "I will come again". Sometimes we make promises we can't keep due to circumstances. But Jesus Christ's promises are sure – they WILL come to pass, and if there is one thing absolutely certain, it is the fact that Christ will one day return to this earth.

a. The Manner of Jesus' Return

i. A Visible Event

There are many people who believe in the coming of Jesus, but many are confused about how it will actually take place. Some believe that Jesus will come secretly and privately, but notice carefully what the Bible says:

> **Act 1:9-11** And when he had spoken these things, while they beheld, he was taken up; and a cloud received him out of their sight. **10** And while they looked stedfastly toward heaven as he went up, behold, two men stood by them in white apparel; **11** Which also said, Ye men of Galilee, why stand ye gazing up into heaven? this same Jesus, which is taken up from you into heaven, shall so come in like manner as ye have seen him go into heaven.

This is the record of the ascension. The disciples saw Him ascend, and the two men in white apparel (probably angels) said "this same Jesus" would return the same way. The disciples saw Jesus ascend with their eyes. It was a visible event; His return will not be secret, but visible.

> **Matt 24:30** And then shall appear the sign of the Son of man in heaven: and then shall all the tribes of the earth mourn, and they shall see the Son of man coming in the clouds of heaven with power and great glory.

It will not only be visible to God's faithful children but also to those who reject God. Notice carefully what the book of Revelation says:

> **Rev 1:7** Behold, he cometh with clouds; and every eye shall see him, and they *also* which pierced him: and all kindreds of the earth shall wail because of him. Even so, Amen.

ii. A Glorious Event

When Jesus comes it will be extremely bright. No one will miss it.

> **Matt 25:31** When the Son of man shall come in his glory, and all the holy angels with him, then shall he sit upon the throne of his glory:

The Bible speaks about the countenance of one angel being like the brightness of lightning. Can you imagine the brightness of all the angels combined with the brightness of the Father and the Son? It will be impossible to miss, it will be wonderfully bright.

iii. A World Changing Event

When Jesus comes the world will be turned upside down.

> **Rev 6:14-17** And the heaven departed as a scroll when it is rolled together; and every mountain and island were moved out of their places. **15** And the kings of the earth, and the great men, and the rich men, and the chief captains, and the mighty men, and every bondman, and every free man, hid themselves in the dens and in the rocks of the mountains; **16** And said to the mountains and rocks, Fall on us, and hide us from the face of him that sitteth on the throne, and from the wrath of the Lamb: **17** For the great day of his wrath is come; and who shall be able to stand?

Every island and mountain will be moved out of their place. This is not a secret event. Notice also the prophecy given to King Nebuchadnezzar:

> **Dan 2:44-45** And in the days of these kings shall the God of heaven set up a kingdom, which shall never be destroyed: and the kingdom shall not be left to other people, *but* it shall break in pieces and consume all these kingdoms, and it shall stand for ever. **45** Forasmuch as thou sawest that the stone was cut out of the mountain without hands, and that it brake in pieces the iron, the brass, the clay, the silver, and the gold; the great God hath made known to the king what shall come to pass hereafter: and the dream *is* certain, and the interpretation thereof sure.

This prophecy clearly tells us that when Jesus comes again, no earthly government will continue to exist. They shall be broken in pieces and the seed of the woman will triumph over the serpent's lie.

b. God Claims His Faithful Children

The Bible says that as Jesus draws near to the earth, that He will shout and all those who have fallen asleep believing in Jesus will be raised to life and will be caught up to meet Jesus in the air.

> **1 Thess 4:16-17** For the Lord himself shall descend from heaven with a shout, with the voice of the archangel, and with the trump of God: and the dead in Christ shall rise first: **17** Then we which are alive *and* remain shall be caught up together with them in the clouds, to meet the Lord in the air: and so shall we ever be with the Lord.

Many have been in their graves for hundreds of years, but now the faithful are raised to eternal life. Some living at the time of Christ's return, and who have of course never experienced death, are caught up in the air with the Lord. These now have eternal life, and will never taste death and will live forever with the Father and the Son.

There are some who believe that Jesus will come again to the earth and work miracles and heal people, but notice the Bible says that the righteous are caught up to meet the Lord IN THE AIR. In another place Jesus comments:

> **Matt 24:30-31** And then shall appear the sign of the Son of man in heaven: and then shall all the tribes of the earth mourn, and they shall see the Son of man coming in the clouds of heaven with power and great glory. **31** And he shall send his angels with a great sound of a trumpet, and they shall gather together his elect from the four winds, from one end of heaven to the other.

The angels gather God's people from the earth like harvesters gathering precious grain.

c. God's Children Permanently Connected to the Life Source

As we have stated several times, man does not have immortal life on this earth. His life is dependent moment by moment upon the gift of the life of Jesus on his behalf. When Jesus comes and the serpent's lie is dead and there is nothing to lead us away from God, the channel of life will flow to us permanently, directly from the throne of God. We will live forever.

> **1 Cor 15:51-54** Behold, I shew you a mystery; We shall not all sleep, but we shall all be changed, **52** In a moment, in the twinkling of an eye, at the last trump: for the trumpet shall sound, and the dead shall be raised incorruptible, and we shall be changed. **53** For this corruptible must put on incorruption, and this mortal *must* put on immortality. **54** So when this corruptible shall have put on incorruption, and this mortal shall have put on immortality, then shall be brought to pass the saying that is written, Death is swallowed up in victory.

What a wonderful thought; to live forever with our wonderful God without fear of death, without sickness and without the loss of loved ones. Relationships will never be broken and everyone will have perfect love and care for one another.

Family Reunion – The Second Coming (The Stone)

The lie of the serpent is conquered, we will drink freely of the waters of life flowing from God's heavenly throne and the law of God will be permanently sealed in our minds. It is interesting to note that it is the symbol of the source of life that is sealed into our minds to ensure we never stray away again and fall into the terrors of sin.

>**Rev 14:1** And I looked, and, lo, a Lamb stood on the mount Sion, and with him an hundred forty *and* four thousand, having his Father's name written in their foreheads.

It is the Father's name that is sealed into our thinking. We will ever remember to honour and give glory to Him always remembering that from Him all life flows.

Chapter 27

Living in God's Family Kingdom in the Last Days

In the first chapter, after examining a tragic situation within a family, I made this comment:

> What principles are at play in society that is causing this breakdown in building a family treasure of memories? What is driving the rising levels of isolation, depression and suicide? We might offer some surface level response of needing to spend more time together and I could give you a list of things to do (which you already know) that could greatly benefit your family treasure building but I guess that would be like offering a mop to clean up the mess rather than pointing to the place to turn off the tap. I believe the issues are much deeper than a simple list of things to do.

We have had a very comprehensive look at the driving forces that are tearing families apart. With these principles in place we can now offer some suggestions and pointers for building a family treasure of memories.

a. The Husband and Wife Relationship

As we have clearly shown, everything depends on the correct structuring of the husband and wife relationship into a blessing structure. This blessing structure is established by the husband realizing his role as the head, blesser and seeder of the home, and the wife realizing her critical role as the submissive nurturing agent that draws down that blessing. So how do we bring this about in day to day life?

i. The Husband and Father

Recognize your privilege and responsibility to bless your wife and children. You have authority from heaven to pray and speak blessing into their lives. Pray each day that the lives of your wife and children will be filled with blessing and peace. Pray for their protection and wisdom and success. Your attitude and self perception in this prayer process is vital. Pray with a sense of purpose; that this is a critical part of your role in the home and that God will indeed bless your family.

Remember the power of your words. Your words are powerful seeds that will reap a harvest in your wife and children.

> **Prov 18:21** Death and life *are* in the power of the tongue: and they that love it shall eat the fruit thereof.

Take every opportunity to speak words of encouragement to your wife and children. Your family needs to hear these seeding words, they depend on them. Avoid the temptation to withdraw your blessing when your authority is challenged. Remember that your worth and value comes from God. Teach your family the Biblical principles of the channel of blessing and the importance for them to stay in that channel.

At the end of each day, intercede for your children and ask the Lord to forgive the errors of your children. This is a vital headship principle. You are responsible for their conduct until they reach the age of accountability and you must act on their behalf.

Remember that your family kingdom rests upon the attitude of submission that your wife has to you. Make her life sweet and joyful. Make every effort to appreciate her work in the home and support her in whatever ways you can. Pray for your wife and pray for wisdom as to best lead her. Remember that she is trusting that your leadership will be directed by God and that she will be blessed under your headship. Pray before you ask her to do things, ensure that what you ask her to do is what God would want.

Do not yell or loudly raise your voice at your family in anger. The raising of your voice indicates a loss of identity on your part. Words spoken in anger by a husband and father are extremely detrimental to the emotional health of your family. Your word is seed and a word sown in anger will reap a whirlwind in your children. Satan will tempt you regularly to speak in anger and to curse your wife and children. If you are constantly feeling the need to do this, you must assess whether you are truly finding your value in your heavenly Father and see yourself as the leader of your home.

You may be in a situation where your wife seeks to dominate and control you. Rather than respond in the same manner, assume your leadership role and pray blessing into the life of your wife. A woman who controls and dominates is really feeling insecure. She needs blessing and appreciation to help heal the wounds she may have received from her father or from your poor leadership in the past. This will take much patience and prayer, but the rewards are worth it.

Remember that it is your responsibility to teach your family about the channel of blessing principles. Bring your family together on a regular basis to teach them the principles found in the Bible. Teach them concerning God the source of all life and how we stay connected to that source. Teach them about the serpent's lie and the dangers of acting independently.

Keep the Sabbath as special family day to worship God and remember all the wonderful things that He has done for you and your family. The Sabbath provides a regular reminder that all life comes from God and we only have life in a relationship with Him.

Teach your family concerning the Sanctuary journey from the Court to the Most Holy Place and how that God has promised to write His protective Ten Commandment Law into our hearts so that we will be permanently connected to Him.

Keep your home as free as possible from New World Order inspired movies, music and educational programs that will undermine the channel of blessing. Watch for TV programs that undermine the headship of the father's role.[65] Keep this text in mind as you assess material coming into your home:

> **Phil 4:7-8** And the peace of God, which passeth all understanding, shall keep your hearts and minds through Christ Jesus. **8** Finally, brethren, whatsoever things are true, whatsoever things *are* honest, whatsoever things *are* just, whatsoever things *are* pure, whatsoever things *are* lovely, whatsoever things *are* of good report; if *there be* any

---

65 The very popular program "The Simpsons" is a clear example of this. You will find that most programs will undermine true family values in some way.

virtue, and if *there be* any praise, think on these things.

Are the things being watched or read true and honest? Most fictional programs do not qualify as true. Are they just, pure and lovely? How many programs are filled with filthy language, immoral conduct and violence? It is important to remember that even if you prevent your children from watching these things, but watch them yourself, the spirit that attends these films will filter through you to your children anyway.

In the earlier years, it is easy to keep these things out, but as your children grow work with them to see the dangers rather than just prevent them having access to things. As children grow, they must start making their own decisions, you can't make all their decisions for them.

Remember that as the head of the house, when you engage in worldly activities, you open the door for your whole family to be affected by a worldly spirit. Remember that if you watch material that has a spirit of rebellion, you may sow a spirit of rebellion into your children. Then when they rebel against you, it may be your fault rather than their fault. Discern carefully the importance of your role as the protector of the family against outside influences.

Above all, stay close to your example and Master – Jesus Christ. As you stay connected to Him in prayer and study, you will be filled with the needed wisdom, grace and peace to lead your family. If your job prevents you from having enough time to pray and meditate – find another job. It is much better to lose a job than to lose your family. Your family is everything to you.

ii.   The Wife and Mother

As we have noted several times before, the key to success for the family kingdom rests upon the pivotal role of the wife and mother. The demonstration of submission in the home both establishes the blessing authority of her husband and demonstrates powerfully to her children the principle of submission. As God is the source of all life, legitimate submission is the key to life in the family.

The role of the wife and mother is to nurture the seed of her husband both physically and spiritually. A wise wife will draw down the blessing of her husband upon herself and her children.

The best way a wife can secure a blessing for herself and her children is to pray for her husband, that he might lead with wisdom and discretion. Pray for him to make carefully considered decisions that will benefit the whole family.

A wise wife will not challenge the decisions of her husband or assume the responsibility of having the final say. She will not seek to manipulate her husband with tears or flattering words or marital favours. Such deception and manipulation will reap a harvest in your children and teach them to be cunning in getting their own way.

Sometimes the Lord will show you things that He will not immediately show your husband, even as the Lord allowed Rebekah to discern that Jacob was a more spiritual boy than Esau. This is a test to see if you will pray for your husband and submissively appeal to him or whether you will trust in your "superior knowledge" to effect change even as Rebekah did in causing Jacob to deceive his father. The result was that she never saw her favoured son again.

In submitting to your husband, you are submitting to the Lord for His sake. If your husband is not a believer, take every opportunity to establish his leadership by demonstrating your submission. As the Bible states:

> **1 Pet 3:1-6** Wives, in the same way be submissive to your husbands so that, if any of them do not believe the word, they may be won over without words by the behaviour of their wives, **2** when they see the purity and reverence of your lives. **3** Your beauty should not come from outward adornment, such as braided hair and the wearing of gold jewellery and fine clothes. **4** Instead, it should be that of your inner self, the unfading beauty of a gentle and quiet spirit, which is of great worth in God's sight. **5** For this is the way the holy women of the past who put their hope in God used to make themselves beautiful. They were submissive to their own husbands, **6** like Sarah, who obeyed Abraham and called him her master. You are her daughters if you do what is right and do not give way to fear. (NIV)

Remember, submission is not a passive process of just doing whatever the husband says, it is an active process of praying for your husband's wisdom, appealing to him concerning issues that are important to you. Seek his advice and guidance in matters and trust the Lord will give your husband wisdom to guide you. If your husband specifically asks you to violate the commandments of God, gently appeal to him that these commandments are very important to you and that in asking you to violate them, he is asking you to violate your conscience and is this really what he wants. If he will not relent, then you must quietly and firmly say that you can't do this and pray that he will cease his request. Do not challenge him, nor yell at him or try and manipulate him to change his mind. Trust that God will not allow you to be tempted above what you are able to bear.

Do not speak badly of your husband to others under any circumstance. Do not criticize him or belittle him; for this is the surest path to bring about your own destruction. If there are problems, appeal to your husband and beyond this appeal to the leaders of your church or family community to assist – not for the purpose of vindication, but for peace.

If your husband is not taking up his priestly duty to teach and lead the family in spiritual matters, do not assume this role automatically. Ask your husband permission to fill this role if he feels he can't do it. And continue to pray that he will resume or commence that role as soon as possible.

You are the queen of your home and you can do a lot to make the home a beautiful place. Through the nurturing gifts of hospitality, you can make your home a place where your husband, children and friends love to be. Be as cheerful in your work and remember that the tidiness of your home, while important, is not more important than the closeness of your family relationships: The home was made for man, not man for the home.

Seek wisdom from the Lord, and through your husband, to teach your children, especially in the early years. It is your privilege to set the tone and groundwork of their characters. Impress upon them the importance of the commandments, the channel of blessing and the need to respect and honour their father. As the Bible states:

> **Titus 2:3-5** The aged women likewise, that *they be* in behaviour as becometh holiness, not false accusers, not given to much wine, teachers of good things; 4 That they may teach the young women to be sober, to love their husbands, to love their children, 5 *To be* discreet, chaste, keepers at home, good, obedient to their own husbands, that the word of God be not blasphemed.

There is a special work to do for mothers with their daughters and spiritual women with young women in the church; and that is to preserve the family kingdom principles of Biblical submission. The family kingdom depends on this teaching and you are in the best place to keep this kingdom active. This is why the Father sent His Son as the principle agent to save the family kingdom, because no-one knows better the principles of submission than the Son of God.

In this modern age, when the world is seeking to train young women to be independent and not submissive at all, you have a sacred duty to raise young women to thwart Satan's plans for the New World Order. Much depends on this vital work of training young women. Even as the universe depends completely on the submission of Jesus to the Father, our families depend on the development of young wise women who understand the power of submission for the family kingdom.

Above all, watch your Saviour closely and study His example of submission. In many respects you have been made in His image and have the joy of powerfully revealing His character to the world.

b. Special Blessing Times and Events

The greatest joy and responsibility for parents is to raise happy, wise and productive children. The success of the family kingdom depends on blessed seed being planted in the hearts of your children by the father and nurtured by the mother. This work can be done day by day but there are a number of special times when a formal blessing ceremony can be performed to seal the blessed seed in the hearts of your children.

i. Conception and Pregnancy

Though the child has not been born, the blessing channel is still very active. Your attitude towards your unborn child is still seeding the foundations of the emotional stability of that child. Both husband and wife should seek the Lord together in thanks for the unborn child, even if the child was an "accident" on their part, it was not an accident on God's part. The first blessing is the attitude of desire and joy for the child. It would be well to have a special celebration of the event for which you can video or take pictures to show the children when they are older of your excitement of their conception and development in the womb.

ii. Birth

The birth of a child is a most joyful event. Do not fall into the temptation to desire either a boy or a girl. Accept the gender of the child as God's gift to you. Any hint of disappointment will immediately flow through the channel into the emotional memory and will curse them.

As soon as is possible arrange for a special dedication ceremony to pledge yourselves to raise this child in the principles of God's family kingdom. You can arrange to do this in a church or a community group or simply with your extended family.

iii. Toddler and Early Years

Provide your child with plenty of love and affection and provide a home environment as best you can free from conflict and discord. During these years a child will test your resolve to carry out your commands. Do not shout at or threaten your children, so behaviour comes from a lack of knowing who you are. Calmly and firmly point the duty of your children and ensure that they follow through. Sometimes this will take more time than you are willing to give, but it is vitally important. Remember that when your child is slow to obey or refuses to obey, Satan is at work to enslave their will. Rather than scold them, pray constantly that God will set their will free, so they can obey your commands. In some cases Satan will try to use fear in the heart of your child to cause them to disobey – this is often the case with eating certain foods. Again, in some cases it is not the child desiring to disobey, but fear through Satan has gripped them and made it hard to obey. Patiently lead them in prayer concerning such fears and encourage them to trust God.

During these years, the morning and evening worship is an excellent time for blessing. I suggest that on the eve of each Sabbath, when you conduct a worship program in the home that you bring your children to you as fathers and lay hands on them and bless them. Tell them they are special and that you love them and God loves them. These events will help seal the seeds of blessing in your children.

iv. Adolescence

The beginning of adolescence or the teen years is an extremely important time. It signals transition from childhood to adulthood. It is during this time that a child will begin to change physically into a man or woman. It is also around this time that a child will seek special validation concerning their identity, purpose and destiny. It is during these years that the role of the father becomes extremely important. Remember the Bible verse which states:

> **Prov 17:6** Children's children *are* the crown of old men; and the glory of children *are* their fathers.

As a child enters the teen years, I suggest that a special ceremony of recognition be arranged for the child in the presence of family and friends; something along the lines of a confirmation or Bar Mitzvah ceremony. The crucial part of the ceremony is the statements of love and appreciation by the father in front of the gathering. This will plant strongly the seeds of God's family kingdom and help preserve them from the many dangers teens face as they seek to establish themselves as adults.

v. Adulthood

A child will reach adulthood typically around the age of 18 to 21 years but this varies according to each child. Many cultures recognize a need to celebrate something like a 21st birthday. Again the father can play a key role in such a celebration and release his son or daughter into manhood or womanhood. When our father tells us we are now a man or woman, it is extremely significant and it would be wise to have such a celebration at this time.

vi. Marriage

The continuation of the family kingdom depends completely in the choice of a right marriage partner for your child. If you have been diligent to bless your child and teach them the principles of headship and submission, they will more likely choose a partner that also holds these values. Pray earnestly for your children that they will make a wise choice and pray that they might seek your counsel concerning a partner. Avoid forcing your opinion concerning a life partner and when they make a choice be careful not to heavily criticize their choice of a potential companion.

When your child makes a decision for marriage and after consultation and prayer, they have decided to move forward, support your child's decision, do not undermine them as this could destroy the marriage from the beginning.

Seek to become close to the son or daughter in-law and welcome them into your family and keep your door open for them. The wedding day should be an extremely joyful event. It takes much prayer and effort to make it so. Bless your children when they marry because without your blessing, their marriage will struggle. Even if you feel there are problems, cursing them will only bring rebellion once they have decided and will cut you off from being close to them. Do everything to keep the channels of blessing open because your children still need your blessing when they have their own children.

vii. Grandchildren

A grandparent has a role to play in blessing. Remember that the crown of old men is their grandchildren. If you are close to your son or daughter they hopefully will come to you for advice on how to deal with their child in certain situations. Because our children are like ourselves, grandparents have special insights into the traits of character of a grandchild. Avoid offering advice concerning child raising when it is not asked for. Bless your grandchildren at every opportunity and encourage them in spiritual things. Grandchildren can be such a blessing to grandparents and spending time with grandchildren that love you can be the greatest blessing.

c. Country Living

You will remember that we have made several comparisons between the philosophy of Abraham and Nimrod. Here is the chart once again.

Abraham	Nimrod
1. Family Structure (Gen 18:19)	1. Individual Dictator/Tyrant (Gen 10:10)
2. Nomadic Rural Dwellers (Heb 11:8-10)	2. City Builders and Defenders (Gen 11:4)
3. Identity by Parental Blessing (Gen 12:2)	3. Identity by Renown (Gen 11:4)
4. Observe Sabbath and Commandments (Gen 26:5)	4. Follow Personal Desires (Rom 1:21-32)
5. Belief in Death and Resurrection (Heb 11:17-19)	5. Belief in Immortality of the Soul (Gen 3:4)
6. Saviour as Humble Life Restorer – Revealed in Slain Lamb (John 11:25)	6. Saviour as Prideful Liberator and Subduer Empowered by Sun and Nature Worship
7. Focus of Worship on the Invisible	7. Focus of Worship on the Visible

One of the points we noted was that a family kingdom works best in rural environment surrounded by the things of God. Cities were first build by Cain and then Nimrod extended these principles. Cities are usually filled with crime, violence and a self pleasing, pleasure loving multitude. The city is not a place to raise children in the family kingdom. The Bible tells us: "Be still and know that I am God." It is hard to be still while living in a bustling city.

When you are surrounded by trees and hills, mountains and rivers, you are constantly reminded of God's channel of blessing system. Rather than depending on man for your water, you depend on the rain from heaven. Your children will be closer to nature and learn to appreciate the things of nature. If you are not living in a country environment, I encourage you to pray about moving out as soon as is reasonably possible. You don't want to be completely isolated from people. Living near a small town would be preferable. As you pray, may God grant you wisdom in these matters as you seek to build your family kingdom.

d. A Treasure of Family Memories

As you prayerfully seek to apply the principles laid out in this book, I am hopeful and confident that you will build a large treasure of memories for you and your children. One thing that I am mindful to do as a father is to record on camera and video, the special family events in our lives and play them to my family at meaningful times like around the holiday season at the end of the year.

I regularly have photos in a slide show playing on my computer as a 'screen saver' and I often see my wife and children stopping and looking at the pictures. It is good to be reminded of the happy times we have spent together over the years. These memories will stay with your children and will protect them against the terrible tragedy that happened to the poor young man in Chapter 1. It will also protect them against the need for many of the vices and rebellion that young people engage in today as they deal with the curses that have come into their lives through the serpent's lie of inherent power.

I want to pray for your family that it will be blessed and joyful and resilient against the attacks of Satan through the global elite. I encourage you to do your part in keeping the commandments of God and the faith of Jesus. I also look forward to the time when all of us as children of God will stand around His throne and worship Him, who is the source of all blessing.

Appendix A

William Miller's Rules of Interpretation

(with full Bible passages included)
From *Memoirs of William Miller* by Sylvester Bliss 1853, Pages 70-72
See also *Review and Herald* March 16, 1868
"That we may proceed intelligently, ...I shall give an extract or two from Mr. Miller's rules of interpretation, which are substantially those of every judicious interpreter of the word of God."
James White – *RH* Sep 16 1951

In studying the Bible, I have found the following rules to be of great service to myself, and now give them to the public by special request. Every rule should be well studied, in connexion with the Scripture references, if the Bible student would be at all benefited by them.

RULE I

Every word must have its proper bearing on the subject presented in the Bible.

PROOF

Matt 5:18 For verily I say unto you, Till heaven and earth pass, one jot or one tittle shall in no wise pass from the law, till all be fulfilled.

RULE II

All Scripture is necessary, and may be understood by a diligent application and study.

PROOF

2 Titus 3:15-17 And that from a child thou hast known the holy Scriptures, which are able to make thee wise unto salvation through faith which is in Christ Jesus. **16** All Scripture *is* given by inspiration of God, and *is* profitable for doctrine, for reproof, for correction, for instruction in righteousness: **17** That the man of God may be perfect, throughly furnished unto all good works.

RULE III

Nothing revealed in the Scripture can or will be hid from those who ask in faith, not wavering.
PROOFS

Deut 29:29 The secret *things belong* unto the LORD our God: but those *things which are* revealed *belong* unto us and to our children for ever, that *we* may do all the words of this law.

Matt 10:26-27 Fear them not therefore: for there is nothing covered, that shall not be revealed; and hid, that shall not be known. **27** What I tell you in darkness, *that* speak ye in light: and what ye hear in the ear, *that* preach ye upon the housetops.

1 Cor 2:10 But God hath revealed *them* unto us by his Spirit: for the Spirit searcheth all things, yea, the deep things of God.

Phil 3:15 Let us therefore, as many as be perfect, be thus minded: and if in any thing ye be otherwise minded, God shall reveal even this unto you.

Isa 14:11 Thy pomp is brought down to the grave, *and* the noise of thy viols: the worm is spread under thee, and the worms cover thee.

Matt 21:22 And all things, whatsoever ye shall ask in prayer, believing, ye shall receive.

John 14:13 And whatsoever ye shall ask in my name, that will I do, that the Father may be glorified in the Son.

James 1:5-6 If any of you lack wisdom, let him ask of God, that giveth to all *men* liberally, and upbraideth not; and it shall be given him. **6** But let him ask in faith, nothing wavering. For he that wavereth is like a wave of the sea driven with the wind and tossed.

1 John 5:13-15 These things have I written unto you that believe on the name of the Son of God; that ye may know that ye have eternal life, and that ye may believe on the name of the Son of God. **14** And this is the confidence that we have in him, that, if we ask any thing according to his will, he heareth us: **15** And if we know that he hear us, whatsoever we ask, we know that we have the petitions that we desired of him.

RULE IV

To understand doctrine, bring all the Scriptures together on the subject you wish to know; then let every word have its proper influence, and if you can form your theory without a contradiction, you cannot be in an error.

PROOFS

Isa 28:7-29 But they also have erred through wine, and through strong drink are out of the way; the priest and the prophet have erred through strong drink, they are swallowed up of wine, they are out of the way through strong drink; they err in vision, they stumble *in* judgment. **8** For all tables are full of vomit *and* filthiness, *so that there is* no place *clean*. **9** Whom shall he teach knowledge? and whom shall he make to understand doctrine? *them that are* weaned from the milk, *and* drawn from the breasts. **10** For precept *must be* upon precept, precept upon precept; line upon line, line upon line; here a little, *and* there a little: **11** For with stammering lips and another tongue will he speak to this people. **12** To whom he said, This *is* the rest *wherewith* ye may cause the weary to rest; and this *is* the refreshing: yet they would not hear. **13** But the word of the LORD was unto them precept upon precept, precept upon precept; line upon line, line upon line; here a little, *and* there a little; that they might go, and fall backward, and be broken, and snared, and taken. **14** Wherefore hear the word of the LORD, ye scornful men, that rule this people which *is* in Jerusalem. **15** Because ye have said, We have made a covenant with death, and with hell are we at agreement; when the overflowing scourge shall pass through, it shall not come unto us: for we have made lies our refuge, and under falsehood have we hid ourselves: **16** Therefore thus saith the Lord GOD, Behold, I lay in Zion for a foundation a stone, a tried stone, a precious corner *stone*, a sure foundation: he that believeth shall not make haste. **17** Judgment also will I lay to the line, and righteousness to the plummet: and the hail shall sweep away the refuge of lies, and the waters shall overflow the hiding place. **18** And your covenant with death shall be disannulled, and your agreement with hell shall not stand; when the overflowing scourge shall pass through, then ye shall be trodden down by it. **19** From the time that it goeth forth it shall take you: for morning by morning shall it pass over, by day and by night: and it shall be a vexation only *to* understand the report. **20** For the bed is shorter than that *a man* can stretch himself *on it*: and the covering narrower than that he can wrap himself *in it*. **21** For the LORD shall rise up as *in* mount Perazim, he shall be wroth as *in* the valley of Gibeon, that he may do his work, his strange work; and bring to pass his act, his strange act. **22** Now therefore be ye not mockers, lest your bands be made strong: for I have heard from the Lord GOD of hosts a consumption, even determined upon the whole earth. **23** Give ye ear, and hear my voice; hearken, and hear my speech. **24** Doth the plowman plow all day to sow? doth he open and break the clods of his ground? **25** When he hath made plain the face thereof, doth he not cast abroad the fitches, and scatter the cummin, and cast in the principal wheat and the appointed barley and the rie in their place? **26** For his God doth instruct him to discretion, *and* doth teach him. **27** For the fitches are not threshed with a threshing instrument, neither is a cart wheel turned about upon the cummin; but the fitches are beaten out with a staff, and the cummin with a rod. **28** Bread *corn* is bruised; because he will not ever be threshing it, nor break *it with* the wheel of his cart, nor bruise it *with* his horsemen. **29** This also cometh forth from the LORD of hosts, *which* is wonderful in counsel, *and* excellent in working.

Isa 25:8 He will swallow up death in victory; and the Lord GOD will wipe away tears from off all faces; and the rebuke of his people shall he take away from off all the earth: for the LORD hath spoken *it*.

Prov 19:27 Cease, my son, to hear the instruction *that causeth* to err from the words of knowledge.

Luke 24:27,44-45 And beginning at Moses and all the prophets, he expounded unto them in all the Scriptures the things concerning himself... **44** And he said unto them, These *are* the words which I spake unto you, while I was yet with you, that all things must be fulfilled, which were written in the law of Moses, and *in* the prophets, and *in* the psalms, concerning me. **45** Then opened he their understanding, that they might understand the Scriptures,

Rom 16:26 But now is made manifest, and by the Scriptures of the prophets, according to the commandment of the everlasting God, made known to all nations for the obedience of faith:

James 5:19 Brethren, if any of you do err from the truth, and one convert him;

2 Pet 1:19,20 We have also a more sure word of prophecy; whereunto ye do well that ye take heed, as unto a light that shineth in a dark place, until the day dawn, and the day star arise in your hearts: **20** Knowing this first, that no prophecy of the Scripture is of any private interpretation.

RULE V

Scripture must be its own expositor, since it is a rule of itself. If I depend on a teacher to expound it to me, and he should guess at its meaning, or desire to have it so on account of his sectarian creed, or to be thought wise, then his guessing, desire, creed or wisdom is my rule, not the Bible.

PROOFS

Psa 19:7-11 The law of the LORD *is* perfect, converting the soul: the testimony of the LORD *is* sure, making wise the simple. **8** The statutes of the LORD *are* right, rejoicing the heart: the commandment of the LORD *is* pure, enlightening the eyes. **9** The fear of the LORD *is* clean, enduring for ever: the judgments of the LORD *are* true *and* righteous altogether. **10** More to be desired *are they* than gold, yea, than much fine gold: sweeter also than honey and the honeycomb. **11** Moreover by them is thy servant warned: *and* in keeping of them *there is* great reward.

Psa 119:97-105 O how love I thy law! it *is* my meditation all the day. **98** Thou through thy commandments hast made me wiser than mine enemies: for they *are* ever with me. **99** I have more understanding than all my teachers: for thy testimonies *are* my meditation. **100** I understand more than the ancients, because I keep thy precepts. **101** I have refrained my feet from every evil way, that I might keep thy word. **102** I have not departed from thy judgments: for thou hast taught me. **103** How sweet are thy words unto my taste! *yea, sweeter* than honey to my mouth! **104** Through thy precepts I get understanding: therefore I hate every false way. **105** Thy word *is* a lamp unto my feet, and a light unto my path.

Matt 23:8-10 But be not ye called Rabbi: for one is your Master, *even* Christ; and all ye are brethren. **9** And call no *man* your father upon the earth: for one is your Father, which is in heaven. **10** Neither be ye called masters: for one is your Master, *even* Christ.

1 Cor 2:12-16 Now we have received, not the spirit of the world, but the spirit which is of God; that we might know the things that are freely given to us of God. **13** Which things also we speak, not in the words which man's wisdom teacheth, but which the Holy Ghost teacheth; comparing spiritual things with spiritual. **14** But the natural man receiveth not the things of the Spirit of God: for they are foolishness unto him: neither can he know *them*, because they are spiritually discerned. **15** But he that is spiritual judgeth all things, yet he himself is judged of no man. **16** For who hath known the mind of the Lord, that he may instruct him? But we have the mind of Christ.

Ezek 34:18-19 *Seemeth it* a small thing unto you to have eaten up the good pasture, but ye must tread down with your feet the residue of your pastures? and to have drunk of the deep waters, but ye must foul the residue with your feet? **19** And *as for* my flock, they eat that which ye have trodden with your feet; and they drink that which ye have fouled with your feet.

Luke 11:52 Woe unto you, lawyers! for ye have taken away the key of knowledge: ye entered not in yourselves, and them that were entering in ye hindered.

Mal 2:7-8 For the priest's lips should keep knowledge, and they should seek the law at his mouth: for he *is* the messenger of the LORD of hosts. **8** But ye are departed out of the way; ye have caused many to stumble at the law; ye have corrupted the covenant of Levi, saith the LORD of hosts.

RULE VI

God has revealed things to come, by visions, in figures and parables, and in this way the same things are oftentime revealed again and again, by different visions, or in different figures, and parables. If you wish to understand them, you must combine them all in one.

PROOFS

Psa 89:19 Then thou spakest in vision to thy holy one, and saidst, I have laid help upon *one that is* mighty; I have exalted *one* chosen out of the people.

Hos 12:10 I have also spoken by the prophets, and I have multiplied visions, and used similitudes, by the ministry of the prophets.

Hab 2:2 And the LORD answered me, and said, Write the vision, and make *it* plain upon tables, that he may run that readeth it.

Acts 2:17 And it shall come to pass in the last days, saith God, I will pour out of my Spirit upon all flesh: and your sons and your daughters shall prophesy, and your young men shall see visions, and your old men shall dream dreams:

1 Cor 10:6 Now these things were our examples, to the intent we should not lust after evil things, as they also lusted.

Heb 9:9 Which *was* a figure for the time then present, in which were offered both gifts and sacrifices, that could not make him that did the service perfect, as pertaining to the conscience;... **24** or Christ is not entered into the holy places made with hands, which are the figures of the true; but into heaven itself, now to appear in the presence of God for us:

Psa 78:2 I will open my mouth in a parable: I will utter dark sayings of old:

Matt 13:13 Therefore speak I to them in parables: because they seeing see not; and hearing they hear not, neither do they understand... **34** All these things spake Jesus unto the multitude in parables; and without a parable spake he not unto them:

Gen 41:1-32 And it came to pass at the end of two full years, that Pharaoh dreamed: and, behold, he stood by the river. **2** And, behold, there came up out of the river seven well favoured kine and fatfleshed; and they fed in a meadow. **3** And, behold, seven other kine came up after them out of the river, ill favoured and leanfleshed; and stood by the *other* kine upon the brink of the river. **4** And the ill favoured and leanfleshed kine did eat up the seven well favoured and fat kine. So Pharaoh awoke. **5** And he slept and dreamed the second time: and, behold, seven ears of corn came up upon one stalk, rank and good. **6** And, behold, seven thin ears and blasted with the east wind sprung up after them. **7** And the seven thin ears devoured the seven rank and full ears. And Pharaoh awoke, and, behold, *it was* a dream. **8** And it came to pass in the morning that his spirit was troubled; and he sent and called for all the magicians of Egypt, and all the wise men thereof: and Pharaoh told them his dream; but *there was* none that could interpret them unto Pharaoh. **9** Then spake the chief butler unto Pharaoh, saying, I do remember my faults this day: **10** Pharaoh was wroth with his servants, and put me in ward in the captain of the guard's house, *both* me and the chief baker: **11** And we dreamed a dream in one night, I and he; we dreamed each man according to the interpretation of his dream. **12** And *there was* there with us a young man, an Hebrew, servant to the captain of the guard; and we told him, and he interpreted to us our dreams; to each man according to his dream he did interpret. **13** And it came to pass, as he interpreted to us, so it was; me he restored unto mine office, and him he hanged. **14** Then Pharaoh sent and called Joseph, and they brought him hastily out of the dungeon: and he shaved *himself*, and changed his raiment, and came in unto Pharaoh. **15** And Pharaoh said unto Joseph, I have dreamed a dream, and *there is* none that can interpret it: and I have heard say of thee, *that* thou canst understand a dream to interpret it. **16** And Joseph answered Pharaoh, saying, *It is* not in me: God shall give Pharaoh an answer of peace. **17** And Pharaoh said unto Joseph, In my dream, behold, I stood upon the bank of the river: **18** And, behold, there came up out of the river seven kine, fatfleshed and well favoured; and they fed in a meadow: **19** And, behold, seven other kine came up after them, poor and very ill favoured and leanfleshed, such as I never saw in all the land of Egypt for badness: **20** And the lean and the ill favoured kine did eat up the first seven fat kine: **21** And when they had eaten them up, it could not be known that they had eaten them; but they *were* still ill favoured, as at the beginning. So I awoke. **22** And I saw in my dream, and, behold, seven ears came up in one stalk, full and good: **23** And, behold, seven ears, withered, thin, *and* blasted with the east wind, sprung up after them: **24** And the thin ears devoured the seven good ears: and I told *this* unto the magicians; but *there was* none that could declare *it* to me. **25** And Joseph said unto Pharaoh, The dream of Pharaoh *is* one: God hath shewed Pharaoh what he *is* about to do. **26** The seven good kine *are* seven years; and the seven good ears *are* seven years: the dream *is* one. **27** And the seven thin and ill favoured kine that came up after them *are* seven years; and the seven empty ears blasted with the east wind shall be seven years of famine. **28** This *is* the thing which I have spoken unto Pharaoh: What God *is* about to do he sheweth unto Pharaoh. **29** Behold, there come seven years of great plenty throughout all the land of Egypt: **30** And there shall arise after them seven years of famine; and all the plenty shall be forgotten in the land of Egypt; and the famine shall consume the land; **31** And the plenty shall not be known in the land by reason of that famine following; for it *shall be* very grievous. **32** And for that the dream was doubled unto Pharaoh twice; *it is* because the thing *is* established by God, and God will shortly bring it to pass.

Daniel Chapter 2, 7 & 8 (Image, unclean beasts, clean beasts)

Acts 10:9-16 On the morrow, as they went on their journey, and drew nigh unto the city, Peter went up upon the housetop to pray about the sixth hour: **10** And he became very hungry, and would have eaten: but while they made ready, he fell into a trance, **11** And saw heaven opened, and a certain vessel descending unto him, as it had been a great sheet knit at the four corners, and let down to the earth: **12** Wherein were all manner of fourfooted beasts of the earth, and wild beasts, and creeping things, and fowls of the air. **13** And there came a voice to him, Rise, Peter; kill, and eat. **14** But Peter said, Not so, Lord; for I have never eaten any thing that is common or unclean. **15** And the voice *spake* unto him again the second time, What God hath cleansed, *that* call not thou common. **16** This was done thrice: and the vessel was received up again into heaven.

RULE VII

Visions are always mentioned as such.
PROOF

2 Cor 12:1 It is not expedient for me doubtless to glory. I will come to visions and revelations of the Lord.

RULE VIII

Figures always have a figurative meaning, and are used much in prophecy, to represent future things, times and events; such as mountains, meaning governments; beasts, meaning kingdoms. Waters, meaning people. Lamp, meaning Word of God. Day, meaning year.

PROOFS

Dan 2:35 Then was the iron, the clay, the brass, the silver, and the gold, broken to pieces together, and became like the chaff of the summer threshingfloors; and the wind carried them away, that no place was found for them: and the stone that smote the image became a great mountain, and filled the whole earth...**44** And in the days of these kings shall the God of heaven set up a kingdom, which shall never be destroyed: and the kingdom shall not be left to other people, but it shall break in pieces and consume all these kingdoms, and it shall stand for ever.

Dan 7:8 I considered the horns, and, behold, there came up among them another little horn, before whom there were three of the first horns plucked up by the roots: and, behold, in this horn *were* eyes like the eyes of man, and a mouth speaking great things…**17** These great beasts, which are four, *are* four kings, *which* shall arise out of the earth.

Psa 119:105 Thy word *is* a lamp unto my feet, and a light unto my path.

Eze 4:6 And when thou hast accomplished them, lie again on thy right side, and thou shalt bear the iniquity of the house of Judah forty days: I have appointed thee each day for a year.

RULE IX

Parables are used as comparisons to illustrate subjects, and must be explained in the same way as figures by the subject and Bible.

Mark 4:13 And he said unto them, Know ye not this parable? and how then will ye know all parables?

RULE X

Figures sometimes have two or more different significations, as day is used in a figurative sense to represent three different periods of time.
PROOFS

    1. Indefinite. Ecc 7:14

    2. Definite, a day for a year. Ezek 4:6

    3. Day for a thousand years. 2 Pet 3:8

If you put on the right construction it will harmonize with the Bible and make good sense, otherwise it will not.

RULE XI

How to know when a word is used figuratively. If it makes good sense as it stands, and does no violence to the simple laws of nature, then it must be understood literally, if not, figuratively.
PROOFS

Rev 12:1-2 And there appeared a great wonder in heaven; a woman clothed with the sun, and the moon under her feet, and upon her head a crown of twelve stars: **2** And she being with child cried, travailing in birth, and pained to be delivered.

Rev 17:3-7 So he carried me away in the spirit into the wilderness: and I saw a woman sit upon a scarlet coloured beast, full of names of blasphemy, having seven heads and ten horns. **4** And the woman was arrayed in purple and scarlet colour, and decked with gold and precious stones and pearls, having a golden cup in her hand full of abominations and filthiness of her fornication: **5** And upon her forehead *was* a name written, MYSTERY, BABYLON THE GREAT, THE MOTHER OF HARLOTS AND ABOMINATIONS OF THE EARTH. **6** And I saw the woman drunken with the blood of the saints, and with the blood of the martyrs of Jesus: and when I saw her, I wondered with great admiration. **7** And the angel said unto me, Wherefore didst thou marvel? I will tell thee the mystery of the woman, and of the beast that carrieth her, which hath the seven heads and ten horns.

RULE XII

To learn the true meaning of figures, trace your figurative word through your Bible, and where you find it explained, put it on your figure, and if it makes good sense you need look no further, if not, look again.

RULE XIII

To know whether we have the true historical event for the fulfilment of a prophecy: If you find every word of the prophecy (after the figures are understood) is literally fulfilled, then you may know that your history is the true event. But if one word lacks a fulfilment, then you must look for another event, or wait its future development. For God takes care that history and prophecy doth agree, so that the true believing children of God may never be ashamed.

PROOFS

Psa 22:5 They cried unto thee, and were delivered: they trusted in thee, and were not confounded.

Isa 45:17-19 *But* Israel shall be saved in the LORD with an everlasting salvation: ye shall not be ashamed nor confounded world without end. **18** For thus saith the LORD that created the heavens; God himself that formed the earth and made it; he hath established it, he created it not in vain, he formed it to be inhabited: I *am* the LORD; and *there is* none else. **19** I have not spoken in secret, in a dark place of the earth: I said not unto the seed of Jacob, Seek ye me in vain: I the LORD speak righteousness, I declare things that are right.

1 Pet 2:6 Wherefore also it is contained in the Scripture, Behold, I lay in Sion a chief corner stone, elect, precious: and he that believeth on him shall not be confounded.

Rev 17:17 For God hath put in their hearts to fulfil his will, and to agree, and give their kingdom unto the beast, until the words of God shall be fulfilled.

Acts 3:18 But those things, which God before had shewed by the mouth of all his prophets, that Christ should suffer, he hath so fulfilled.

RULE XIV

The most important rule of all is, that you must have faith. It must be a faith that requires a sacrifice, and, if tried, would give up the dearest object on earth, the world and all its desires, character, living, occupation, friends, home, comforts, and worldly honors. If any of these should hinder our believing any part of God's word, it would show our faith to be vain. Nor can we ever believe so long as one of these motives lies lurking in our hearts. We must believe that God will never forfeit his word. And we can have confidence that he that takes notice of the sparrow, and numbers the hairs of our head, will guard the translation of his own word, and throw a barrier around it, and prevent those who sincerely trust in God, and put implicit confidence in his word, from erring far from the truth, though they may not understand Hebrew or Greek.

These are some of the most important rules which I find the word of God warrants me to adopt and follow, in order for system and regularity. And if I am not greatly deceived, in so doing, I have found the Bible, as a whole, one of the most simple, plain, and intelligible books ever written, containing proof in itself of its divine origin, and full of all knowledge that our hearts could wish to know or enjoy. I have found it a treasure which the world cannot purchase. It gives a calm peace in believing, and a firm hope in the future. It sustains the mind in adversity, and teaches us to be humble in prosperity. It prepares us to love and do good to others, and to realize the value of the soul. It makes us bold and valiant for the truth, and nerves the arm to oppose error. It gives us a powerful weapon to break down Infidelity, and makes known the only antidote for sin. It instructs us how death will be conquered, and how the bonds of the tomb must be broken. It tells us of future events, and shows the preparation necessary to meet them. It gives us an opportunity to hold conversation with the King of kings, and reveals the best code of laws ever enacted.

This is but a faint view of its value; yet how many perishing souls treat it with neglect, or, what is equally as bad, treat it as a hidden mystery which cannot be known. Oh, my dear reader, make it your chief study. Try it well, and you will find it to be all I have said. Yes, like the Queen of Sheba, you will say the half was not told you.

The divinity taught in our schools is always founded on some sectarian creed. It may do to take a blank mind and impress it with this kind, but it will always end in bigotry. A free mind will never be satisfied with the views of others. Were I a teacher of youth in divinity, I would first learn their capacity and mind. If these were good, I would make them study the Bible for themselves, and send them out free to do the world good. But if they had no mind, I would stamp them with another's mind, write bigot on their forehead, and send them out as slaves!

www.ingramcontent.com/pod-product-compliance
Lightning Source LLC
Chambersburg PA
CBHW070541160426
43199CB00014B/2329